DOCUMENTA MISSIO

FACULTAS MISSIOLOGICA - PONT. UN

HINDU SPIRITUALITY

MARIASUSAI DHAVAMONY, S.J.

EDITRICE PONTIFICIA UNIVERSITA' GREGORIANA

ROMA 1999

IMPRIMI POTEST
Romae, die 16 januarii 1999
R.P. Franco Imoda, S.J.
Rector Universitatis

IMPRIMATUR
dal Vicariato di Roma, 27 gennaio 1999
† Luigi Moretti, *Segretario Generale*

ISBN 88-7652-818-0

Editrice Pontificia Università Gregoriana
Piazza della Pilotta, 35 - 00187 Roma, Italia

TABLE OF CONTENTS

INTRODUCTION

Hinduism makes a clear distinction between morality and spirituality, for its aim is not merely to help become a perfect human being but to make him or her one with the ultimate Reality, the eternal universal Spirit, the personal God or the Absolute. This goal cannot be reached by merely improving or reforming human personality but by trasforming human consciousness. Though moral paths prepare the person for a higher spiritual path which alone is capable of realizing liberation from bondage of spiritual ignorance and egoism, spiritual paths of higher wisdom and love of God are necessary to open a new realm of consciousness. The transformation of human consciousness into divine consciousness which is the final destiny of human being is not possible in the course of a single life. Therefore, Hindus believe in a series of rebirths; men and women are in different stages of their journey and are in different grades of spirituality from the ordinary devotional practices to the mystic experience. The different stages of spirituality are characterized by the doctrine of spiritual competence (*adhikhāra*) and the doctrine of the chosen Deity (*ishta-devatā*). The first requires that the religious discipline prescribed should correspond to the spiritual competence. The second means that out of the many forms of the Supreme Being recorded in the Hindu Scriptures, the worshipper is taught to choose that which satisfies his spiritual longing and to make it the object of knowledge and love. The more of such spiritual qualities as goodness, justice, mercy, love and kindness a person has, the nearer he or she is to the Supreme Being who is the source and perfection of all spiritual qualities. The first chapter on the religious quest of Hinduism precisely outlines the signifi-

known passage: "Scriptural texts are not the only means of knowledge in the enquiry into Brahman, as they are in the enquiry into Dharma. But both scriptural texts and spiritual experience are to be taken as authorities, indispensable for any spiritual progress, firstly because spiritual experience is the final goal of all enquiry into Brahman, and secondly because the object of the inquiry is an already existing Reality." (*Brahma-Sūtra-Bhāsya 1.1.1*) Two things are necessary to acquire the higher knowledge: namely, the authority of the *Śruti* and the testimony of one's own spiritual experience. Without conformity to the teaching of Scriptures there is no guarantee of truth in religion; without an earnest spiritual quest, there is no vitality in religion. Faith in a living spiritual teacher (*guru*) is of fundamental importance. Not the mere book-knowledge, but whatever a preceptor of realization imparts directly to a true disciple, a branch of learning, a mode of sādhana, or a *mantra*, becomes effective. The guru himself must possess an illumination in the experiential and practical sphere in order to radiate the light of truth which he possesses. The guru is the supreme God in the visible form. (chapter 3) The character of the good man (*sādhu*) can be described thus: Compassionate, unharmful, and forebearing towards all, having truth as his strength, equal and helpful to all, with a mind not ruined by desires, subdued, mild, clean, unburned by possessions, without craving, moderate in acquisition, quiet, firm, silent and meditative, with a spirit surrendered to God, friendly and merciful. (Chapter 4) Hindu tolerance is a virtue that is practised towards equals or towards inferiors; this means the recognition that the Absolute or God expresses itself or himself in many ways, and that none should seek to force on others his own views or his own methods. All paths by which people seek God lead to him. (Chapter 5) Hospitality is a virtue on which great stress is put, and the guest must be honoured as a god. Uprightness, fair dealing, trust, honour, straightforwardness, urbanity, fidelity, cooperation, readiness to forgive injuries are virtues which are necessary for a happy and prosperous social life and peaceful living. Peace belongs to the ideal state of perfection; i.e., perfect peace, harmony, absolute fearlessness, freedom. "May all gods bring me peace. May there be peame auspicious, let everything be beneficial to us". (*Atharva Veda* 19.9) It is through spiritual means (*sādhana*) that we pass from disharmony to harmony, from multiplicity and variety to unity and oneness, and from a state of disturbance to a state of perfect peace. (Chapter 6)

The idea of the adorable Lord of the world, the God who resides in the heart of all beings, plays a most important part in the spiritual life of the Hindu. The experience of deep love for God is called *bhakti*. There are different types of love of God, lower and higher, exterior and interior, active and contemplative. The highest love of God does not seek for the fulfilment of any desire, and is not determined by any conditions, and has no desire for the fruits of one's action. The mystics experience God as master, as friend, as a parent and as a spouse and realize the sphere of God, the nearness of God, the same form of God and the deepest union and oneness with God. (Chapters 7 and 8) Finally we take up the meaning of death in Hinduism (chapter 9). During his earthly life a Hindu consecrates his life by performing various rites (birth, initiation, marriage, etc.) at the different stages of his growth. At his leaving from this world his survivors consecrate his death for his future happiness in his next life. A Hindu text says: "It is well known that through the sacraments after the birth one conquers this earth; through the sacraments after the death heaven" . The kind of rebirth after death depends on the kind of life one led before death. Death is merely a dissolution of the body; the self never dies but migrates from one body to another as a consequence of its past good or bad actions. The *Bhagavad-gītā* (8.2-13) instructs people to direct the thoughts at the hour of death on God and meditate on him in order to obtain salvation from rebirth. Those who love God during their life, especially at the time of death, go to Him and participate in his mode of being. Cosmic eschatology in Hinduism is cyclical and therefore we may begin with the smallest time units, the yugas, and the great yuga (*mahāyuga*) which is composed of four ordinary yugas. The great yuga is the basic cosmic cyclic entity, for it is at this level that we find the great cyclic pattern in its full scope: creation, gradual diminuition in vitality and virtue, final dissolution, recreation

CHAPTER ONE

THE RELIGIOUS QUEST OF HINDUISM

The Declaration[1] of the second Vatican Council on the relationship of the Catholic Church to Hinduism really touches the core of Hinduism which consists in an inquiry into the divine mystery and in seeking after release from human misery. It rightly combines the philosophical inquiry and the religious aspirations, for in Hinduism both go hand in hand and are never separate. The problem of God and of human existence, for the Hindus, far from being an academic and purely intellectual one, is through and through religious and highly practical. The document outlines with reverence the Hindus' searching spirit in mythology and philosophy in which the divine mystery is expressed and brings out clearly the longing of the Hindu soul for reaching the divine, once liberated from fetters by means of asceticism, contemplation and love of God. It inspires respect for what is good and noble in Hinduism and encourages solid study and appreciation of these values.

The main ideas of the Conciliar Declaration such as the divine mystery, liberation, asceticism, contemplation, love of God, myth, philosophy, and the term Hinduism itself have special connotation, different from their Western counterparts. We have to place these ideas in the background of Hinduism, one of the great living religions of the world today, and study what the great classical Hindu seers[2] and *gurus*[3] themselves understand by these terms in their sacred writings.

---

1 The text reads as follows: «In Hinduismo, homines mysterium divinum scrutantur et exprimunt inexhausta fecunditate mythorum et acutis conatibus philosophiae, atque liberationem quaerunt ab angustiis nostrae conditionis vel per formas vitae asceticae, vel profundam meditationem, vel per refugium ad Deum cum amore et confidentia».

2 Seer is an inspired sage (*ṛṣi*) who has received the revelation from the supreme Being.

3 *Guru* is a religious master in whom God resides.

I. The ancient religious heritage

The Hindus divide their sacred writings into two distinct categories which they call *śruti* (hearing) and *Smṛti* (memory). The first comprises the *Veda*[4] (knowledge) itself which is considered to be the eternal *Śabda* (Word) heard by the *ṛṣis* (sages) of immemorial antiquity. The *Veda*, as we have it, is historically divided into three groups: the *Saṁhitās* (collections of hymns and formulas), the *Brāhmaṇas* (sacrificial texts) and the *Āranyakas* (forest-treatises) which culminate in the *Upaniṣads* (esoteric treatises). The Hindus believe that the whole of the *Veda* is uncreated: it is the Word uttered by the Absolute in eternity and "heard" or "memorized" by sages of old. The second category, *Smṛti*, does not have the rank of being eternal truth; it comprises the *Sūtras* (philosophical aphorisms), *Dharma-śāstras* (the Law Books), the *Purānas* (stories about the great gods) and the two great epics, the *Mahābhārata* and the *Rāmāyana*. The *Bhagavad-Gītā*, though not part of the sacred canon of the *Veda*, is in practice at least as highly regarded by all Hindus. These sacred writings do not contain an account of God's dealings with man in history as the Christian Bible does, but are rather a gradual realization by man of the being of God and of man. It is man's search for the Real, the Light and the Immoṛtal, both in himself and in the world that surrounds him:

> «From the unreal lead me to the real;
> From darkness lead me to light;
> From death lead me to immortality»[5].

Hinduism is both a way of life and a highly organized social and religious system. Although it is free from dogmatic assertions concerning the nature of God and so on, still there are certain presuppositions in post-Vedic Hinduism that are in no way disputed and are accepted as self-evident. These are *dharma, karma, saṁsāra, Brahman, mokṣa*.

---

4 The *Veda* used in a wider sense covers the whole or any part of the literature based on one or another of the four *Saṁhitās*; used in a restricted sense, it comprises the four *Saṁhitās:* Rig Veda, Sāma Veda, Atharva Veda and Yajur Veda.

5 *Bṛh, Upan.* 1. 3. 28.

The Hindus themselves call their religion *sanātana dharma*, eternal *dharma*. *Dharma*[6] (from the root *dhṛ*, to hold, to maintain) is the «form» of things as they exist and the «power» that keeps them as they are. It is that which maintains in being the whole universe in the cosmic order and mankind in the moral order in accordance with the eternal law. This *dharma* is set down in the sacred texts particularly in those which deal with Hindu customary law (*Dharma-śāstras*). The term is also applied to the religious assumptions on which these laws are based. *Brahman*[7] is the eternal substrate of the universe from which the "eternal" *dharma* proceeds. It also founds the spiritual prerogative of the *Brahman* caste. In earlier texts it meant «the sacred» and hence whatever was sacred, whether a formula or a chant or sacrificial action, was called *brahman*. Since the sacred as manifested in the sacrificial ritual was considered to be the bond linking temporal man with the eternal, *brahman* came to signify the eternal as it is in itself beyond space and time and as it manifests itself in the phenomenal world. Consequently, the term *brahman* was also applied to the state of the liberated soul (*mokṣa*); to the source from which all phenomenal existence derives its being; to the link between the world of *saṁsāra*[8] conditioned by space and time, cause and effect, and the *mokṣa*[9] which transcends these; to the eternal being which is the unchanging source of all change; and finally to the eternal *dharma*, the law which is based on the eternal and which governs the world of *saṁsāra*.

Karma (from the root *kṛ*, to do or to make) is the universal law according to which every action is the effect of a cause and is in its turn the cause of an effect. The whole process is called *saṁsāra*, the cycle of births and deaths to which all phenomenal existence is subject. The world of experience is in bondage to the fetters of time and desire because desire to do and to live implicates the doer in the wheel of *saṁsāra*. Escape from this cycle of time and action is possible and is called *mokṣa* (release or liberation). Time is conceived as a revolving wheel returning ever again to the point from

---

6 See Prof. R. C. Zaehner, *Hinduism* , Oxford, 1962, pp. 2 ff.

7 See H. Grassmann, *Wörterbuch zum Rig Veda*, s. v. *bráhman*. For an extensive study of the whole problem of *bráhman,* see J. Gonda, *Notes on Bráhman*, Utrecht, 1950.

8 The cycle of rebirth.

9 *Mokṣa* is the state of a liberated soul.

which it started[10] and in which there can be neither purpose nor salvation.

Hindu Mythology can be defined as the body of stories which give an account of gods and heroes, describing their origin and surroundings, their deeds and activities. Vedic mythology conceives of gods who are originally mortal, as having overcome death by the practice of austerity or by drinking *soma*[11]. They appear as supernatural beings, varying in character and power. They are usually stated to be thirty-three in number and from the earliest times we find them divided into terrestrial gods (Agni, Pṛthivī, Sarasvatī), space gods (Indra, Rudra, Maruts etc.) and celestial gods (Dyaus, Varuna, Mitra, Sūrya etc.). The Vedic pantheon can also be classified according to the functions they symbolize into ruler-gods, warrior-gods, and gods of economic life; or better in accordance with the three[12] classes of Vedic society: *Brāhmans* (priests), *kṣatriyas* (warriors) and *Vaiśyas* (peasantry and artisans). But Vedic mythology is concerned not only with nature-myths or with functional deities or with the social structure of a tribal society but also with a combination and integration of all these three into an ordered whole (*ṛta*). The term *ṛta* is a designation of the cosmic order on which human order, ethics and social life depend. Thus there is correspondence between the world of men, the perfomers of the sacrifice and the world of gods, the recipients of the sacrifice. The Vedic worshippers had to see to it that perfect balance is kept between these two orders by means of the right performance of sacrifice which is really the meeting-ground between men and gods.

Unlike the *Veda,* the two great Indian national epics, the *Mahābhārata* and the *Rāmāyana,* contain much of the developped Hinduism in many respects and continually preach the Hindu ideal and the Hindu ethics, caste duties and so on. In the *Mahābhārata* we have the whole of Hinduism in all its myriad aspects and in the *Rāmāyana* we are given an idea of what the Hindus conceive to be a perfect life as lived by the God Viṣṇu in his incarnation as Rāmā. The Purànic mythology concerns itself with the great Goddess's battles with demons, Śiva's martial or ascetical achievements, Krishna's

10 That is to say, time is a cycle without beginning or end.

11 *Soma* is an intoxicating juice extracted from the soma plant.

12 Śūdra ('servant') caste is a later addition.

life story. Different from the Vedic mythology the *Purānas* claim to be historical and set down the history of royal dynasties, citing an immemorial ancient cosmogony and theogony as the basis of this history. Some of the *Purānas* are sectarian and the eighteen major ones are traditionally dedicated to Viṣṇu, Śiva or Brahmā. The most famous of them, the *Bhāgavata Purāna* relates the life of Krishna, an incarnation of Viṣṇu and gives a fairly good account of the Vaishnavite religion.

Hindu sacrificial ritualism is also essential: The *Vedas* and more specially the *Brāhmaṇas* describe the sacrificial worship that was prevalent in those days and its essential features are as follows. Vedic sacrifice consists in paying homage to the gods in the form of a lengthy ceremony culminating in offerings made to the sacred Fire (Agni)[13]. Its purpose is to commune with the gods whose help is sought for general well-being or some particular advantage. The offering is usually some product of the land (melted butter or grains) or parts of an animal victim (usually a he-goat). The most dominant offering is *soma,* a plant the juice of which possesses intoxicating properties. The means of sacrifice is the fire on which the ceremony hinges. The *brāhman*[14] watches in silence and points out any mistake in the performance of sacrifice, while the *hotṛ,* the priest in charge of the "invocations" of the gods recites passages from the Rig-Veda; the *udgātṛ* chants aloud verses from the Sāma-Veda; and the *adhvaryu* performs the sacred action or sacrifice itself as prescribed in the Yajur-Veda.

In later Hinduism, this Vedic ritual gives place to the inward worship in the form of mental adoration and symbolic gestures become widespread. Prayer in the form of the *mantra* (sacred formula) on special occasions of initiation, expiation, etc., and the practice of *japa* (mental recitation) become universally established. Adoration called *pūja* is the form par excellence of Hindu religious practice. In a series of operations partly based on Vedic models, the image of a deity is anointed, dressed, adorned; food and drink are offered to it; flowers are placed and lamps are lighted. Annually the image is carried out of the temple precincts in processions (*yātras*)

---

13 Agni is the God who, as fire, consumes the sacrifice, and as priest presents it to the gods above; Agni is the mediator between gods and men.

14 *Brāhman* is the priest in charge of vigilance over perfect performance of the sacrifice.

in which the image is installed in a chariot and immersed in some sacred river.

The deeper meaning and purpose of the Hindu ritual and myth is to abolish "profane time" and to situate man in an eternal setting. For every myth, whatever its nature», recounts an event that happened *in illo tempore* and constitutes as a result, a precedent and pattern for all actions and "situations" later to repeat the event. Every ritual repeats a mythical archetype; and this repetition involves the abolition of profane time and the placing of man in a magico-religious time which without succession in the strict sense forms the "eternal now" of mythical time[15].

There is much in Vedic religion that is purely sacrificial, hieratic and ritualistic; but even here a certain personal relationship between the worshipper and the god is undoubtedly manifested in many of the Rig Vedic hymns[16]; one finds in them together with a healthy fear of the gods' wrath an inner piety to the main gods in whose benevolence the worshipper places his faith, whom he profusely praises, whom he confidently invokes in all his needs. The prayer for forgiveness of guilt is characteristic of the Varuna hymns[17] which are the most exalted and ethical in the whole *Veda*.

Finally, with regard to the Hindu and specially Vedic polytheistic mythology, it should be noted that the frequent practice of invoking individual gods as the highest or the supreme has made scholars[18] call it "Henotheism" or "Kathenotheism", which is defined as the belief in individual gods alternately regarded as the highest, the god addressed being for the moment treated as supreme Deity. This practice led to an identification of one god with another and even with all. «What is but one the wise call [by] manifold [names]. They call it Agni, Yama, Mātariśvan»[19].

15 See M. Eliade, *Patterns in Comparative Religion*, Eng. Tr., London, 1958, pp. 429-30. On the symbolism of the Vedic altar and every movement in the building of it, see the same author's study, *The Myth of the Eternal Return,* New York: Pantheon, 1954,

16 1. 31. 10 and 16; 1. 67. 1; 5. 1. 9; 5. 25. 4; 6. 2. 7; 10. 7. 3.

17 1. 25; 2. 28; 7. 86; 7. 87; 7. 89.

18 See Max Müller, *Six Systems of Indian Philosophy,* Oxford, p. 40; see also Prof. R. C. Zaehner, *Hindu and Muslim Mysticism*, London, 1960, p. 22.

19 *Rig Veda* 1. 164. 46.

2. - Theistic currents

Already towards the end of the Rig-Vedic hymns, the early Indian speculates on how the world began and sees only an unfathomable mystery. As he tries to account for the origin of the world and the development of multiplicity out of unity, the Vedic man stands before the mystery of existence. From now on Indian philosophy wrestles with the problem of the *relationship of the one to the many* and its main theme has been the possibility of restoring the primal unity through mystical insight or mystical love.

In the Creation hymns of the Rig-Veda, creation is regarded as the transition from a chaos to a diversified order through a pre-existent creator-god or not. The seer asks:

«What was the basis, what the beginning, how was it - that from which Viśvakarman, the all-seeing, generated the earth and unfolded the heavens in their greatness?»[20].

The answer is: It is Viśvakarman who «welds them together with his arms and wings» or who carves them out of the primal wood. As "creator" *(dhātā)* and "orderer" *(vidhātā)* God is distinct from the primeval matter[21]. In other hymns of creation the supreme principle appears both as efficient cause of the universe and its material cause or it is the "golden seed" *(hiraṇyagarbha)* which is born as the only Lord of creation[22]. The author of the famous Creation hymn (Rig-Veda X. 129), seems to conceive of primal existence as a formless and moving mass (water, darkness, the void, or non-being). The quest for the Absolute has begun but the riddle as yet remains unsolved. Is this Absolute an impersonal principle or is it a personal God?

This reverent inquiry is carried on more metaphysically in the *Upaniṣads* where the word used for the Absolute is *Brahman*. What is *Brahman?* What is the innermost Self (*ātman*) of all things and of the individual human beings? Some[23] said that *Brahman* was food in the sense of matter in a constant state of transforma-

---

20 *Rig Veda* 10. 81. 2.
21 *Rig Veda* 10. 82. 2.
22 *Rig Veda* 10. 121. 1.
23 *Taitt. Upan.* 3. 1 (2) and 3. 7; *Bṛh. Upan.* 1. 5. 1.

tion, for one cannot live unless one eats and one cannot eat unless one takes other lives whether animal or vegetable. The process of eating and being eaten constitutes the unity underlying the diversity of existence. Others[24] said *Brahman* was the breath of life. Yet others[25] said it was mind in the human being. Still others[26] said it was ether or space, which, since it pervades everything, can well be considered to be the ground of all things of the external world. Or again, it would be better to say no more of it than "Not this, not this", since once you define it, you limit it, and whatever it is, it is certainly not limited or circumscribed[27]. Or again, if living creatures are "real" in spite of their being subject to change and mortality, then *Brahman*, the true "self" of all things must be the "Real of the real" (*satyasya satya*)[28]. It is the "inner controller"[29], the "inmost self"[30], the "unseen seer", the unheard hearer, the unthought thinker, the un-understood understander[31], the warp and woof of all things[32], other than the world but controlling it from within[33].

In brief, *Brahman* is both eternal Being and the source of all the phenomenal universe; besides, it is also the inmost self within the essence of man. Thus is reached the famous identification of the eternal essence of man (*ātman* or self) with the changeless Absolute that indwells and controls the whole universe. The *Bṛhadāraṇyaka-Upaniṣad* declares: «whoso knows: "I am *Brahman*", becomes this All»[34]. The *Māṇḍūkya* opens with the words, «This whole world is *Brahman*: the self is *Brahman*»[35]. One has only to recall Yājñavalkya's teaching as contained in the *Bṛhadāraṇyaka-Upaniṣad*: «*ayam ātmā brahma* (this self is Brah-

---

24 *Bṛh. Upan.* 3. 9. 9; *Kaus. Upan.* 3. 2.
25 *Chànd. Upan.* 1. 13. 1-3.
26 *Ibid.* 3. 12. 7 and 7. 24.
27 *Kena Upan.* 9; 11-13; *Isà Upan.*
28 *Bṛh. Upan.* 3. 7
29 *Ibid.* 3. 7. 5
30 *Ibid.*
31 *Bṛh. Upan.* 3.8. 11.
32 *Ibid.*
33 *Bṛh. Upan.* 3.7.
34 1. 4. 10.
35 See also *Chānd. Upan.* 7. 25.

man)[36]; and Uddālaka's in the *Chāndogya*-Upaniṣad: «*tat tvam asi* (that thou art)[37].

Although this tendency towards pure non-duality is to be found in all the *Upaniṣads,* however a tendency towards the conception of the supreme Being in personal terms, distinct from the universe is not absent in the earlier ones and becomes more prominent in the later ones. Perhaps the first formulation of the Hindu idea of God is found in the so-called *Śāndilya-Vidyā* (wisdom of *Śāndilya*)[38] in which *Brahman* is called "this whole" world, which also transcends the world, for it is "greater than the great" and indwells the human soul as what is "smaller than a grain of rice". The idea of God as origin, sustainer, and indweller of the universe and of the human self slowly begins to emerge as something distinct from them[39]. *Brahman* is the cause of the phenomenal world as the spider is the cause of its web, fire of smoke. «As a spider might prolong itself in the threads [of its web], or as small sparks rise up separately from fire, even so do all breathing spirits, all worlds, all gods, all beings rise separately up from the self. The secret interpretation (*Upaniṣad*) of this is "the Real of the real". Living spirits are the real. He [the self] is their [own most] real»[40] Similarly God (the self) as final cause is compared to the ocean into which all rivers flow[41] or He is that which pervades all things yet is other than they like salt dissolved in water[42]. All this shows a tendency towards a conception of God - whether He be called *Brahman,* Self, or Person as efficient, material, final, and formal cause of the universe.

In the *Kaṭha-Upaniṣad,* the figure of a personal God emerges, who is the Lord of both the ideal world (*Brahman*) and the world of becoming.

---

36 2. 5. 19.
37 6. 8. 7.
38 *Chānd. Upan.* 3. 14. 3-4.
39 *Bṛh. Upan.* 2. 5. 14-15; 3, 8. 6-8.
40 *Ibid.* 2. 1. 20.
41 *Chānd. Upan.* 6. 10.
42 *Ibid.* 6. 13.

> «More minute than the minute, yet greater than the great
> Is the Self hidden in the depths of a creature.
> Him does one who lets go of his will behold, all sorrow gone,
> By the grace (*prasāda*) of the Creator (*dhātuh*) he beholds the greatness of the Self»[43].

God and Self are one. As Self, God is immanent in the human soul; as God and Creator, He is dispenser of the grace which opens the dwelling of the soul to His presence[44]. In the *Śvetāśvatara Upaniṣad* a fairly clear and consistent theism is proposed. In the first chapter the *Brahmavādins'* identification of *Brahman* with time, fate, chance etc. are rejected. God (Rudra Śiva) is the One "who presides over all causes endowed with time and self"[45]. God and his power (*śakti*) form an indissoluble unity. As God He is unmoved, as *śakti* He is the mover; as God the self of all things, as *śakti* He who causes motion. *Śakti* is the creative principle in God[46] "by whom all things were made". God is the source (or "womb") of the imperishable *Brahman*[47], as well as of all things[48] and transcends both these categories[49]. Souls as fragments of God[50] must therefore be of the same substance as He, and will be merged into Him at the end of time[51]. God is regarded as Lord and Creator of the universe, immanent as well as transcendent, who loves righteousness and hates evil, and who has positive qualities and a distinct personality[52]. He is the beginning and the end; from Him all things proceed[53] and to Him do they return[54].

The *Bhagavad Gītā* is the crowning of Indian theism. *Brahman,* for the *Gītā*, is cosmologically primal matter (*prakṛti* or *māyā*); psy-

43 *Kaṭha Upan.* 2. 12.
44 See also *Muṇḍ. Upan.* 2. 1. 1-2 and 3. 1. 3.
45 1. 3.
46 4. 1 and 6.8.
47 5. 6.
48 5. 5.
49 3. 7.
50 4. 10.
51 4. 1 etc.
52 6. 5-11.
53 3. 4 and 5. 5.
54 4. 1.

chologically, it is the realization of immortality[55]. God is creator, sustainer, and destroyer of the universe, its begining, middle, and end[56], transcendent as the Highest Person as well as immanent, and dwells in the hearts of men[57] as the essence of all things[58] and their seed[59]. Though some passages of the *Gītā* are pantheistic[60], yet some key passages do not imply pantheism and understand the divine immanence correctly. Of the *guṇas* (constituents) of nature, Krishna says, «Know that these are from Me: I am not in them but they are in Me»[61]. Similarly God sustains all creatures but does not subsist (*-stha*) in them. «All creatures subsist in Me, but I am not established in them. And yet creatures do not subsist in (-side) Me. Behold my sovereign power (*yoga*). My own Self sustains creatures without subsisting in them; it causes them to exist»[62]. God generates the world from Himself, He Himself being the seed[63]. «Though I am unborn and of changeless substance (*ātman*), though I am the Lord of creatures, yet do I by my creative power (*māyā*) draw near to Nature (as mother) which is of Me and thus grow together (as son)»[64]. The world is then totally dependent on Him while He is utterly independent of the world.

The real message of the *Gītā* is that God is not an impersonal Absolute but the lover of man's soul, indeed Love itself. Krishna says: «I am that love in created things which is not contrary to righteousness»[65]. He is father, comrade, and beloved[66]. The relationship between man and God is one of grace (*prasāda*) and love (*bhakti*). «With strong desire I have desired (*iṣṭo*) thee; therefore shall I tell thee thy salvation (*hitam*). Think of Me, worship Me, sacrifice to Me, pay Me homage: so shalt thou come to Me. I promise thee truly, for I love thee well. Give up all things of the law (*dharmān*),

55 Chapters 1-6.
56 10. 20.
57 15. 15.
58 7. 8 ff.
59 7. 10; 9. 18.
60 9. 16 ff; 7. 8 ff.
61 7, 10; 9. 18; 10, 39.
62 9, 4-5,
63 7. 10; 9. 18; 14. 3.
64 4. 6.
65 7. 11.
66 11. 44.

turn to Me only as thy refuge. I will deliver thee from all evil; have no care»[67]. For the first time, in the long history of Indian religious experience God seems to be speaking directly to man - a God of love, mercy and terror[68].

3. - Philosophical Hinduism

Turning now to the two great Hindu philosophers, Śaṅkara and Rāmānuja, we notice that the philosophical Hinduism has been developing along two main lines of absolutism and theism, already contained in the *Upaniṣads*, as we have seen.

Śaṅkara is the classical teacher and interpreter of *advaita* (non-dualism) in its most strict and subtle form. He starts his inquiry into the nature of *Brahman* (the Absolute) from the famous text of the *Chāndogya Upaniṣad:*

Sat eva idam agra āsīt, ekam eva advitīyam[69].

(Being only was this in the beginning, One only, secondless). The entire philosophy of Śaṅkara as deduced from this Upaniṣadic doctrine assumes three basic positions: the non-duality of *Brahman,* the non-reality of the world, and the non-difference of the self from *Brahman.*

True Being is *Sat* alone (Being itself), the eternal *Brahman*, unchanging and unchanged, indivisible and without parts (*Ekam eva advitīyam*). Because in itself *Brahman* or Being is absolutely and immutably "One only" (*ekam eva*), without multiplicity of differences and delimitations (*nirguṇam, nirviśeṣam*), it is non-dual (*advitīyam*) both inwardly and outwardly. Reality cannot be two, for if it were not non-dual, then it would be limited and conditioned and thus cease to be real; every limitation is a negation. *Brahman* is opposed to all alteration (*vikāra*); hence, it is opposed to all beginning (*utpāda*) and becoming (*sambhava*).

But this does not mean that Brahman is *niḥsvarūpa* (without his own form or nature). In its own nature, this eternal One is wholly and purely *Átman* (Self). This cannot be denied, for it is the Self

---

67 18, 64-66.
68 11, 24-30.
69 6. 2. 1.

of even the one who denies. We know *that* the Self exists but we do not know *what* it is. It is pure Consciousness (*cit*), pure Knowledge (*jñāna*), pure Bliss (*ānanda*). If it were non-conscious, it could not be even known; and even to say that reality is non-conscious a fundamental consciousness is needed. Because Brahman is indivisible and simple, this consciousness goes beyond the threefold antithesis of knower, known and the act of knowing itself. It is pure Bliss without the distinction of enjoyer, the enjoyed and the act of enjoying itself.

No form can express *Brahman*, for it is neither this nor that (*neti, neti*). We can negatively say that it is beyond space and time (*kāladesa-animittam*) without distinction (*nirviśeṣam*), opposed to the many (*nānātva*), opposed to all inequality (*ekarasa*), infinite (*ananta*), non-temporal (*nitya*), without adjuncts (*upādhi*), without anything foreign to itself (*anyad*), without quality (*nirguṇa*), without form (*amūrta*). All we can say about it is: absolutely real (*nispanna*), solely it is (*sanmātra*), pure consciousness, pure Bliss; in brief, *Saccidānanda*.

The soul of man, the inward self, is nothing else than this One, eternal, immutable *Brahman* (*ātmā ca brahma*). Through the power of *māyā* there arises in the soul *avidyā* (false knowing). *Māyā* from the point of view of *Brahman* is unreal; from the point of view of empirical knowledge, it is real; from the point of view of the metaphysician, it is the indeterminable (*anirvacanīya*), principle which veils the true and projects the untrue. *Māyā* superimposes (*adhyāropa*) upon the reality of the One Being the deceptive multiplicity of the phenomenal world. So Being which is One only, appears to the soul as world, as manifoldness, as many objects (*prapañcha*) and the soul beholds itself as separate from other souls, engaged in the cycle of rebirth.

Although from the absolute standpoint (*pāramārthika*) *Brahman* is non-dual and *nirguṇa* (attributeless), from the relative point of view (*vyāvahārika*) *Brahman* becomes personal and *saguṇa* (endowed with attributes). This personal *Brahman* is *īśvara* (God), the creator and sustainer of the world. Śaṅkara's doctrine of causality is known as *vivarta-vāda* (the theory of phenomenal appearance); i.e., the world is but an illusory appearance in *Brahman* just as the snake is in the rope which, when mistaken, has the appearance of a snake.

Rāmānuja rejected Śaṅkara's pure *advaita* as being destructive of religion and proposed his own system *visistādvaita* (non-duality in difference). Its most striking feature is the attempt to unite personal theism with the philosophy of the Absolute.

"Created" reality is divided into the spiritual (*cit*) and the material (*acit*) that is the substrate not only of all change but also of all thinking and feeling. There exist an unlimited number of souls. Souls and matter are dependent on God (*īśvara*) just as human body (*śarīra*) depends on the soul (*śarīrī*). Both together are regarded by Rāmānuja as the body of God. Between God and creatures as between body and soul there is an intrinsic relation (*apṛthak-siddhi*). This relation is central to Rāmānuja's philosophy. For instance, when we say "Krishna is a man", a mode (*prakāra*) or quality (*viśeṣana*) is predicated of a substance (*prakārin, viśeṣva*). The relation between substance and mode, qualified and qualification is inseparable, though distinct. God as qualified (*visista*) by the world of souls and matter is non-dual (*advaita*). Thus the kingdom of God consists of three different abodes: the abode of unconscious matter (inanimate world), the abode of conscious spirit (liberated souls) and the abode of beings composed of both matter and spirit (living human beings and animals).

The human soul of its very nature eternal, timeless, unchangeable, purely spiritual, is of the same substance as God: its essence is knowledge and bliss. But this does not imply that each soul comprises the whole creation but that there exists an identity between the soul and other creatures when freed from material adjuncts (*prakṛti*) in that they all have one form, consciousness. This is what is meant when the *Upaniṣads* say that *Brahman* is the same in all creatures; that is to say, as "-soul-thing" (*ātmavastu*) it is the stuff of all souls. Or, what comes to the same, *Brahman* is the category of existence which characterises the soul. The individual soul's connection with the body is not illusory as Śaṅkara maintained but real and is effected by *māyā* which by no means denotes illusion but God's mode of operation in the material universe. Causality for Rāmānuja implies transformation (*pariṇāma*) and consists in making patent what is latent, for in the cause the effect is latent (*sat-kārya*). Hence, creation and dissolution are the appearance and disappearance respectively of the world.

God (*īśvara*) is endowed with the eternal attributes of truth, goodness, beauty and bliss. He is the support (ādhāra) of all beings, their inner controller (*niyantṛ*), their goal (*śeṣin*). He is the great Lord of souls and material beings. Being the very opposite of all that is imperfect or evil (*heya*) and the unique source of indefectible, perfect, and incommensurable good (*kalyāna*), and having omnipotence (*niyamana*) as his personal nature, God is different in kind both from non-intelligent matter which is ruled by the laws of cause and effect, and from the intelligent soul-stuff whether in a state of bondage or liberation, from all in fact which is subject to his rule. Therefore, whosoever is free of the delusion that God is not wholly different in kind from all else and knows God as such, is released from all ills.

4 - Religious Hinduism

If philosophical Hinduism seeks to vindicate the existence and to ascertain the nature and attributes of the ultimate Reality, whether personal or impersonal, and of man's relation to it, religious Hinduism seeks to find out the way for the imperfect man to return to this ultimate Reality and to realize his ultimate goal (*paramā gatiḥ*).

What for the Hindus constitutes liberation (*mokṣa* or *mukti*) is release not from sin as in Christianity but from the human conditions; i. e., release from action (*karma*) of any kind, whether good or evil; liberation into a condition where time and space are abolished and all is seen as One. Liberation for the non-dualist Upaniṣadic seers means merging into *Brahman*, the supreme principle, as a river merges into the sea, by which man is freed from the fetters of phenomenal life and passes into a mode of being which is infinite, omnipresent (because space is transcended), and deathless (because time is transcended); this is precisely to be *Brahman*. The *Sāṁkhya-Yoga* is content to define liberation as *kaivalyam*, isolation of the individual soul in its eternal essence. But theistic *bhakti* sects see the path-way to God as loyalty and love between the soul and God and liberation means union with a personal God in an ecstacy of total surrender.

As to the way of liberation, the Hindus traditionally speak of three *mārgas* (paths): *karma-mārga* (ascetical and religious observance), *jñāna-mārga* (transcendental knowledge of true Reality) and *bhakti-mārga* (loving devotion and surrender to a personal God). The distinction between these three *mārgas*, though helpful to understand the Hindu spirituality, is never adequate, for they interpenetrate one another in actual practice.

a - *Hindu asceticism*: The early Brahmanic asceticism consists mainly of sacrifices and rituals. The word *yoga* (from the root *yuj*, to yoke, link) is used in the sacrificial context. The performer of sacrifices "yokes" the heavenly powers to the offering or "yokes" by mental concentration his own thought to the spiritual formula or action[70]. After a ritual bath the performer of sacrifice undergoes a rigorous fast, sitting in ascetical immobility in embryo posture, in the dark, between sacred fires, and thus communes with the gods[71]. *Tapas* (internal asceticism) among other purposes is used to attain union with the deity. Sacred recitation (*svādhyāya*), accompanied by meditation (*dhyāna*) may be purely mental (*manasā*) or vocal (*japa*). During the *Āranyaka* period, the *vanaprasthas* (forest ascetics) put the emphasis not on sacrificial ritualism but on austerity (*tapas*) and meditation (*dhyāna, upāsana*) as the means of realizing the supreme Being.

It is the *Bhagavad Gītā* that gives a deeper meaning to the Indian asceticism[72]. If man's goal is to pass beyond all action into a timeless peace, then why should he act at all? The *Gītā* answers that it is not action, strictly speaking, that binds, but attachment to action and to its fruits. When action is performed with complete detachment, it ceases to bind one to the world. Right action moreover automatically leads to a state of detachment of the mind, and detachment in its turn leads to a higher stage of spirituality in the way of liberation. The *Gītā* says in its last chapter: «By giving up self, force, pride, lust, anger, and acquisitiveness, with no thought of "mine", at peace, so is a man fitted to realize his eternal essence».

b - *Hindu mysticism of Knowledge (jñāna)*: In the *Patañjali's Yogasūtras,* along with a strict bodily discipline and the repetition of spells, devotion to God is considered to be efficacious as a step towards final liberation[73] which is the complete isolation

70 *Taitt.* S. IV. 1. 1.

71 *Atharva Veda* 8. 5. 15 and 19. 40. 1-3.

72 Chapters 1-6.

73 2. 1.

(*kaivalyam*) of the individual self from all that is other than itself, and this implies the total suppression of all discursive thought[74] God or Lord is described thus: «The Lord is a special type of soul which is untouched by care, works, the fruits of works, or desire. In him the seed of omniscience is perfect. He is the *guru* even of the ancients since he is not limited by time»[75]. But the God of the *Yogasūtras*, though unaffected by the world, is nonetheless, through his association with *sattva* and through his omniscience, permanently aware of the world and thus committed to it. Devotion to this Lord is only the third method in the Yoga technique. The first of these is bodily discipline or asceticism from which results perfection of the bodily senses from impurity and decay. Secondly, from the study of Hindu scriptures and the repetition of spells (*svādhyāya*) results the knowledge (*samprayoga*) of the deity of one's choice (*ista-devatā*). From the third method of devotion to God (*īśvara*) results the perfection of concentration (*samādhi*)[76]. The Yogin's aim is neither deification nor participation in the divine but the attainment of the supraphenomenal mode of existing; i. e., to reach the immortal substrate of his own soul.

Quite other than the Yogic mysticism is the advaitic which consists in knowing the difference (*viveka-jñāna*) between eternal being (*brahman*) and illusory being (*māyā*). This type of Hindu mysticism proposes, as the method besides others of renunciation and devotion which are only preparatory to it, transcendental knowledge of one's own inner self *(ātman)*. «*Átmani, Átmanam, Átmana*: know the self in the self alone through the self. Knowledge based on the Hindu scriptures is merely the finger which points to the object and which disappears when it is itself looked upon. The real knowledge is that which is one's own vision (*darsan*), an awareness of identity with Brahman in the sense of *"intuitus mysticus"*. This awareness cannot be "produced", cannot be reasoned out, for it is not a "work". The way to this vision may be prepared by the words of the Veda and by the loving devotion (*bhakti*) to a personal God,

74 1. 2.

75 1. 24-26.

76 2. 43-45; see Bhojaràja's commentary.

and by meditation (*pratyaya*) on the ultimate truth; in the end it is the seeing of the identity itself of *Brahman* and *Átman*.

c - *Hindu mysticism of love (bhakti): Bhakti* (from the root *bhaj*, to participate, to share) is Godward love of a religious person in utter self-surrender. It is expressed in loving devotion to a *guru* in whom God resides and to God Himself. It implies an affective participation of the devotee in the divine. It can be both the way to the union with God and the goal itself, namely, the union with God. *Bhakti* in the latter sense of union with God is the "*unio mystica*" realized by the *bhakta* in the ultimate state of *mukti*. The object of *bhakti* is *Bhagavān*, the gracious Lord, whether Viṣṇu or Śiva, according to different sects. The God of *bhakti* is gracious to men and has compassion (*kārunya, kṛpā*) for all; but He is specially benevolent to those who love Him; His devotees are "dear to Him", as the *Gītā* says. *Bhakti* is man's loving response to this divine graciousness on which he acknowledges himself utterly dependent for his liberation. In the *bhakti* religion liberation is not expected from yogic techniques or ritual practices or from transcendental knowledge, though these may precede *bhakti*, but from God's grace (*prasāda*). The doctrine of *avatāra* (incarnation) illustrates the priority of the divine initiative.

«Think on me, worship me, sacrifice to me, pay me homage: so shalt thou come to me. I promise thee truly, for I love thee well. Give up all things of the law, turn to me only as thy refuge. I will deliver thee from all evil. Have no care»[77]. So does the incarnate God Krishna declare the secret of God's love for man and summon his *bhakta* to share in his life. Again, «By love and loyalty to me he comes to know me as I really am. How great I am and who; and once he knows me as I am, he enters me forthwith. Let him then do all manner of works, putting his trust in me; for by my grace he will attain to an eternal, changeless state»[78]. The *Bhagavad Gītā* thus marks a turning point in the history of Hinduism. Man now no more turns exclusively inwards in search of the eternal ground of his soul which is also the eternal ground of the whole universe; he al-

77 18. 65-66.
78 18. 55 ff.

so turns outward to meet his transcendent God in trust and love and devotion, and he finds, in return, an amazing trust and love which never lets him down.

Through the Tamil saints of Śaivism and Vaishnavism the same mysticism of love has penetrated India more intensely and deeply. These saints sang the praises of their God in terms of ecstatic love. It is not any longer the absorption in the still centre of the self that is the ideal but total self-surrender to a loving and all-powerful God. The soul ever conscious of its unworthiness and sinfulness trusts absolutely in the mercy of God. In these Tamil saints a new note creeps in which has not been present before in Hinduism; namely, the sense of sin[79]. For Tukārām, the great Marāthī saint *bhakti* mysticism consists in surrendering all actions to God and feeling the greatest misery in forgetting God, and in clinging affection of the heart for a personal God. Tulsi Dās, the most famous mystic of the Hindi speaking people, conceives the supreme Being, Rāmā, as absolute knowledge and love and advocates utter self-surrender to and loving confidence in Rāmā's power to save men from the world of *saṁsāra*.

Unlike the other types of Hindu mysticism, *bhakti* mysticism believes in and strives for real union with a personal God through pure love of Him. Although there has been among some sects a tendency towards regarding *bhakti* in purely emotional terms and showing a sentimental devotion to God, the real religious *bhakti* as manifested by genuine mystics is love in the best sense of the term, including knowledge as well. Through love the religious soul comes to know God, who and how great He is in His Being. Thus knowing God in His essence, he forthwith enters into union with Him. This highest state of participation in God's essence is realized by the help of God's grace. Mānikkavāsakar, the greatest of the Śaivite mystics, expresses this love in touching terms:

> «The light superne deep plunged me in love's sea!
> How sweet His mercy is, sing ye, and beat Te%o%o|nam»[80].

79 *Hymns of the Tamil Saivite Saints*, Tr. hy F. Kingsbury and G. E. Phillips, Calcutta, 1921, pp. 43-47; 97, 99, 101.

80 *Tiruvācakam, Tiruttell|nam* 12. Tell|nam is an imitative word borrowed from the popular *kummi* songs. *Kummi* is a folk-dance.

CHAPTER TWO

SEERS AND GOD-MEN AS "FOUNDERS" OF HINDUISM

Introduction

When we speak of the "founder of religion" and apply the term to Hinduism without qualifications, we run the risk of falsifying the nature of Hinduism itself. For the Indian languages do not have any single word to express the wider idea of religion which includes the various religions of the world. Besides Hinduism had no historical founder in the sense that the founder is a human person who has given a specific, historical form under divine influence to a religious experience which has concretized in a religion and has been continued by his disciples and followers in the course of time. A religious founder is not an establisher of a religion in the sense that he organizes a body of men to be maintained for a particular purpose, as for instance an army, a navy, a civil service; he is not an originator of religion in the sense of the originator of socialism, for instance; nor is he a great inventor in the sense of devising a new method or instrument to realize a special end. For religions are neither invented nor imposed by purely human effort; they appear "founded". Every experience of God is certainly original in the sense that God is its originator; still it is also the outcome of some stimulus and is derived from some predecessor. Whenever this originating experience becomes very intense and consequently arouses many experiences and continues to operate historically, then we can speak of the "foundation of a religion". Although every genuine religious experience is a foundation from which new experiences can arise, we speak of the foundation of a religion only when its historical effects are visible on a large scale[1].

---

1 G. VAN DER LEEUW, *Religion in essence and manifestation*, Tr., Vol. 2, Harper & Row, New York, 1963, chapter 101.

The most comprehensive term for "religion" in Sanskrit is *Dharma* which is translated in general as law, teaching, truth, religion, morality, righteousness, duty[2]. It has also the meaning of what is characteristic of a thing, the attribute of a genus, the mark of a species. The rules of human conduct, for instance, which every one is expected to follow constitutes man's dharma *(mānavadharma)*. Besides, for each individual man there are particular *dharmas* deriving from his civil status, his caste, his rank, his occupation, and the stages of his life. The universal *dharma*, valid for and obligatory on all men of all castes is summarized by Manu as follows: "Abstention from injuring others, veracity, abstention from unlawfully appropriating others' goods, purity, and self-control"[3]. One knows the general and particular *dharma* from the following sources according to Manu: "The whole Veda is the first source of *dharma;* next, the smṛtis (the traditions contained in the Law Books) and the Śīla (the rules of morality) of those who know the Veda; also the customs of holy men; where no definite rule has been laid down, the independent judgement of the virtuous has to be followed[4]. *Mārga* ("the path or the way") is used to indicate the conduct prescribed for attaining salvation; a Hindu must tread the

---

2 From the religious point of view there is also the distinction between *Pravrtti Dharma* and *Nirvrtti Dharma* which is of particular interest here. *Manusmṛti* defines them thus: "The acts prescribed by the Veda are of two kinds, such as procure an increase of happiness and cause a continuation (of mundane existence, *nirvrtti*). Acts which secure (the fulfilment of) wishes in this world or in the next are called *pravrtti* (such as cause a continuation of mundane existence); but acts performed without any desire (for a reward), preceded by the acquisition of true knowledge, are declared to be *nirvrtti* (such as cause eventually the cessation of mundane existence)." (12.88-89) In the above text the next world in which acts are supposed to secure the fulfilment of desires refers to heaven, i.e., acts performed with the view of attaining heaven. *Pravrtti Dharma* is that which leads men to pursue worldly aims, and consequently to deeper bondage and ignorance while *Nirvrtti Dharma* is the action performed unselfishly for the good of the whole; it is performed without attachment to the results.

3 *Manusmṛti* 10.63; "Harmlessness, truthfulness, absence of the tendency to steal, to be free from the passions of desire, anger and covetousness, activity in the direction of what is agreeable and good to beings, form the course of *dharma* common to all *varṇas*." *Bhāgavata Purāṇa* 11.17.21; "Contentment, forgiveness, self-control, abstention from unrighteously appropriating anything, (obedience to the rules of) purification, coersion of the organs, wisdom, knowledge (of the Supreme Self), truthfulness, and abstention from anger, (form) the tenfold dharma." *Manusmṛti* 6.92.

4 *Manusmṛti* 2.6. The last source of *dharma* in this text, namely, the independent judgement of the virtuous is one's own personal experience, inner approbation, which is the result of one's conscience.

three ways (which are mutually inclusive of one another) of works, of knowledge and love of God. The term *mata* which literally means "thought" is also used to indicate the teaching of a master of any religious sect within the Hindu fold. The chief authority on which depends every Hindu belief and practice is the great tradition embodied in the Veda and the many branches of its literature.

The Hindu method of appealing to tradition is to see if the propriety of a particular belief or custom finds support in the sacred literature. They inquire whether that belief or custom is mentioned approvingly by the learned treatises (Śāstrokta or Śāstra-sammata), or mentioned in the Vedas (*Vedokta*), or mentioned in the Purāṇas (*Purāṇokta*). If the belief or conduct has the backing of any of these three, then it is to be followed, because these indicate the path by which good peple have gone; Śāstras, Vedas and Purāṇas constitute the final authority in religious matters in different degrees, since they are based on Śruti or Smṛti. The phrase *Śrutismṛtipurāṇokta* is of frequent occurrence in the Hindu ritual. If no support is to be found in any of these three, then that belief or conduct is to be abandoned; if all the three support it, then it should be held in greatest respect.

A founder of religion is primarily a witness to revelation. He has seen or heard something divine and transmits it to his followers. "To the Numen pertains a seer". It is in this sense that we can speak of the inspired sages as founders of Hindu religion. For the inspired sages are the authors of Śruti (primary revelation) and Smṛti (tradition) on whose authority depend the whole Hindu religion and social structure[5]. *Āgama* in general means anything handed down and fixed by tradition; a traditional doctrine or precept, a collection of such doctrines, a sacred work. In this sense it is usually referred to the Vedic tradition. *Āgama* is also a generic name of a Tantra or the work which inculcates the mystical worship of Śiva and Śakti; in which text a dialogue is found between the Goddess who interrogates as the disciple and Śiva who replies as the master. Finally *Āgama* is a generic name of religious texts which are at the basis of Hinduism and which are divided into Vaishṇava Āgamas,

---

5 Strictly speaking, the inspired sages are distinguished in two categories: Ṛishis proper are those who composed the Śruti texts while other sages are authors of Smṛti (secondary revelation).

generally called Saṁhitās; Śaivāgamas, which are the Āgamas in the proper sense of the term; and the Āgamas of adepts of Durgā or Śaktāgamas, which are more often called Tantras. The name of Tantra designates also by extension the whole of Āgama. Unlike the Vedas, the Āgamas are emphatically sectarian in character; namely, relating to the three sects: Śaiva, Vaishṇava and Śakta[6].

For the sake of clarity we shall speak of the Vedas as the basic text of Hinduism common to all Hindu sects, of the Āgamas as the sacred texts of the Śaivites, of the Saṁhitās as the sacred texts of the Vaishṇavas, and of the Tantras as the sacred texts of the Śaktas[7]. It is generally believed that the Vedas were composed around 1000 B.C.; that the Āgamas originated in Kashmir and South India which date from the 7th century A.D. and even earlier; that the Saṁhitās in various parts, particularly in Bengal and South India around the 7th century A.D. The Tantras of the Śaktas are dated from the 5th century A.D. Ṛṣis are the authors of the Vedas; Śaivāgamas were originally revealed by Śiva himself to his devotees who wrote them in Sanskrit and Dravidian languages. The Pāñcarātra Saṁhitās were composed by different sages; the presumed founder-sage is Pañchasikha; according to others Śāndilya. The Pāñcarātra literature like that of the other sects is divided into two categories: works of inspired or divine origin and works of human authorship. The latter is entirely dependent on the former. According to tradition God Vishṇu, Goddess Lakṣmī and the divine messenger Visvaksena are the foremost and first revealers of Vaishṇavism to the composers of Pāñcarātra literature. The Tantras belong to the Śakti cult. They glorify Śakti (energy) aspect of God and prescribe numerous courses of ritualistic worship of the Divine Mother in various forms. The texts are actually in the form of dialogues between Śiva and Pārvatī. The authors are believed to have been inspired by Śakti, the creative power of Lord Śiva.

---

6 The sectarian scriptures are known simply as Āgamas or Tantras; these two names are used indiscriminately; they belong to the three main sects of Śaivism, Vaishṇavism and Śaktism. Generally they are arranged in four parts: they deal with theological beliefs, meditative exercises, the building of temples and making of images, and their use in worship, and finally conduct.

7 A fourth sect called Smārtas consists of worshippers who do not belong to the Śaivas or Vaishṇavas or Śaktas nor do they follow their sectarian scripture but who follow the ancient traditions (Smṛtis) and worship all the gods without any exclusive preference to one or the other.

The relation between the general revealed texts such as the Vedas and the special texts such as the Āgamas, the Saṁhitās, and the Tantras are explained thus in the sectarian Hinduism. The Śaivas explain the relation between the Vedas and the Āgamas as one of transition from the general revelation to the special.[8] No Āgama that goes again t the Vedas will be acceptable to the Śaivas. Śrīkaṇṭha Śivacarya held that there was no difference between the Vedas and the Āgamas (*na vayam vedaśivāgamayor bhedaṁ paśyāmaḥ*) and that the Vedas may properly be called Śiva Āgamas, as revealed by, or as having come down (*āgama*) from, Śiva.[9] While the Vedas are general and meant for all, the Āgamas are special and revealed for the benefit of the blessed and they contain the essential truths of the Vedas and the Vedānta, as remarks Aru%onanti Śivacarya.[10]

The Vaishṇavas look upon the Veda including the Upanishads and the Bhagavad-gītā as the main revelation śruti, while Smṛti, Itihāsa and Purāṇa and the Saṁhitās are referred to as exegetical or expository literature, illustrative of the great truths embodied in the Veda and the Upanishads.[11] While Veda is impersonal (*apauruṣeya*) the rest are personal (*pauruṣeya*); but the *pauruṣeya* character of these will no way lessen their importance and authoritative character in so far as they have emanated from inspired seers like Parāsara, Vyāsa and Vālmīki. Yamunācārya, a predecessor of Rāmānuja wrote a work Āgama Pramāṇya in order to establish the authenticity of Pāñcarātra Saṁhitās as scripture.

The Śaktas admit four classes of sacred scriptures (śāstras). (1) Śruti which commonly includes the four Vedas and the Upanishads; (2) Smṛti such as the Dharma Śāstra of Manu and other works on family and social duty, which prescribe *pravrtti-dharma*, while the Upanishads have revealed the *nirvṛtti-dharma*; (3) The

8 For instance, Tirumūlar says: The Vedas and the Āgamas are both true and both are the word of God. The first is a general treatise and the second a special one. When examined and where difference is perceived by some between the Vedānta and the Siddhānta, the wise will perceive no such difference." See the *Tirumantiram*, n. 2358, Śaiva Siddhanta Society Edition.

9 See his *Brahmāsūtra* Bhāṣya 2.2.38.

10 See his *Śivañāna Cittiyār,* Cupakkam, 8.15.

11 On Vaishṇava sctiptute see F. OTTO SCHRADER, *Introduction to the Pāñcarātra and the Abirbudhnya Sambitā,* Adyar Library, Adyar, 1916, especially pp. 1-26.

Purāṇas, of which eighteen are regarded as principal; (4) the Tantras. The Veda is the root of all Śāstras (*mūla-Śāstra*); all others are based on it. The Tantra is spoken of as the fifth Veda. According to Kulluka-Bhaṭṭa, Śruti is of two kinds: Vaidik and Tantrik (*vaitikī-tāntrikī chaiva dvi-vidhā śrutikīrttitā*). The various śāstras are different presentiments of śruti appropriate to the humanity of the age (*yuga*) for which they are given. Hence the Tantra is that presentiment of śruti which is modelled as regards its ritual to suit the need of the kind of men that are found in the Kali-yuga.[12]

We can say that as far as Hinduism is concerned the inspired sages of the Veda (in the comprehensive sense of the four Vedas, the Brāhmaṇas, the Āraṇyakas, the Upanishads and the Bhagavadgītā), of the Śaivāgamas, of the Vaishṇava Pāñcarātras and of the Śakta Tantras are considered to be the founders of the various religious traditions within Hinduism itself. The authors of the Smṛti texts are held in great veneration but come next in merit with regard to the foundation of the Hindu belief and practice.

1. Terminology

The Sanskrit equivalents for "founder" reveal certain meanings that are interesting to know when we deal with the subject of religious foundation. Although we should not be satisfied with the dictionary meanings, still they help us determine the more accurate terms and meanings when we speak of the religious founders.[13]

Sthāpakaḥ has the meaning of "causing to stand, placing, fixing, the erector of an image, an establisher". Prathamasthāpakaḥ would be the principal establisher or erector. Saṁsthāpakaḥ and Pratisthāpakaḥ have the same meaning.

12 See ARTHUR AVALON, *Tantra of the Great Liberation,* Dover Publication, New York, 1972, pp. xlix f.

13 I have made use of the following standard dictionaries in the analysis of the Sanskrit terms: MONIER MONIER-WILLIAMS, *A Sanskrit-English Dictionary,* The Clarendon Press, Oxford, 1964 (reprint); Idem, *English-Sanskrit Dictionary,* Munshiram Manoharlal Publishers, New Delhi, 1976 (Indian Edition); VAMAN SHIVRAM APTE, *The Student's Sanskrit-English Dictionary,* Motilal Banarsidass, Delhi, 1965; Idem, *The Student's English-Sanskrit Dictionary,* Motilal Banarsidass, Delhi, 1972.

Nirmmāti means "one who builds, creates, produces". Nirmāṇa has the sense of "measuring, forming, creating, making".

Ādikarttāḥ or Ādikartṛi signifies "the creator", ādikara meaning "the first maker", "the prime producer".

Ārambhakaḥ connotes "causing to begin or commence". Hence it means any initiator or stimulator or animator of a movement.

Pravarttakaḥ has the sense of "one who acts, proceedes, sets in motion; founder, author, originator of anything".

Prayojakaḥ has the meaning of "causing, effecting, leading to, prompting, instigating"; hence instigator, promoter, author, composer, a founder or institutor of any ceremony.

Pravarttakācāryaḥ is mentioned by Monier-Williams as signifying "the founder of a religion". Ācārya simply means "one who knows or teaches the *ācāra* "rules"; a special guide or teacher; especially the one who invests the student with the sacrificial thread and instructs him in the Vedas, in the law of sacrifice and religious mysteries. More generally one who propounds a particular doctrine, a spiritual guide or preceptor.

As a general rule, *ācārya*, meaning "a teacher, a preceptor" is not necessarily founder of a religion or even of a sect, if we depend strictly on the real meaning of the term. There are founders who are at the same time teachers or preceptors but not necessarily all teachers or preceptors are founders. Another important term is *muni* which signifies "any one who is moved by inward impulse, an inspired or ecstatic person, an enthusiast"; hence it denotes also a saint, a seer, ascetic, monk, sage, devotee, hermit, especially the one who has taken the vow of silence. A religious founder may also be a muni but not necessarily all munis are founders.

We can speak of two classes of "founders" in the context of Hinduism: the sages who composed the sacred revealed texts, generally called *ṛṣis;* the *avatārs,* especially Krishṇa and Rāma, in Vaishṇavism; lastly, the Śiva-gurus who embody Śiva himself and teach Śaiva religion. We know from the Hindu tradition that Vaishṇavas believe that the Supreme God assumes the form of *avatārs* to bring home to mankind the facts and features of true religion affirmed in the comprehensive concept of *dharma*. The purpose of the divine *avatāra* is not only the protection of the good and the destruction of the wicked; but their real purpose was to rectify the spiritual disequilibrium of the cosmos by establishing among men the reign of righteousness. The establishment of *dharma* (*dharma-samsthapana*), more than the protection of the good (*sādhuparithrana*) or destruction of the evil-doers (*duṣṭanigraha*) has determined the scope of the periodical *avatārs* of God. The record of what the *avatārs* said and did constitutes what is foundational in the religious sect , since by *avatārs* God's will is made manifest and the religious man has to follow and realize in him what the *avatārs* said and did.

2. Ṛṣis, the inspired seers

Ṛṣi is a singer of sacred hymns, an inspired poet or sage; any person who alone or with others invokes the deities in rythmic speech or song of a sacred character. These are the inspired poets or sages to whom the hymns of the Vedas were revealed, and under whose names they stand. They came from well-known families but advanced in spiritual power through personal efforts; they were not confined to any one place but wandered in woods, hills, to practise asceticism and religious life in order to enhance their sacred character. They are the seers of truths recorded in the Vedas. The Vedas are believed to derive from a "hearing" (*śruti*), i.e., a revelation; they are held to have emanated from Brahman, to have been "breathed" by God in the form of "words", while their human authors, the *ṛṣis* or inspired sages, did no more than receive them by direct "vision"

Tradition has handed down the names of the reputed authors or the inspired seers (*ṛṣis*) of most of the hymns of the Ṛig Veda:[14]

> Maṇḍalas 2-7 are ascribed to different families of *ṛṣis*; whence are usually called the six "family" books.

14 See ADOLF KAEGI, *The Ṛig Veda: The oldest Literature of the Indians*, Tr. Ginn and Company, Boston, 1886, pp. 21, 79, 80; especially note 73.

Maṇḍala 2 is ascribed to the Bhārgavas, whose principal poet is Gṛtsamada.
Maṇḍala 3 is asctibed to the Viśvāmitras or Kuśikas.
Maṇḍala 4 is ascribed to the Gautamas, whose principal poet is Vāmadeva.
Maṇḍala 5 is ascribed to the Ātreyas.
Maṇḍala 6 is ascribed to the Bhāradvājas.
Maṇḍala 7 is ascribed to the Vāsiṣṭhas.
Portions of Maṇḍalas 1, 8, 9, 10 are ascribed to the Āngirasas.
Portions of Maṇḍalas 1, 8, 9 are ascribed to the Kāṇvas.

The epithets used in the Vedic texts themselves to indicate the composers of the Vedic hymns, past and present, and the sages who instituted the Vedic rites of worship and those who continue to conduct these rites, are the following: *ṛṣi* (seer), *kavi* (wise, poet in laser Sanskrit), *medhavin* (intelligent), *vipra* (wise, a Brahman in later Sanskrit), *vipaschit* (learned), *vedhas* (wise), *dirghaśrut* (a man who has heard much), *muni* (one moved by inward impulse, a sage in modem Sanskrit). The Böhtlingk and Roth's Lexicon defines the *ṛṣis* as "persons who, whether singly or in chorus, either on their own behalf or on behalf of others, invoked the gods in artificial language, and in song"; and the word is said to denote especially "the priestly bards who made this art their profession".

The *ṛṣis* are in some cases mentioned in the Ṛig Vedic hymns themselves. The name of the author may have been read into some word or other occuring in the verse. In any case these names tell us nothing about the personality they refer to. We can safely say that they are a body of priest-bards attached to a princely family; the Ṛig Vedic hymns are a collection or at least a selection from their works.

The later generation of the Hindus regarded the *ṛṣis* as patriarchal sages, occupying the same position in Indian history as the heroes and patriarchs of other countries. They constitute a peculiar class of beings in the early mythical system as distinct from gods, men and asuras, etc. They are the inspired sages to whom revelation has been made directly. So to say, an expression as "The *Ṛṣi* says" is equivalent of "So it stands in the sacred texts".

The Hindu tradition says that the Vedas had been produced

by the Creator God Brahmā from his different mouths or by the intervention of the Gāyatṛi, or to have sprung from the Goddess Śarasvatī. *Manusmṛti* says:

> "He (Brahmā) in the beginning fashioned from the words of the Veda the names, functions, and conditions of all (creatures). That Lord also created the subtle order of active and living deities, and of Sadhvas, and eternal sacrifice. And in order to the performance of sacrifice, he drew forth from fire, from air, and from the sun, the triple eternal Veda, distinguished as Ṛik, Yajush, and Sāman".[15]

Vishṇu Purāṇa expresses the same idea thus:

> "In the beginning he (Brahmā) ordained, from the words of the Veda, the names, forms, and functions of the gods and other creatures. He also assigned the names and the respective offices of all the ṛishis, as handed down by the Vedas».[16]

The *Mahābhārata* repeats the similar idea:

> "Through austerity the ṛishis studied the Vedas both day and night. In the beginning wisdom, without beginning or end, divine speech, formed of the Vedas, was sent forth by Svayambhu (the self-existent): from her all activities (are derived). It is from the words of the Veda that the Lord in the beginning frames the names of the ṛishis, the creations

---

15 Manusmṛti 1.21-23:
Sarveṣāntu sa nāmāni karmānica pṛthak pṛthak /
Veda-śabdebhya evādau pṛthak saṁsthāśca nirmame //
Karmātmanāñca devānāṁ so 'sṛjat prāniṇām prabhuḥ /
Sādhyānāñca gaṇaṁ sūkṣmaṁ yajñañcaiva sanātanam //
Agni-vāyu-ravibhyastu trayam brahma sanātanam /
Dudoha yajñasiddhyartham ṛg-yajuḥ-sāma-lakṣaṇam. //

16 Vishṇu Purāṇa 1.5.58 ff.:
Nāma rūpanca bhūtānāṁ kṛtyānāñca pravarttanam /
Veda-śabdebhya evādau devādīnāṁ cakāra saḥ //
Rśīṇāṁ nāmadheyāni yathā-veda-śrutāni vai /
Yathā-niyoga-yogyāni sarveṣām api so'karot. //

which are (recorded) in the Vedas, the various forms of beings, and species of works".[17]

The *Bhāgavata Purāṇa* narrates that the Vedas are said to have been created by the four-faced Brahmā from his several mouths:

> "Once the Vedas sprang from the four-faced creator, as he was meditating "how shall I create the aggregate worlds as before?"... He formed from his eastern and other mouths the Vedas called Ṛik, Yajush, Sāman, and Atharvan, together with praise, sacrifice, hymns, and expiation".[18]

According to the *Bṛhadāraṇyaka Upanishad*, the Vedas as well as other scriptures are the breath of Brahmā:

> "As clouds of smoke surge up in all directions from a fire kindled from damp fuel, so too, I say, was this (whole universe) breathed forth from that great Being (*bhūta*), – Ṛig Veda, Yajur Veda, Sāma Veda, the Atharva Veda, (the hymns of) the Aṅgirasas, the collection of stories (*itihāsa*), the ancient tales (*purāṇas*), wisdom (*vidyā*), the secret doctrines (*upaniṣad*), the verses (*śloka*), aphorisms (*sūtra*), commentaries and commentaries on commentaries, – all these were breathed forth from it".[19]

The above passage is rather strange because the Vedas are classed in the same category as the other works such as sūtras and

---

17 Mahābhārata 12.232:
Ṛṣayas tapasā vedān adhyaiṣanta divāniśam /
Anādinidhanā vidyā vāg utsṛṣṭā svayambhuvā //
Adau vedamayī divyā yataḥ sarvah pravṛttayaḥ /
Ṛśīṇāṁ nāmadheyāni yāśca vedeṣu sṛṣṭayaḥ. //
Nānārūpañca bhūtānām karmaṇāñca pravarttayan /
Vedaśabdebhya evādau nirmimīte sa īśvaraḥ. //

18 Bhāgavata Purāṇa 3.12.34 and 37 ff.:
Kadācit dhyāyataḥ sraṣṭur vedā āsaṁś caturmukhāt /
Kathaṁ srakṣyāmyahaṁ lokān samavetān yathā purā //
....
Ṛg-yajuḥ-sāmātharvākhyān vedān pūrvādibhir mukhaiḥ /
Śāstram ijyāṁ stutistomam prāyaścittam vyadhāt kramāt. //

19 Bṛhadāraṇyaka Upanishad 2.4.10.

bhāṣyas whereas the later writers clearly distinguish between the Vedas (including the Brāhmaṇas, Āraṇyakas and the Upanishads) which are of superhuman origin (*apauruṣeya*) and the other works which are represented as *pauruṣeya* (merely human composition). The Mahābhārata speaks of the Goddess Śarasvatī as the mother of the Vedas: "Behold Śarasvatī, mother of the Vedas, abiding in me".[20] In the *Vishṇu Purāṇa* we have the following assertion of the eternity of the Veda: "The Śruti (Veda) derived from Prajāpati (Brahmā) is eternal: these (the Sākhas), O Brahman, are only its modification".[21]

Having shown the supernatural origin of the Veda, we have to explain in what manner the *ṛṣis,* the ackowledged utterers of the hymns, should be considered as authors of these hymns. Indian writers have always maintained that the *ṛṣis* were merely seers of the pre-existing sacred texts. The ṛṣis did not compose but only saw the hymns and other parts of the Vedas which had in reality pre-existed from eternity. It is said:

> "These ṛishis were seers of things beyond the reach of the bodily senses. The fact of their seeing the Vedas is recorded in the Smṛti: "The great ṛishis, empowered by Svayambhu, formerly obtained, through austerity, the Vedas and the Itihāsas which had disappeared at the end of the (preceding) yuga".[22]

---

20 Mahābhārata 12.331:

Vedānām mātaraṁ paśya matsthām devīṁ sarasvatīm.

21 Vishṇu Purāṇa 3.6:

Iti śakhāḥ prasaṇkhyātāḥ śākhābhedās tathaiva ca /
Karttāraścaiva śākhānām bhedahetus tathoditaḥ //
Sarvamanvantareṣveva śākhābhedāḥ samāḥ smṛtāḥ /
Prājāpatyā śrutir nityā tadvikalpās tv ime dvija. //

22 Vedārtha Prakāsa on the Taittirīya Samhitā: Atīdriyārtha-draṣṭāra ṛṣayaḥ / Teṣāṁ vedadraṣṭṛtvaṁ smaryate // Yugānte 'ntarhitān vedān setihāsān maharṣayaḥ // Lebhire tapasā pūrvam anujñātāḥ svayambhuvā. //

Manusmṛti in a similar vein affirms:

> "Prajāpati created this Śāstra (the Institutes of Manu) by austerity and by austerity did the *ṛṣis* obtain the Vedas".[23]

We can resume the view of the Hindus with respect to the different Śāstras thus: they clearly draw a distinction between the Vedas and other Śāstras; the former is considered to be infallible and to possess an independent authority; while the latter derive their authority from the Veda alone, and in theory are infallible guides only in so far as they coincide with the Veda. All the Śāstras other than the Vedas are of human origin; nevertheless they possess authority, as being founded on the Veda. It is true that the Indian tradition does point to certain *ṛṣis* as the authors of the Vedic hymns; but these *ṛṣis* are said to have only seen the hymns which were eternally preexistent and in this sense they were not their authors. The whole character of the compositions of the hymns and the circumstances in which they appear to have arisen indicate clearly that these *ṛṣis* though assisted by the superhuman, divine power were expressing their own personal hopes and feelings. But this does not mean to say that the hymns were ordinary productions of the *ṛṣis'* own minds, for this would be contrary to the expression "seeing" which is applied to the mental act by which the hymns were created. The *ṛṣis* are said to have had an intuitive insight into truths contained in the Vedas.

There are many passages in the Ṛig Veda which either expressly or in indirect reference speak of contemporary *ṛṣis* as distinct from the ancient ones. This recognition of the succession of *ṛṣis* really constitutes one of the historical elements in the Veda; the *ṛṣis* themselves acknowledge that there existed before them persons who were the composers of the hymns; this only shows that the ṛṣis were historical persons even though some of them belonged to the distant antiquity. "Agni who is worthy to be celebrated by former, as well as modern, *ṛṣis,* will bring the gods hither".[24]

---

23 Manusmṛti:
Prajāpatir idam śastraṁ tapasaivāsṛjat prabhuḥ
Tathaiva vedān ṛṣayas tapasā pratipedire.

24 Ṛig Veda 1.1.2: Agniḥ purvebhir ṛṣibhir īḍyo nūtanair uta sa devān eha vakṣati.

"The former *ṛṣis* who invoked thee for succour".[25] "In the ceremony (or hymn) which Atharvan, or our father Manu, or Dadhyanch performed, the prayers and praises were, as of old, congregated in that Indra..."[26]. The ancient *ṛṣis* were Bhṛigu, Aṅgiras, and others who are not named in a special way; in some places we find the names of Atharvan, Manu, Dadhyanch.

Bhṛgu is the name of one of the chief Brahmanical families of ancient times, to which the Aitasayanas are said to belong. It is also the name of a *ṛṣi* regarded as the ancestor of the Bhṛgus. He is enumerated among the ten mahaṛṣis created by the first Manu.[27]

Aṅgiras is considered as one of the seven, *ṛṣis* of the first manvantara, as a Prajāpati, as a teacher of the Brahmavidyā, which he had learned from Satyavaha, a descendant of Bharadvāja.

Atharvan is the name of the priest who is said to have been the first to institute the worship of fire and offer Soma and prayers; he is represented as a Prajāpati, as Brahmā's eldest son, as the first learner and earliest teacher of the Brahmā-vidyā, as the author of the Atharva Veda.

Dadhyanch is the name of an ancient *ṛṣi* or sacrificer.

Manu is regarded in the Ṛig Veda as the first to have instituted sacrifices and religious ceremonies, and associated with *ṛṣis* Kanva and Atri. The name Manu is especially applied to forteen successive mythical progenitors and sovreigns of the earth, as creating and supporting this world through successive long periods of time (*manvantara*). The first Manu is called Svayambhu, a sort of secondary creator who produced ten Prajāpatis or Mahaṛṣis, of whom the first was Marīci; to this Manu is ascribed the Manusmṛti, Kalpa and Gṛhya Sūtras (sacrificial and domestic rites). The seventh Manu is regarded as the progenitor of the present race of living beings, and is said to have been preserved from a great flood by Vishṇu in the form of a fish; he is also described as one of the Ādityas and as author of some of the Vedic hymns.

---

25 Ibidem 1.48.14: Ye cid hi tvām ṛṣayaḥ pūrve ūtaye juhūre ityādi.

26 Ibidem 1.80.16:
Yām atharvā manuṣ pitā dadhyaṇ dhitam atnata
Tasmin brahmāṇi pūrvathā indre ukthā samagmata ityādi.

27 Manusmṛti 1.35.

The *ṛṣis* refer to themselves as the authors of the Vedic hymns besides the fact that they are proved to have been the real authors of the hymns by the content itself of the hymns. For numerous events which had occurred in time are unquestionably mentioned in the Vedas. The *ṛṣis* describe themselves as the makers, fabricators, or generators of the hymns.

> "This hymn, conferring wealth, has been made to the divine race, by the sages, with their mouth (or, in presence of the gods)".[28] "Grow, O Agni, by this prayer which we have made to thee through our power, or our knowledge".[29]
> "Thus have we made a prayer for Indra, the productive, the vigorous, as the Bhṛgus (fashioned) a car ... A new prayer has been made for thee, O Lord of steeds. May we, through our hymn (or rite) become possessed of chariots and perpetual wealth".[30]

The *ṛṣis* appear to have imagined themselves to be inspired by the gods in the expression of their religious emotions and ideas. They speak of supernatural attributes attaching either to themselves or to their composition. A superhuman character or supernatural faculties are attributed to the earlier *ṛṣis*. There are also passages in the Ṛig Veda where it is said that the praises and ceremonies of the *ṛṣis* were suggested or directed by the gods in general, or by the goddess of speech in particular. The ancient seers are represented by the group of seven seers. They are called divine and are associated with the gods:

> "They who were versed in ritual and metre, in hymns and rules, were the seven God-like *ṛṣis*. Viewing the path of those of old, the sages have taken up the reins like chariot-drivers".[31]

The knowledge of the ritual is derived from the divine priests; the sages or *ṛṣis* have followed them in sacrificing.

---

28 Ṛig Veda 1.20.1.
29 Ibidem 1.31.18.
30 Ibidem 4.16.20-21.
31 Ibidem 10.130.7.

> "Thus spake of her those gods of old, seven *ṛṣis* who sate them down to their austere devotion...".[32]

The earlier *ṛṣis* are credited with supernatural power:

> "The pious sages who lived of old, and who conversed about sacred truths with the gods, led a conjugal life..."[33].
> "The *ṛṣis* are various in character, profound in emotion; they are the sons of Aṅgiras; they have been born from Agni"[34].
> "And Vasiṣṭha, thou art the son of Mitra and Varuṇa, born, O priest, from the mind of Ūrvasi ... Born at the sacrifice, and impelled by adorations, they (Mitra and Varuṇa) let the same procreative energy fall into the jar; from the midst of this Mana (Agastya) issued forth; from this men say the *ṛṣi* Vasiṣṭha was produced"[35].

Certain passages clearly indicate a certain mysterious knowledge possessed by the *ṛṣis*. For example,

> "A wise *ṛṣi*, a leader of men, skilful, and prudent, is Usanas, through his insight as a seer; he has known the hidden mysterious name applied to these cows".[36]

However we have to admit that the *ṛṣis* did not appear to have had clear and definite ideas of inspiration, although they appear to have been conscious of divine assistance or at least implored it while composing the hymns. That the hymns as prayers possessed a certain efficacy which iṣ supernatural, and which is more than what is due to the efficacy of ordinary prayers addressed to the gods no one can call into question. But the idea of divine inspiration which the *ṛṣis* had in their composition of the hymns is very vague and far distant from that of the later Hindu believers with regard to the supernatural origin and authority of the Vedas. The gods like Agni, Indra, Varuṇa who were supposed to have inspired

32 Ibidem 10.109.4
33 Ibidem 1.179.2.
34 Ibidem 10.62.5.
35 Ibidem 7.33.11 ff.
36 Ibidem 9.87.3.

the *ṛṣis* disappeared in the Hindu pantheon in later Hinduism. The only deity who is said in the Ṛig Veda to be the source of illumination and who is identified with the Supreme Brahman in later Hinduism is Vāk or Śarasvatī. "By Speech, O monarch, Brahman is known. Speech is the Supreme Brahman"[37].

The teaching of the Upanishads on the origin of the Veda is expressed in two tendencies: non-dualist and theist. The earlier Upanishads especially emphasize the non-dualist trend as follows:

The *Bṛhadāraṇyaka Upanishad* teaches that as from a fire laid with damp fuel, clouds of smoke separately issue forth, so from the great Being (*Bhūta*) has been breathed forth that which is Ṛig Veda, Yajur Veda, Sāma Veda, hymns of the Atharvans, and Aṅgirases, Upanishads[38]. The *Maitri Upanishad* is very clear in its affirmation of the origin of all scriptures from the All-One:

> "From this indeed do all living things, all worlds, all the Vedas, all the gods and all contingent beings issue forth, (though it abides ever) in itself. Its secret meaning (*upanisad*) is: The real of the real"[39].

The Veda then originated from or rather is identified with the Absolute Brahman. The theist trend explains that the Vedas proceed from God:

> "He who alone presides over every place of production, over all forms, and all sources of birth, who formerly nourished with various knowledge that *ṛṣi* Kapila, who had becn born, and beheld him at his birth".[40]
>
> "By the power of austerity, and by the grace of the Veda, the wise Śvetāsvatara declared perfectly to the men in the highest of the four orders, the supreme and holy Brahman, who is sought after by the company of the *ṛṣis*".[41]
>
> "This (doctrine) Brahmā declared to Prajāpati, Prajāpati declared it to Manu, and Manu to his descendents. Having re-

37 Bṛhādiraṇyaka Upanishad 4.1.2.

38 Ibidem 4.5.11.

39 6.32.

40 Śvetāsvatara Upanishad 5.2.

41 Ibidem 6.21.

ceived instruction in the Veda from the family of his religious teacher in the prescribed manner, and in the time which remains after performing his duty to his preceptor; and when he has ceased from this, continuing his religious studies at home, in his family, in a pure spot, communicating a knowledge of duty (to young men)... a man attains to the world of Brahmā...".[42]

What is the teaching of the Upanishads themselves with respect to the sources from which the true knowledge of Brahman is to be derived? Bṛhadāranya Upanishad[43] asserts that like all natural phenomena, the products of the mind also throughout the universe are derived from Brahman. The sacred texts (including the Smṛti) are explained as Speech (Vāk)[44]; but the existimg Vedic lore is insufficient to obtain the true knowledge which is taught only in the Upanishads[45]. The Veda and the Upanishads with them are regarded as sources of the highest knowledge. If the Veda is explained to be nectar, the Upanishads are the nectar of the nectar[46].

The *Bhagavad-gītā* speaks of seven great *ṛṣis*[47], the chief of whom is Bhṛgu[48]. They are at times identified with the Prajāpatis (progenitors of the human race), and the "mind-born sons of Brahmā". The title Prajāpati is given to Manu Svayambhu as the son of Brahmā and as the secondary creator of the ten *ṛṣis* who are called "mind-born-sons" of Brahmā, from whom mankind has descended. They are Marīci, Atri, Aṅgiras, Pulastya, Pulaha, Kratu, Vasiṣṭha, Pracetas (or Daksha), Bhṛgu and Nārada. Ānandagiri remarks that the maharṣis from Bhṛgu to Vasiṣṭha were omniscient, and were the original teachers of the traditional wisdom. In the *Bhagavad-gītā* Arjuna says:

"Supreme Brahman, Supreme Abode, Supreme Vessel of purity are you. All seers *(ṛṣis)* agree that you are the Person eter-

42 Chāndogya Upanished 8.15.
43 2.4.10.
44 Bṛhadāraṇyaka Upanishad 4.1.2.
45 Chāndogya Upanished 7.1; 6.1.
46 Ibidem 3.5.4.
47 10.6.
48 10.25.

nal and divine, Primeval God, unborn and all-pervading Lord. So too Nārada, the godly seer, Asita, Devala, and Vyāsa (have declared); and You yourself tell me so"[49].

Nārada is a ṛṣi to whom some of the Ṛig Vedic hymns are attributed. He is one of the Prajāpatis and one of the seven great *ṛṣis*. To Vyāsa is attributed the compilation of the Veda in its present form and the authorship of many sacred books such as the Mahābhārata and the Purāṇas. Again Arjuna observes:

"O God, I behold in your body the gods and all the hosts of every kind of being; Brahmā, the lord, throned on the lotusseat, divine serpents and all the (ancient) seers (*ṛṣis*)"[50].

The above passage is set in the account of the tremendous vision in which Arjuna sees the universe in all its variety as Krishṇa's body, all its multiplicity converging onto One. At the beginning of each world-aeon a lotus emerges from the navel of reclining Vishṇu and Brahmā is seated on it. The divine serpents are those who live in Pātāla. Their king is Vāsuki who was used by the gods and asuras for a coil round the mountain Mandara at the churning of the ocean. It is worth noticing that *ṛṣis* are specially mentioned in this vision of Arjuna. The last explicit reference in the *Bhagavad-gītā* is the following: Krishṇa says,

"In many ways has it been sung by seers, in varied hymns each in its separate way, in aphoristic verses concerning Brahman, well reasoned and conclusive"[51].

---

49 10.12-13. *Param brahma* is identified with *akṣaram* (imperishable) in 8.3: *akṣaraṁ brahma paramaṁ*. *Paraṁ dhāma* is identified with the Unmanifest beyond the Unmanifest; the first Unmanifest is the material Nature (*prakṛti*); the second Unmanifest is God; identified also with the imperishable and the highest way; cfr 8.21: *avyakto 'ksara ity uktas; tam āhuḥ paramāṁ gatim... tad dhāma paramaṁ mama*. *Dhāma* can also mean 'light'. The highest vessel of purity; the word *pavitra* is used for knowledge in 4.38. *Puruṣaṁ śāśvataṁ divyam* is identified with the highest person, with the imperishable and the highest way. 8.22. *Ādi-devam:* the Supreme God.

50 Arjuna describes what he sees in the vision he had of Krishṇa. He sees gods in Krishṇa's body; which indicates that other gods together with all other kinds of beings are subordinate to Him. Brahmā the Creator-God is also subordinate to Him.

51 13.4 The *Bhagavad-gītā* tells here that it identifies its own thought with earlier concepts

The context is the discussion about the "field" and the "knower of the field". The field is the body and every thing that derives from material nature. The "knower of the field" is God. What that field is and what it is like, what are its changes and which derives from which, and who the knower of the field is, what his powers are: all these have been declared by the *ṛṣis* in many ways and in hymns, and in the *Brahmā Sūtras*. The *Bhagavad-gītā* traces its doctrine back to the Vedas, hymns sung by the *ṛṣis* and to the Brahmasūtra which probably refers to the doctrine of the later *Brahmasūtra* of Bādarāyana but currently known at the time of the *Bhagavad-gītā*; some take it to mean the Upanishads or the Vedānta as referred to in 15.15. What is to be noted here is that the authority of the *ṛṣis* as forming the foundation of the Hindu revelation is recognized by the *Bhagavad-gītā*, itself being admitted in later Hinduism as a Śruti text. The following verse can be discussed as contrary to the above statement:

"As much use as there is in a tank flooded with water on every side, so much is there in all the Vedas for the Brahman who discerns"[52].

Although the above verse is rather obscure and the commentators have differred among themselves very widely, it can be said that there is no undermining of the Vedas. It can mean, as some hold, that there are certain uses that the enlightened Brahman alone can detect in the Vedas, or as others interpret, that the uses of the Vedas are limited to the aspirants just beginning the way of works (*karma-mārga*), while for the truly enlightened Brahman the utility of the Vedic ritual is comprehended in right knowledge, just as the utility of the tank is comprehended in that of the all-spreading flood of water. The second view is more probable. The Veda is of use just as the tank. But Krishṇa's doctrine is the widely spreading flood. To worship the gods of the Vedas is to worship Krishṇa,

by interpreting them in terms of its own thinking. It is conscious of the traditions that existed in its own time and wishes to be in accord with this tradition while at the same time establishing something new of its own. Thus it makes appeal to the hymns *(chandas)* which were sung *(gītām)* by seers.

52 2.46.

for Krishṇa *is* the gods. It was Krishṇa who made the Upanishads or Vedānta (the end of the Veda), for Krishṇa says:

> "I am the father of this universe, the mother, the ordainer, the grandsire; that which is to be known, and that which purifies; Oṁ; the Ṛig-, Sāma-, and Yajur-Vedas too"[53].

At times Krishṇa in the *Bhagavad-gītā* says that he is the Sāma Veda[54] because that Veda receives special honour in the *Chāndogya Upanishad*[55] as being the essence of the Ṛig Veda, from which nearly all its verses are derived. The fact that its verses are also chanted gives it special value. More specially, Krishṇa says:

> "I make my dwelling in the hearts of all; from me stem memory, wisdom, the dispelling of doubt. Through all the Vedas it is I who should be known, for the maker of the Vedānta am I, and I know the Vedas"[56].

Very significantly Krishṇa describes himself as the maker of the Vedānta, i.e., the Upanishads, the end of the Veda. Hence Krishṇa's teaching in the *Bhagavad-gītā* is an epitome of the essentials of the whole Vedic teaching as contained in the Upanishads; and a knowledge of its teaching leads to the realization of all human aspirations.

So far we have studied the authority of the *ṛṣis* in matters of Hindu revelation or revealed sacred texts. What has the *Mahābhārata*[57] to say on this important subject?

---

53 9.17. Krishṇa is conceived of and worshipped in manifold ways: as father or mother of the universe, for he is the Lord of the universe (9.10); and his lower nature is its womb (9.7-8;14.3). Similarly he may be seen as the ordainer of the universe (8.9: *dhata*). The three Vedas are seen as forms of Krishṇa.

54 10.22.

55 1.1.

56 15.15. Krishṇa says that, having entered into the heart of everyone as the true self (15.7), he is the cause of memory, knowledge, and reasoning. He says that it is about him that the Vedas speak, or he is the one who is known by the study of the Vedas. His interpretation of the Vedas is accurate for ultimately he is the knower of the Vedas and the end of the Veda itself.

57 Mahābhārata 12.166.

Brahmā's creation of the *ṛṣis* is narrated vividly in the Śānti Parvan: Brahmā, assuming a visible form, after creating the wind, fire, the Sun, sky, the heavens, the earth, etc., begot by the power of his will some sons possessed of great energy: they are the sages Marīci[58], Atri[59], Pulastya[60], Pulaha[61], Kratu[62], Vasiṣṭha[63], Aṅgiras[64], and the mighty Rudra[65] and Prachetas[66]. The last begot Daksha[67] who in his turn begot sixty daughters. The sages took all these daughters for the purpose of begetting children upon them, from whom sprang all the creatures of the universe, including gods, pitṛis, gandharvas, apsaras, rākshasas, birds and animals and fishes, and all other beings. Brahmā then promulgated the eternal religion laid down in the Vedas. That religion was accepted by the gods and *ṛṣis* of different kinds, Bhṛgu, Atri, Aṅgiras, Vasiṣṭha, Gautama, Agastya, Nārada, etc. 12.166.

In another story of creation in the same Śānti Parvan we come across interesting details which throw much light on the nature of

58 Marīci: name of one of the Prajāpatis (mind-born sons of Brahmā). He is sometimes represented as springing directly from Brahmā; He was father of Kasyapa, and one of the seven great *ṛṣis*.

59 Atri, a *rsi* and author of many Vedic hymns. In the Epic period he is considered as one of the lords of creation engendered by Manu for the purpose of creating the universe. Later on he appears as one of the Prajāpatis and one of the seven great *Ṛṣis*, who preside over the reign of Swayambhuva. He married Anasuya, daughter of Daksha, and their son was Durvasas.

60 Pulastya is one of the Prajāpatis and one of the great *Ṛṣis*. He was the medium through which some of the Purāṇas were transmitted to man. Brahmā communicated the Vishṇu Puràna to him who passed it on to Parāsara who promulgated it to the whole mankind.

61 Pulaha is also one of the great *ṛṣis* and prajāpatis. Married to Kṣama, he had three sons by her.

62 Kratu is also reckoned among the great *ṛṣis* and prajāpatis.

63 Vasiṣṭha, a celebrated Vedic sage to whom many Vedic hymns are ascribed. There arose a special rivalry between him and the sage Visvāmitra, who raised himself from the state of kshatriya to that of the brāhman. He possessed the cow of plenty called Nandinī which was able to grant him all that he desired; hence his name Vasiṣṭha.

64 Aṅgiras, a *rsi* to whom many hymns are assigned as author of them. He was one of the great *ṛṣis* and in later times was one of the inspired law-givers and also a writer on astronomy.

65 In the Vishṇu Purāṇa the god Rudra is said to have sprung from the forehead of Brahmā and to have separated his nature into male and female.

66 One of the Prajāpatis; an ancient sage and law-giver; the ten Prachetas are said to be the progenitors of mankind.

67 Daksha is a son of Brahmā, one of the Prajāpatis, and sometimes is regarded as their chief.

the vision of the *ṛṣis* in their perception of the eternal truths of revelation: "Those whose vision is directed to truth regard Brahmā as the cause. Penance is the highest good for living creatures. The roots of penance are tranquillity and self-restraint. By penance one obtains all things that one wishes for in one's mind. By penance one attains to that Being who creates the universe. He who (by penance) succeeds in attaining to that Being becomes the puissant master of all beings. It is by penance that the *ṛṣis* are enabled to read the Vedas ceaselessly. At the outset the Self-born caused those excellent Vedic sounds, that are embodiments of knowledge and that have neither beginning nor end to (spring up and) flow on (from preceptor to disciple). From those sounds have sprung all kinds of actions, the names of the *ṛṣis,* all things that have been created, the varieties of form seen in existent things, and the course of actions, have their origin in the Vedas[68]. Indeed, the Supreme Master of all beings, in the beginning created all things from the words of the Vedas. Truly the names of the *ṛṣis,* and all else that has been created, occur in the Vedas. Upon the expiration of his night (i.e., at the dawn of his day), the uncreated Brahmā creates from prototypes that existed before, all things which are of course well-made by him. In the Vedas hath been indicated the topic of the soul's emancipation, along with the ten means constituted by study of the Vedas, adoption of the domestic mode of life, penances, observance of duties common to all the modes of life, sacrifices, performance of all such acts as lead to pure fame, meditation which is of three kinds, and that kind of emancipation which is called success (*siddhi*) attainable in this life. This incomprehensible Brahman which has been declared in the words of the Vedas, and which has been indicated more clearly in the Upanishads by those who have an insight into the Vedas, can be realised by gradually following the practices referred to above. Unto a person who thinks he has a body, this consciousness of duality, fraught again with that of pairs of opposites, is born only of acts in which he is engaged. That person however who has attained to emancipation, aided by his

68 It appears that what the author intends to say by this statement is that the Vedas are Speech or Words, and the Creator has to utter words symbolizing his ideas before creating anything. Since the Vedas represent the words of Brahmā, all modes of life with the duties of each and the modes of worship are also included in his creative act.

knowledge, forcibly drives off that consciousness of duality. Two Brahmans should be known, viz., the Brahman represented by sound (i.e., the Vedas), and secondly that which is beyond the Vedas and is supreme. One that is conversant with Brahman represented by sound succeeds in attaining to Brahman that is Supreme".[69] Those whose vision is directed to truth are those who depend upon the really existent, and these regard Brahmā as the sole cause of the production of all effects. As the Vedas are speech or Words, the creator had to utter words which symbolize his ideas before creating anything. Brahman is twofold: Śabda Brahman and Parā Brahman. The Vedas are Śabda Brahman. The Supreme Brahman is Parā Brahman. One who is well-versed in Śabda Brahman knows Parā Brahman[70]. God created Logos, reason (*vidyā*) or word (*Vāk*), which is without origin or end. The Vedas sprang out of Logos. God is their creator[71]. The word for penance is *tapas* which originally means "heat, fervour" but can be best translated as asceticism. In cosmogonic context it can suggest the creative warmth that is symbolized by brooding over eggs; the idea of a cosmic egg out of which the world comes out is common in the early sacred writings. In the religious context the word means religious, devotional fervour, the inspiration of priests and hence is related to Brahman, the holy word. Hence the term occurs in the meaning of cosmic force, as the first principle; the creator god exercises *tapas* in creating the world. In the period of the Upanishads the term acquires the meaning of asceticism in the context of *Sannyāsa* (renunciation) and meditation which help in the search for higher knowledge.

3. Śrī Krishṇa

Śrī Krishṇa is not only the Supreme God, the object of worship and religious experience, of the Vaishṇava sect, called Krishṇaism but is considered as its "founder".

The historical Krishṇa was born in the Vṛṣṇi branch of the Sātvata family of the Yādava tribe. The Yādavas are descendants of

69 Mahābhārata 12.232.

70 Ibidem 12.270.1-2.

71 Ibidem 12.232.24-26.

an eponymous ancestor Yadu; among their clans were the Sātvatas who worshipped Vāsudeva, eternal, beneficient and loving. The Ṛig Veda refers to the family of the Yadus. The Sātvatas are the original worshippers of Vāsudeva (*vāsudevakas*) and hence we can presume that Krishṇa himself was originally the worshipper of Vāsudeva. Krishṇa was undoubtedly a powerful chief of the Yādava tribe, who were probably Rajputs occupying the region of Central India, south of Mathura. The real date of his birth cannot be fixed with any certainty.

The Vedic tradition refers to Krishṇa as one of the Vedic seers (*ṛṣis*) who is said to be the composer of the Ṛig Veda hymn 8.74:

> "Here Krishṇa is invoking you, O Asvins, Lords of ample wealth, to drink the savoury Soma juice.
> Listen, heroes, to the singer's call, the call of Krishṇa lauding you, to drink the savoury Soma juice"[72].

The Anukramaṇi, a table of contents, index to a collection of Vedic hymns, calls him an Aṅgirasa or descendant of Aṅgiras. The Aṅgirasas are sons of heaven, seers (ṛṣis) who are sons of gods; they are also in a general way connected with other groups of divine beings like the Ādityas, Vasus, Maruts. The *Kauśitaki Brāhmaṇa*[73] contains an allusion to Krishṇa:

> "The conclusion day by day is by Krishṇa; Krishṇa Aṅgirasa saw this third pressing for the Brahmanacchansin's office; thereby day by day the conclusion is by Krishṇa".

This belongs to the litany of the Hotrakas at the third pressing in the Soma sacrifice. Krishṇa Aṅgirasa is represented as having seen the evening libation in its connection with the Brahmanacchansin priest.

A later Krishṇa, son of a mother Devakī, appears as pupil of a sage called Ghora. The *Chāndogya Upanishad* says:

> "Ghora, the descendant of Aṅgiras, having declared this (the preceding mystical doctrine) to Krishṇa, the son of Devakī,

72 Verses 3-4.
73 30.9

said to him that (which when he heard), he became free from thirst (i.e., desire), viz.: 'let a man at the time of his death have recourse to these three thoughts, "You are the undecaying[74], you are the imperishable[75], you are the subtle principle of breath".[76]

As the commentator on this verse explains, a person, Ghora by name, and an Aṅgirasa by family, declared the doctrine of sacrifice to Krishṇa, the son of Devakī. Having heard this doctrine Krishṇa became free from desire for any other kind of knowledge. In this way he praised the knowledge of the Purusha sacrifice by saying that it was so distinguished that it destroyed all thirst in Krishṇa for any other knowledge[77].

Now in the great Epic (the Mahābhārata) Krishṇa is represented as the son of Vāsudeva and Devakī. He certainly is not the hero of this epic. He appears merely as a powerful chief who sides with the real heroes; namely, the Pāṇḍavas. His claims to divine rank are often disputed during the development of the story of his life. In the various parts of the Epic Krishṇa is represented in many different ways. Krishṇa appears merely as human in some parts (the oldest portions); in some others, as a demigod; in others as the tribal deity of the Yādavas; in others (especially in the Bhagavad-gītā) as the Supreme God, identified with Vishṇu.

Krishṇa as man was Arjuna's cousin, since Vāsudeva was the brother of Kuntī, wife of Pāṇḍu. Hence Krishṇa was cousin of the sons of Pāṇḍu, brother of Dhṛita-rāshtra, representing two kshatrya races contending for supremacy. Though Krishṇa refused to take arms on either side, he consented to act as Arjuna's charioteer. He had an elder brother Balarāma or Samkarsana. Vāsudeva, Krishṇa's father had two wives, Rohinī and Devakī. The latter had eight sons of whom the eighth was Krishṇa. It was predicted that one of the eight would kill Kaṁsa, the king of Mathura and cousin of Devakī. Kaṁsa not only imprisoned Vāsudeva and Devakī but also killed their first six children. Balarāma the seventh child was abstracted

74 *Akṣita.*
75 *Acyuta*
76 3.17.6.
77 See J. Muir, Original Sanskrit Text, Vol. IV, London, 1973, p. 184.

from Devakī's womb and transferred to that of Rohinī and was thus saved. As soon as Krishṇa was born, Vāsudeva escaped from Mathura with the child and found a herdsman, Nanda, whose wife had lately given birth to a child. He entrusted Krishṇa to his care. Nanda settled first in Gokula and then in Vrindāvana, where Balarāma and Krishṇa grew up. Krishṇa is portrayed as sporting with gopīs, wives and daughters of cowherds, the most favourite of him being Rādhā. Krishṇa killed Kaṁsa and transported the inhabitants from Mathura to Dvāraka. Krishṇa is reputed to have worked many miracles to give proof of his divine origin.

Krishṇa was a demigod chieftain who receives invulnerability and other boons as gifts of gods. As the *Mahābhārata* says:

> "Krishṇa has been obtained by me (Arjuna) for the destruction of those wicked ones. I see the hand of the gods in all this. The person whose success is only wished for by Krishṇa, without the latter's actually taking up arms in his behalf, is certain to prevail over all enemies, even if those be the celestials with Indra at their head, while anxiety there is none if they be human... It was this favourite of the gods, who having speedily smashed the Gandharvas and conquered all the sons of Nagnajit, forcibly liberated from confinement king Sudarsana of great energy. It was he that slew king Pāṇḍya by striking his breast against his, and moved down Kaliṅgas in battle..."[78].

Krishṇa is pictured as possessed of extraordinary prowess and superhuman powers. In order to show little prospect of winning the battle against the Pāṇḍus who were aided by Krishṇa, Dhṛtarāshtra gives an account of the divine exploits of Krishṇa: as a boy he slew the king of the Hayas by the force of his arms; in his childhood he destroyed with his arms the Dānava; he slew Pralambha, Naraka, Jambha, Pitha and Mura. Through his valour he overthrew in battle Kaṁsa, etc.

Krishṇa is also presented as the founder of a religion which started with the Yādavas but soon spread beyond the tribal com-

---

78 5.48.86.

munity. This is the non-Brahmanic monotheist sect, called Bhāgavata religion, which sprang independent of the Vedic tradition. Later they called themselves Pāñcarātras and worshipped the Supreme Being as Bhāgavat (the exalted One), from which is derived the term Bhāgavata, i.e., worshipper of Bhāgavat. The God exalted by this religious movement was known as Harī, which afterwards became a familiar name of Vishṇu. His worship was based on love of God (*bhakti*). The *Mahābhārata* gives the story of the origin of the Pāñcarātra cult. It records a tradition that seven citrasikhandin *ṛṣis* had proclaimed a Śāstra on par with the four Vedas. Krishṇa was originally the chieftain of the Yādava tribe; endowed with extraordinary qualities, he was soon deified and then integrated into Vishṇu. We can indicate the three strands that appear to have contributed to the emergence of Krishṇa as the Supreme God of the Vaishṇava sect. God Vāsudeva of the Sātvatas and the Bhagavān Vishṇu of the Bhāgavatas and Nārāyana, the God of the Pāñcarātras were fused into Krishṇa, being variously named as Vāsudeva-Krishṇa, Bhagavan Krishṇa, Nārāyana-Krishṇa. In the process of apotheosis of the founder of a religious sect, quite in accordance with the Indian mentality, he became identified with the deity whom he had proclaimed. Thus Krishṇa, his patronymic Vāsudeva (son of Vāsudeva), and Nārāyana became other names of the same deity. Thus the Sātvata current, the Bhāgavata current and the Pāñcarātra current of early Hinduism, especially of Vaishṇavism, merged into one religious sect which later on came to be called Krishṇaism. It is only in the *Bhagavad-gītā* that Krishṇa reveals his pervading supremacy in every department of life and being, and gives Arjuna an awe-inspiring vision of his universal form, showing the whole universe to be contained in him.

Krishṇa in some passages of the *Mahābhārata* does not appear as a person of high morality. He is repeatedly denounced not only as a deceitful person but as a low person, cowherd and coward[79]. As fighter he is blamed for ignoble conduct[80]. Bhīma, instigated by Krishṇa, fells Duryodhana by an unfair blow on the thigh, and kicks him with his left foot. For this he is condemned by Baladeva

79 Mahābhārata 2.44.26; 9.60.26, etc.
80 Ibidem 5.160.52; 6.65.40; 66.19; 18.47.32.

and others, but justified by Krishṇa. Duryodhana reproaches Krishṇa for having in unfair ways brought about the fall of five of the Kaurava leaders. Although Krishṇa tries to justify himself, an invisible voice confirms the words of Duryodhana[81].

Krishṇa defends Bhīma's action on the ground that for the sake of the advancement of one's own self, or of one's friends, or for the sake of the fall of one's enemy one should apply the efficacious remedy which is the blow inflicted by Bhīma on Duryodhana's thigh. But the argument of Krishṇa is characterized by Sanjaya as *dharmacchalam*, or in other words, Krishṇa is said to be a pious hypocrite. Rāma's words are very significant: "Morality is well practised by the good. Morality however is always afflicted by two things, viz. the desire of profit entertained by those that covet it, and the desire for pleasure cherished by those that are wedded to it. Whoever without afflicting morality and profit, or pleasure and profit, follows all three, viz., morality, profit and pleasure, always succeeds in obtaining great happiness. In consequence however of morality being afflicted by Bhīmasena, this harmony of which I have spoken has been disturbed, whatever, O Govinda, you tell me!" Rāma departs in disgust, and the virtuous heroes "became very joyless". Then Krishṇa who has all along been approving the ignoble act, turns to Yudhiṣṭhira who reproved it, and says, "Why do you sanction this unrighteous act?" Yudhiṣṭhira answers, "I am not pleased with it, but (because we were so badly treated by this man therefore) reflecting on all this, I overlook it. Let Pāṇḍu's son take his pleasure whether he does right or wrong".[82]

Krishṇa is openly charged with violating all rules of honour and noble conduct. Duryodhana says to Krishṇa: "You have, it seems, no shame, for have you forgotten that I have been struck down most unfairly, judged by the rules that prevail in encounters with the mace? It was you who unfairly caused this act by reminding Bhīma with a hint about the breaking of my thighs! Having caused thousands of kings who always fought fairly to be slain through diverse kinds of unfair means, feel you no shame or no abhorrence for those acts?... If you have fought me and Karṇa and

81 Ibidem 9.60-61.
82 Ibidem 9.60.

Bhīsma and Droṇa by fair means, victory then without doubt would never have been yours. By adopting the most crooked and unrighteous of means you have caused many kings observant of the duties of their order and ourselves also to be slain." To which Krishṇa replies by pointing out the sinful deeds that the Kuru brothers have done to the Pāṇḍus and hence that they merited to be slain. Finally he says, "King Duryodhana could never be slain in a fair encounter! The same is the case with all those mighty car-warriors headed by Bhīsma. From desire of doing good I repeatedly applied my powers of illusion and caused them to be slain by diverse means in battle. If I had not adopted such deceitful ways in battle, victory would never have been yours, nor kingdom, nor wealth".[83]

There is also a group of texts in the *Mahābhārata* that refer to the denial of his divine qualities by Śiśupāla, Duryodhana, Karṇa and Salya. Yudhishṭhira, about to perform the Rājasuya sacrifice, is joined by Krishṇa who is designated as Harī, the *ṛṣi*, the ancient, identified with the Veda, invisible to those who know him. On this occasion Bhīsma proposes to honour Krishṇa in a special way as the most eminent of the chiefs to receive gifts indicative of his superiority. Śiśupāla protested against this very vehemently but Bhīshma defends Krishṇa's claims to the honour which he had received. Duryodhana also manifests a similar disbelief of Krishṇa's divine character. These texts, it appears, indicate the existence of a strong rivalry between the adherents of Krishṇa and those of Mahādeva or Śiva[84].

The acts of Krishṇa as man suggest that he was a mere man. The *Mahābhārata* repudiates this view. "Foolish is he who says that Vāsudeva is only a man".[85] Krishṇa's divine dignity is denied by his enemies and asserted by his partisans. However in many passages of the Epic Krishṇa is identified with Vishṇu who is himself identified with the Supreme Spirit. It appears rather clear from the texts that Krishṇa was originally a mortal, a tribal chief, brought up in concealment by shepherds in order to be protected from his uncle, the cruel king Kaṁsa. This is interpreted as a folklore theme but not removed from the events of everyday life. He sides with the Pāṇḍu brothers in the

83 Ibidem 9.61.
84 Ibidem 2.40 f.
85 Ibidem 5.160.52.

great war; becomes a cunning and unscrupulous counseller; is instrumental in bringing about the success of the Pāṇḍavas. In the end he is killed unintentionally by a hunter's arrow. In the portrayal of Krishṇa another strand is introduced; namely, that of Krishṇa-Gopāla, a pastoral demigod who dallies with shepherdesses. There are many obscure points in the legends of Krishṇa; for instance, how Krishṇa-Gopāla becomes Vāsudeva-Krishṇa or how Vāsudeva-Krishṇa is accepted as one of the *avatārs* of Vishṇu? Anyway all the three are merged into one and Krishṇa becomes the Supreme God of the Vaishṇavas.

The theory of the *avatār* is very congenial to the Indian mentality, for India has considered its great men as some kind *of avatārs* of God. Krishṇa who is probably the most ancient of the *avatārs* of Vishṇu is not the only *avatār* under which Vishṇu manifests himself in the world. Every time, as he says in the *Bhagavad-gītā*, that religion (*dharma*) is in danger and that non-religion (*adharma*) triumphs, he issues forth; for the defense of the good and the suppression of the wicked, for the establishment of justice, he manifests himself from age to age[86]. As A. Barth observes,"

> "In fact, by permitting the worship of the deity under a series of hypostases no longer abstract, such as those which the ancient theology had conceived, but such as were highly concrete, highly personal, and what is better still, human, they resolved in a new manner the old problem, so often attempted, of reconciling aspirations after a certain monotheism with an irresistible tendency to multiply forms of worship. In a way which surpasses the clumsy device of divine genealogies, or the conception of different "forms" of the same god, which still prevails in the Śaivite religions, it responded by its elasticity and its affection for mystery to all the instincts of this people. ... An avatāra, in the highest and fullest sense of the word, is not a transitory manifestation of the deity, stili less the procreation, by the connection of a god with a mortal, of a being in some sense intermediate; it is the presence, at once mystic and real, of the supreme being in a human individual..."[87].

86 Bhagavad-gītā 4.7-8.

87 A. Barth, *The Religions of India*, London, 1882, pp. 169-70.

In other words the theory of the *avatāra* is a means of reconciling the belief in One Supreme Being (monotheism) and the acceptance in practice of the plurality of divine manifestations and of the principle of divine interventions in the human life or providence.

The clearly worded doctrine of the *avatāra* appears for the first time in the *Bhagavad-gītā*, in which Krishṇa replies to the question of Arjuna who, not knowing that Krishṇa is All-God, is perplexed by Krishṇa's saying that he declared the changeless mode of life to Vivasvat (the Sun) who declared it to Manu, and Manu to kingly seers:

> "Many a birth have I passed through, and (many a birth) have you: I know them all but you do not.
> Unborn am I, changeless is my Self, of (all) contingent beings I am the Lord! Yet by my creative energy *(māyā)* I consort with Nature – which is mine – and come to be (in time). For whenever the law of righteousness withers away and lawlessness arises, then do I generate myself (on earth).
> For the protection of the good, for the destruction of evil-doers, for the setting up of the law of righteousness I come into being from age to age.
> Who knows my godly birth and mode of operation thus as they really are, he, his body left behind, is never born again; he comes to me"[88].

Krishṇa is thus represented as God, the highest Brahman in personal form, and therefore beyond all forms of opposites, above all men, beyond all gods. The climax of the *Bhagavad-gītā* is the theophany in which Krishṇa reveals his supreme form as Lord to Arjuna. For Krishṇa says:

> "Grace have I shown to you, O Arjuna, revealing to you by my own power this my supreme form, glorious, universal, infinite, primal, which none save you has ever seen"[89].

---

88 Bhagavad-gītā 4.5-9.
89 Ibidem 9.49.

The message of the theophany is that while anyone who is completely detached from this world can gain the spiritual, supreme, eternal state of Brahman, only God-lovers can see and experience the fulness of the Godhead as it is tirelessly active in time. He says,

"By worship of love addressed to me alone can I be known and seen in such a form and as I really am: (so can my lovers) enter into me"[90].

Finally at the very end of the *Bhagavad-gītā* Krishṇa reveals the most secret doctrine of all, i.e. that he (God) loves man:

"Hear again the most secret of all, my ultimate word. Because I greatly desire you, therefore shall I tell you your salvation. Think on me, worship me, sacrifice to me, pay me homage, so shall you come to me. I promise you truly, for I love you well. Give up all the things of *dharma,* turn to me only as your refuge. I will deliver you from all evil. Have no care"[91].

The sum total of the revelation in the *Bhagavad-gītā* is that Krishṇa is God, that He manifests his love for man, and that He demands love in return from man in order that man may attain liberation which is a state of union with Krishṇa in perpetual and blissful love.

The following sects of Krishṇaism[92] are prominent in modern India. The Vallabhācharis (also called Rudra Sampradāyis) owes its popularity to Vallabha Ācārya and generally known as the religion of the Gokula Gosains. Its original founder is Vishṇu Swami who first restricted this religion only to the Brāhmans but Vallabha who flourished about the sixteenth century extended it to men of other castes as well. Krishṇa is said to have appeared in vision to Vallabha at Vrindāvana and had enjoined him to propagate his worship under the form of Bāla Gopal (Boy Gopal). The Gosains or gurus

90 Ibidem 11.54.

91 Ibidem 18.64 ff.

92 See W. J. WILKINS, *Modern Hinduism,* London, 1975 (reprint), pp. 297-368. R. G. BHANDARKAR, *Vaisnavism, Śaivism and minor religious systems,* Strassburg, 1913.

have great influence over their disciples and are well cared for by them wherever they go. Most of the adherents of the sect are merchants. The most important temple of Gopal is at Ajmere. The worship of the images of Gopal side by side with those of Rādhā and Krishṇa is common in places where this sect is found.

The Mīrā Bāis is a subdivision of the above sect and is found mostly in the West of India. Mīrā Bai is the authoress of many devotional hymns in honour of Krishṇa which are read and meditated upon by the followers, even of other sects. Mīrā Bai adored Ranachor, a form of Krishṇa, and visited the places sacred to the memory of Krishṇa. She gave protection to the worshippers of Krishṇa in her kingdom. The images of Krishṇa and of Mīrā are to be found in Udaypore.

The Bengal Vaishṇavism owes its foundation to Caitanya (1485-1533) who is popularly believed to be an *avatār* of Krishṇa for the purpose of leading men to the worship of Krishṇa and Rādhā. Impelled by a great enthusiasm, he preached of the immense bliss he found in the contemplation of love to Krishṇa. His followers are in the habit of singing, dancing and talking the praises of Krishṇa for many hours. The followers of Caitanya elaborated a rich experience of love of Krishṇa *(bhakti)*, very emotional and at times even erotic.

The other Vaishṇavas such as the Śrī Sampradāyis or Rāmanujas and the Madhvācharis are not specifically Krishṇa worshippers but include Him in the worship of Vishṇu. The Rāmanujas are the oldest and most respectable of the Vaishṇava sect, founded by Rāmānuja himself in the eleventh century. This sect worships Vishṇu and his consort Lakshmī and their *avatārs*. Besides the temple worship, images are also set up in houses; they also venerate Sālaigrāma and Tulasi. Vishṇu is worshipped in five ways: clearing the images and temples; offering flowers and perfumes for religious rites; making unbloody sacrifice and offerings, repetition of the name of the Deity and meditation and love of Vishṇu *(bhakti)*. Rāmānuja's Vedānta is based on the notion of the "qualified Brahman"; i.e., a personal God endowed with attributes which comprehend human spirits and other things. The individual self is dependent on, and united with, God and forms a part of God. The religious practice consists precisely in experiencing this dependence and union in love and surrender *(bhakti)*.

The Madhvācharis (12th century) form a sect which appears as a sort of connecting link between the Vaishṇavas and Śaivas. Madhva was not a bigot; hence his sect includes among images in temples those of Śiva, Durgā, and Ganeśa, along with that of Vishṇu. The specific character of their belief is that though the human spirit *(jīvātman)* is united to and dependent on the Supreme God, it is not a part of the substance of the Supreme God.

4. Śrī Rāma

The next in importance after Śrī Krishṇa among the divine founders of the prominent Hindu sects within Vaishṇavism is Śrī Rāma.

There are many Rāmas in the early literature of India. We have to distinguish them in order to avoid confusion. It appears at first to have been the name of many mythical personages. In the Vedic literature two Rāmas are mentioned: one Rāma with patronymic Mārgaveya (*Aittirīya Brāhmaṇa*) and another Rāma with patronymic Aupatasvini, a descendant of Upatasvina; it is the name of a ṛisthi. (Cfr. *Ś. Br.* 4) Another Rāma with the patronymic Jāmadagnya is the supposed author of the Ṛig Veda 10.110. In later times three Rāmas are distinguished: Parasurāma who is the sixth *avatār* of Vishṇu and sometimes called Jāmadagnya as son of the sage Jamad-agni by Renuka, and sometimes Bhārgava, as descended from Bhṛigu; Rāmacandra, the son of Dasaratha, the seventh *avatār* of Vishṇu and the hero of the Epic, *Rāmāyana*; Balarāma who is regarded as the elder brother of Krishṇa. Parasurāma became manifest in the world as *avatār* of Vishṇu at the beginning of the Treta-yuga, for the purpose of repressing the tyranny of the Kshatryas. In the *Rāmāyana* he appears as an opponent of Rāmacandra. In the *Mahābhārata* he instructs Arjuna in the use of arms, and has a combat with Bhīsma in which both suffered equally. Balarāma, the elder brother of Krishṇa, is recognized as the seventh *avatār* of Vishṇu in the place of Krishṇa when Krishṇa himself is regarded as the full manifestation of Vishṇu himself. According to this view of the Vaishṇavas Krishṇa is a full divinity and Balarāma an incarnation. He killed the great Asura, Dhenuka and other Asuras.

The story of Rāma is told in the Epic, *Rāmāyana*. Dasaratha, King of Ayodhyā, has three sons, Rāma, Bharata and Lakṣmana, by his three wives Kausalyā, Kaikeyī and Sumitrā respectively. By his prowess in bending the giant bow of Janaka Rāma wins as his bride Śita, Janaka's daughter. When Dasaratha on reaching old age announces his intention of making Rāma heir-apparent, Kaikeyī, wishing her son Bharata to succeed, reminds the king of the two boons he had given her in the past and demands him to appoint Bharata to succeed him and to banish Rāma for forteen years.

When the king informs Rāma of his fate, Rāma obeys him and Śita and Laksmaṇa accompany him on his exile. On the death of the old king Dasaratha, Bharata implores Rāma to return to Ayodhyā as king. Rāma declines to return because he must fulfil his vow of exile. Then Śita is carried away by the demon-king Rāvaṇa to his palace in Laṅka. Rāma with the armies of Hanuman, the king of the monkeys, marches to the South, bridges the straits, overthrows Rāvaṇa, brings home Śita, and is crowned king of Ayodhyā. After she has purified herself from the suspicion of infidelity by the ordeal of fire, Rāma is reunited with her and reigns gloriously in association with his faithful brother Bharata and gladdens his subjects with a new golden age.

Such is the main story of Rāma in the *Rāmāyana*. But by the additions of the first and last books Vālmīki's Epic has been transformed into a work meant to glorify Rāma as an *avatār* of Vishṇu. Rāvaṇa abuses his immunity from any kind of harm from gods, demigods and demons to such an extent that gods become desperate. They finally profit by the fact that Rāvaṇa in his arrogance forgot to ask that he should not be harmed by men, and implore Vishṇu to incarnate as a man to destroy the demon. Vishṇu is born as Rāma and fulfils his task. At the end of the seventh book, Brahmā and other gods pay homage to Rāma and proclaim him as Vishṇu, "the glorious Lord of the discus".

The central theme of the *Rāmāyana* appears to be based on the Vedic mythology itself. The celestial myth of the Veda takes on the shape of a narrative in which the triumph of the good over the powers of evil is depicted amidst many earthly adventures and political intrigues. Śita appears in the Ṛig Veda as the Furrow personified and is invoked as a goddess. In the Ṛig Veda[93] Śita is invoked as presiding over agriculture or the fruits of the earth. In *Vajasneya*

---

93 4.57.6.

Samhita [94] Śita the furrow is again personified and addressed as a goddess. In *Taittiriya Brāhmaṇa* she is called savitri, and in Paskara's *Grhya Sūtra* Indra-patni, "the wife of Indra". In the *Rāmāyana* she is the wife of Rāma and daughter of Janaka, king of Mithila, capital of Videha. She is also considered by some as the incarnation of Lakshmī and of Uma. She was named Śita because she is supposed to have sprung from a furrow made by Janaka while ploughing the "ground to prepare for a sacrifice to obtain a progeny[95]. At last Śita disappears underground in the arms of the goddess earth[96]. Rāma prefigures in the person of Indra; his conflict with Rāvaṇa, the chief demon, would represent the Indra-Vrtra myth as found in the Ṛig Veda. We can see a confirmation of this by the fact that Rāvaṇa's son is called Indrajit (conqueror of Indra) and Indrasatru (Enemy of Indra), an epithet of Vrtra in the Ṛig Veda. The abduction of Śita would have its prototype in the stealing of the cows recovered by Indra. In the figure of Hanuman perhaps survives a reminiscence of Indra's alliance with the Maruts in his conflict with Vrtra, since Hanuman is the son of the wind-god.

The *Mahābhārata* calls Rāma Vishṇu and introduces the story of Rāma which appears to reproduce the main ideas of the *Rāmāyana* itself:

> "And it came to pass that the mighty son of Dasaratha, the heroic Rāma, who is Vishṇu's self in the shape of a huṃan being, took his birth in this world. And in company with his queen and brother, taking his bow, that foremost of bowmen with the view of compassing his father's welfare, began to reside in the Daṇḍaka forest. And from Janasthana, that mighty Rākshasa monarch, the wicked Rāvaṇa, carried his (Rāma's) queen by strategem and force, deceiving, O sinless one, that foremost of men, through the agency of a Rākshasa, Mārīcha, who assumed the form of a deer marked with gemlike and golden spots. ... Having by my own prowess crossed the ocean, I saw in Rāvaṇa's residence the daughter of king Janaka, Śita, like unto the daughter of a celestial ... Then with the

94 12.69-70.
95 Ramayana 1.66.
96 Ibidem 7. 97.

help of Hanuman he crossed the sea and killed those Rākshasas in battle, and also Rāvaṇa, the oppressor of the worlds together with his Rākshasa followers ... Then Rāma recovered his wife even like the lost Vaidic revelation"[97].

Only in some passages Rāma is proclaimed as Vishṇu besides the above one. No doubt he is often spoken of as being divine, as being like Vishṇu, like the sun, etc. with divine powers. But he is also identified clearly with Vishṇu as in the following passage:

"Listen to the history of Rāma (the son of Dasaratha).. For the destruction of Rāvaṇa, O king, Vishṇu in his own body took his birth as the son of illustrious Dasaratha. We saw in Ayodhyā that son of Dasaratha after he had been born"[98].

In both the Epics Rāma was at first no more than a local royal hero-god who has the divinity of such but no more. But gradually Rāma develops into a form of Vishṇu and is finally identified with Vishṇu himself[99]. Rāma is Vishṇu and Śita is Lakshmī.[100]

The *Mahābhārata* has this following account of the incarnation of Vishṇu as Rāma: "Towards the close of Treta and the beginning of Dvapara, I shall take birth as Rāma, the son of Dasaratha in Ikshvāku's royal line. At that time the two Ṛishis, namely, the two sons of Prajāpati, called by the names of Ekata and Dvaita, will in consequence of the injury done by them unto their brother Trita, have to take birth as apes, losing the beauty of the human form. Those apes that shall take birth in the race of Ekata and Dvaita shall become endowed with great strength and mighty energy and will equal Sakra himself in prowess. All those apes will become my allies for accomplishing the business of the deities. I shall then slay the terrible lord of the Rākshasas, that wretch of Pulastya's race, viz., the fierce Rāvaṇa, that thorn of all the worlds, together with all his children and followers"[101].

---

97 Mahābhārata 3.146-47.

98 Ibidem 3.99.35 ff.

99 Rāmāyana 6.120.

100 Ibidem 7.17.35.

101 Mahābhārata 12.339.41.

Rāvaṇa's women came out and surrounding his body, wept. The queen Mandodarī[102] lamented thus: "Alas! you who had vanquished the gods have met with death by human hands. But I do not believe Rāma to be a mere man; even when your brother Khara and his Rākshasas were exterminated at Janasthana, I concluded that Rāma was no mere man; it is clear the Supreme Being, the eternal Lord, greater than the great, who is beyond darkness, the invincible Vishṇu of true valour, has taken human form, and surrounded by all the gods in the form of monkeys, has come for the good of the world, to destroy you with all your Rākshasa followers"[103].

Another episode also clearly shows of Rāma's true identity. All the gods gathered together came to Rāma and asked him why he ignored Śita entering the fire; they praised him also as the Supreme Lord. But Rāma said that he considered himself simply as a man. Brahmā then told Rāma that in reality Rāma was Lord Nārāyana who had taken a human form for the sake of destroying Rāvaṇa[104].

When the Goddess Earth clasped Śita and took her into her womb, there was a shower of flowers from the gods who praised Śita's character. But Rāma sat plunged in grief. God Brahmā who was witnessing the scene with the gods bade Rāma not to grieve and reminded him of his original divine status as Vishṇu and the mission on which he had come on earth and assured him that both he and Śita will be reunited in his own heaven[105].

In the earliest part of the *Rāmāyana* which was probably written in the fourth century B. C. Rāma appears as a hero but in the later additions as an incarnation of Vishṇu, as the above texts amply demonstrate, Rāma at the beginning was the ideal man, loyal, patient in affliction, faithful to duty and higher authority, ideal son, brother, husband, and the chastiser of evil powers. By and by he became a partial incarnation and finally full incarnation of Vishṇu. Thus we see a development in the image of Rāma as presented in the *Rāmāyana*. Rāma, the tribal hero, has been transformed into a national hero, the moral ideal of the people; and the human hero

102 His chief wife.

103 Ramayana 6.3.112 f.

104 Ibidem 7.17.

105 Ibidem 7.97.

of the five genuine books of the Epic (except a few interpolations) has in the first and the last books become deified and identified with the God Vishṇu, his divine nature in these additions being always present in the minds of their authors. The original part of the *Rāmāyana* appears to have been completed before the Epic kernel of the *Mahābhārata* took definite shape.

The stroy of Rāma as narrated in the *Rāmāyana* became so popular that it grew with age. It grew by fresh descriptions of the same scenes and episodes. Generations of poets and literary men enriched the story with new descriptions of the scenes which were dear to the Hindus who in the course of time listened to them with religious reverence and joy. The virtues of Rāma and the faithfulness of Śita were extolled again and again to be emulated by the Hindus. The loving devotion of Rāma's brothers, the sanctity of the saints, and the peacefulness of the hermitages visited by Rāma, were committed to memory with endless reiteration. Kālidāsa conjures up the memories of a golden age, constructs lofty ideals of piety and truth, and describes with delicate pathos the domestic scenes and affections, which endear the work to the modern Hindus.

It is obvious that in India today the Rāmāyana is a living tradition and a living faith. It forms the basis of the moral instruction of a nation and a part of the lives of the Hindus. When the modern languages of India grew up, the Rāmāyana had the greatest influence in inspiring the modern poets, and it was translated into many modern languages throughout the country. Kamban's Rāmāyana in Tamil appeared as early as A.D. 1100. Tulsī Dās's Rāmāyana is the great classic of the Hindi language; Krittibas's Rāmāyana is the classic of the Bengali language; Śrīdhar's Rāmāyana is a classic in the Marāṭha language. The story of Rāma has inspired Hindu religious reformers, and purified the popular faith of the modern Hindus. Rāma, the true and dutiful, was accepted as the Spirit of God descended on earth as an incarnation of Vishṇu, the preserver of the world. The worship of Rāma still holds its "ground especially in North and Central India and he has many worshippers in the South. The name of Rāma, as "Rām! Rām!" is a household form of salutation. The great theologian Rāmanuja (12th century) can be called the founder of Śrī Vaishṇavism, which first blended into full harmony knowledge and love in the worship of Vishṇu. He teaches in his *Śrī Bhāṣya*: "What it (The Bhāgavata system) teaches is that the highest Brahman, called Vāsudeva, from kindness to those devoted to it, voluntarily abides in a fourfold form, so as to render itself accessible to its devotees... That highest Brahman, called Vāsudeva, having for its body the complete aggregate of the six qualities, divides itself in so far as it is either the "Subtle" (*sūkshma*), or "division" (*vyūha*), or "manifestation" (*vibhāva*), and is attained in its fulness by the devotees who, according to their qualifications, do worship to it by means of works guided by knowledge. "From the worship of the Vibhāva-aspect one attains to the vyūha, and from the worship of the vyūha one attains to the "Subtle" called Vāsudeva, i.e., the highest Brahman: such is their doctrine. By the "vibhava" we have to understand the aggregate of beings, such as Rāma, Krishṇa, etc., in whom the highest Being becomes manifest ... Scripture already declares, "Not born, he is born in many ways", and it is this birth – consisting in the voluntary assumption of bodily form, due to tenderness towards its devotees which the Bhāgavata system teaches"[106].

Three principal ideas govern and determine the whole religious vision of Rāmānuja. The first is that the Supreme Being Vishṇu is indeed infinite, but infinite in qualities of goodness. The second is that in his love for his creatures the Supreme Lord becomes incarnate in various blessed forms to save men from sin and sorrow, and lead them to final union with him. The third doctrine is that the Supreme Lord may be reached by any suppliant, whatever his birth or status in life, who worships him in perfect self-forgetting love (*bhakti*).

Rāmānuja's disciple Rāmānanda in the fourteenth century preached in Northern India the doctrine of Rāma's boundless love for men of every race and order. He introduced the purer and more chaste worship of Rāma and Śita instead of that of Krishṇa and Rādhā. He used vernacular languages for the spread of the new creed and began a radical reform to abolish all caste distinctions. Kabīr conceived the bold idea of uniting Hindus and Muslims in the worship of One God Rāma. He said: "The God of the Hindus is

---

106 Śrī Bhāṣya 2.2.42; THIBAUT's translation, pp. 525-26.

the God of the Mahomedans, be he invoked as Rāma or Ali"[107]. "The city of the Hindu God is Benares, and the city of the Mahomedan God is Mecca; but search your hearts, and there you will find the God both of Hindus and Mahomedans"[108]. "If the Creator dwells in tabernacles, whose dwelling is the universe?"[109] The following passage from Kabir indicates clearly his unshakable belief in Rāma and in the salvation wrought in Rāma:

> "The crowds went by the path traversed by the Pundits. Lofty is the ascent to Rāma. Kabir has climbed it. The whole world has gone astray by partiality for one's own system.
> He who, becoming free from partiality, adores Harī, is a wise sage. The great ones are lost in their own greatness; pride peers out through every pore; when they are not familiar with a wise preceptor, all the orders of men are of the Camar caste, i.e., the degraded caste of curriers. The Kali is a wicked age; the world is blind and nobody believes in the true word. He to whom a salutary advice is given becomes an enemy. Three things went to a holy place (the body, the fickle heart, and the mind which is a thief). They did not destroy a single sin, but on the contrary the mind contracted ten others. Men in general polluted the path of bhakti by washing pebbles and stones. Keeping poison within, they have thrown the nectar. "I am the author of the whole creation, there is no other who is superior to me". Kabir says that when one does not know what one is oneself, one thinks everything to be contained in oneself. In this world all have passed away considering themselves to be Rāma, but no one actually became Rāma. Kabir says that those who know Rāma as he truly is, attain all their objects"[110].

Kabir usually calls God "Rāma" despite the fact that he strongly disapproved the Hindu polytheism; which indicates that the de-

---

107 As cited by ROMESH DUTT, in his *The Rāmāyaṇa and the Mahābhārata*, London, 1944, pp. 162-63.

108 Ibidem.

109 Ibidem.

110 As cited by R. G. BHANDARKAR, *Vaiṣṇavism, Śaivism*, op. cit., p. 72.

ification of Rāma was so strong and prevalent among the people of his time that his name had become synonym for "God".

For Tulsī Dās Rāma is the Supreme God who for love of human beings incarnated himself as a fabulous hero. It is worth citing his praise of Rāma as the Supreme God:

> "You are the guardian of the bounds of revelation, O Rāma, you are the Lord of the Universe, and Jānākī is Māyā which creates, preserves and destroys the world at your pleasure, O All Gracious. And Lakshmaṇa is the Serpent with a thousand hoods who supports the earth, sovereign of all things animate and inanimate. You have taken a human body for the good of gods and you have come to destroy the army of demons. Your real form transcends speech and intelligence. You are ineffable and infinite, called ever by the Vedas: "Not this! Not this!". The world is only a drama and you watch it as a spectator, and Brahmā, Vishṇu, and Śiva you make to dance like puppets. They themselves know not the mystery of your character: who else can then understand you as you are? He alone knows you to whom you have granted the power to know you, and knowing you he becomes one with you.
> It is by your grace, O Raghunātha, that your devotees understand you, you touch the heart of the faithful like refreshing sandal-paste. Your true form is pure thought and bliss, free from change. They know it who have been privileged thus. But for the good of gods and the just, you have taken the form of illusion and you speak and act as a prince of this earth.
> O Rāma, when they see your actions and then they hear about them, fools are perplexed, but the saints rejoice; Whatever you say or do is right: like costume, like mimicry"[111].

For Tulsī Dās Rāma is fully deifid, and his name is used to mean simply "God".

Speaking of the Rāmaite sects[112], we can single out first the Śrī Sampradāyis or Rāmānujas. They worship Vishṇu and his consort Lakshmī and their incarnations either singly or conjointly. They are

111 As cited in L. Renou, *Hinduism*, New York, 1967, pp. 196-97.
112 See W. J. Wilkins, *Modern Hinduism*, op. cit., pp. 313 ff.

commonly called Śrī Vaishṇavas. The main ceremony of initiation is the communication of the Vaishṇava mantra by the guru to the disciples. This mantra is said to be "Oṁ Rāmaya nama" (Oṁ salutation to Rāma). Vishṇu is to be worshipped in his many incarnations and this consists in clearing the images and temples, in providing flowers and perfumes for religious rites, in presenting offerings, in repeating the name of the deity, in meditation and love of God, the object of which is to achieve most intimate union of the self with God, and finally to enter into Vaikunṭha, the heaven of Vishṇu.

Rāmānandis or Rāmavats, the followers of Rāmānanda, worship Rāmachandra or Rāma, together with Śita his wife, his half-brother Lakshmaṇa, and his faithful friend Hanuman. Some of the adherents believe in Rāma as their Supreme Deity while others prefer Śita, while still others worship both Rāma and Śita together.

The Kabīr Panthīs or followers of Kabīr say that there is but One God Rāma, the creator of the world, and the Sādhu of the Kabīrs is His living resemblance. Every creature is a part of God; therefore God and man together form everything that lives and moves. They promulgated a high moral code and declared that life was a sacred gift of God and advocated strongly non-violence towards all living beings. They laid great stress on truthfulness and love of God (*bhakti*) which is the most efficacious means of liberation from the cycle of rebirth.

We can summarize the origin and development of Rāmaism as follows. Special devotion to Rāma is first illustrated in the traditions of Rāmānuja in the twelfth century. Madhva in the thirteenth century sent his disciples to Puri in Orissa to bring back what were supposed to be the original images of Rāma and Śita[113]. The worship of Rāma establishes itself and a festival of his birth is described by Hemadri. Then translations of the *Rāmāyana* in different moderna languages appeared in the fourteenth century. In the Adhyātma-Rāmāyana (before the sixteenth century) the story of Rāma is retold with the doctrine that Rāma is God. Thus Rāma was incorporated into the theology of the Vedānta. His nature was Knowledge and the doctrine of *Saccidānanda* (Being, Consciousness and Bliss) was

113 See R. G. BHANDARKAR *Vaiṣṇavism. Śaivism* .... op. cit.. p. 58.

applied to him and he was identified with the Absolute. Śita becomes in her turn the incarnation of Lakshmī. The divine couple, undergoing hardship with patience and rectitude, is interpreted as exhibiting the divine compassion with which God takes his share in the suffering and sorrow of humanity. The *Rāmāyana* is read and meditated upon in this light, which accounts for its profound influence which it exercises in the Hindu mind, especially among the Rāmaites. The spread of Rāma-worship is largely attributed to Rāmānanda, Kabīr, Tulsī Dās and their respective followers throughout India.

5. Conclusion

In many respects Hinduism appears to be a unique phenomenon in the history of religions. Indeed Hinduism is not centred around one single person venerated as its sole founder. Its basic tenets are not revealed to any prophet and then either propagated among or imposed upon people. However, we can with just reason say that Hinduism owes its origin to the utterances of seers (*ṛṣis*) and "god-men" (*avatārs*) like Krishṇa and Rāma and hence these can be called founders of Hinduism in its various developments as Vaishṇavism, Śaivism and Śaktism. They are the fountainheads from which are derived the spiritual currents that animate every Hindu. Their utterances are treasured by the generations that follow and become their spiritual patrimony. The spiritual experiences of these great seers and god-men form the soul of the Hindu religion.

Under the name of seers can be grouped all the authors of the Hindu Sacred Scriptures which are common to all and which are special to different Hindu sects like Vaishṇavism, Śaivism and Śaktism. These authors are regarded by later generations as patriarchal and foundational sages, occupying a position similar to the historical founders of other religions. They are the inspired authors who "saw" the Vedas and Āgamas which were "revealed" to them. There are three kinds of seers (*ṛṣis*): the rājaṛṣi, who is a prince who adopted the life of a spiritual master and saint; the devaṛṣi who is the sage who was also a demi-god such as Nārada; and finally, brahmaṛṣi, the priestly sage. They are certainly a definite group of ancestral sages, some of whom are pre-historical, some others semi-historical, if not mythical, who are believed to have received revelation from the Supreme Being. The Hindu Scriptures (including the Vedas and the Āgamas and the Saṁhitās of different sects) are believed to derive from a "hearing" (*śruti*), i.e., revelation; they are held to have emanated from Brahman, to have been "breathed" by God in the form of "words", while their human authors, the *ṛṣis* or inspired sages, did no more than receive them by a direct "vision".

The God-men of Hinduism are of various kinds, depending on the beliefs of various sects. Some are "incarnations" (*avatārs*) of Vishṇu like Krishṇa and Rāma. Others are Śiva-gurus, the manifestations of Śiva in the human form of saints and ascetics. The auspicious qualities of God are revealed to the loving hearts of the worshippers through the medium of avatārs and gurus; they are also the teachers of the Hindu *dharma*. The ideal characters like Rāma and Śita that we find in them firmly establish Hindu *Dharma* in the minds of the people. The avatārs and gurus summarize for Hindus all the theological and ethical teachings of the Hindu Scriptures. We can recall a popular verse which compares the Upanishads (Vedānta) to cows, the Bhagavad-gītā to milk, Krishṇa to a cowherd, and Arjuna to a calf. The various accounts of the life of Krishṇa and Rāma are intended to give the Hindus an imaginative representation of God's help to man at different stages of his evolution.

Originally the figures of Krishṇa and Rāma appear as human heroes of different tribes; but then they develop into demi-gods and divinized heroes until they become fully divine beings, founding particular religious traditions of sectarian Hinduism. The Hindu theory of avatār is significant from many points of view. The purpose of the avatārs is said to consist in establishing the moral order in the universe. Its aim is also said to be the setting up of a norm that man should follow in his religious quest of God, for the avatār is believed to have come to man in order that man might become divine by following the example of the avatār. It is also a serious attempt to personalize the eternal, impersonal or supra-personal character of God who is transcedent and incomprehensible, so that man in his *bhakti* contemplate the personal God. These God-men thus reveal God and found the original God-experience among men. It is in this way that we can consider the God-men and the inspired seers as founders of Hinduism.

CHAPTER THREE

THE GURU IN HINDUISM

From the time of the Upanishads[1] India ha stressed the importance and necessity of a personal spiritual master or guide, commonly called guru, in one's striving after spiritual and religious perfection. Even in the educational system of ancient India knowledge of the Vedas was personally transmitted through oral teaching from the guru to his pupil. During the classical period of Hinduism the pupil lived at the home of his guru and served him with obedience and devotion[2]. Self-instruction in religious matters was considered dubious. It is the guru who instructs the disciple in the Vedic knowledge, who explains in a personal manner the principles and methods of spiritual life, who prescribes what to do and what not to do. More than this, the example of the guru, who, though human, has achieved spiritual enlightenment has had a powerful influence on the pupil in the effort to make progress in religious life. The plan of this chapter is quite simple. After studying the important Hindu sacred texts which deal with the notion and function of the guru, we select Srī Ramana Maharśi as an exemplary model of the Hindu guru.

1. The religious meaning of the term guru

The term guru means "heavy" as opposed to "light"; hence it signifies "great, large, important, serious; valuable, venerable, respectable; father, mother, any relative older than oneself; a spiritual parent or preceptor from whom a youth receives the initiatory mantra or prayer,

---

1 It is in the Upanishads that we come across for the first time the idea of having a guru at least from the textual point of view; the institution may have existed even before the Upanishads.

2 The *Brabrnacarya* is the first stage in the life of a twice-born Hindu in which a young man is initiated into the religious life by a guru; the student studies the Vedas and learns to recite the mantras and leads a life of continence.

who instructs him in the śāstras and conduct the necessary ceremonies up to that of investiture". The guru is not only a competent authority but a man of influence and who takes initiative in the religious training of a disciple. He is a prestigious person because of a special power possessed by him. Because of this special power, he possesses sacred knowledge and grace so that he can communicate them to his followers[3].

Often in the Hindu sacred texts three words are used to signify "master": *guru, ācārya* and *vaktri.* They are distinguished from one another as follows. The *guru* is the illuminator who shows his disciple what he could not by himself discover. The *ācārya* is the instructor who teaches the doctrine to the crowd. The *vaktri* is the orator who is eloquent and sincere and knows how to convince the hearers. While the *ācārya* reasons with his flash of insight and teaches to the public, the guru establishes a personal relationship with the disciple and guides him in the practical realization of the spiritual goal. The presence, the word uttered in an intimate meeting and, sometimes even the silence, of the guru become the medium of transmitting the spiritual wisdom. Wisdom is revealed by an inexplicable peace which influences the heart. He is the umbelical cord of a birth in the Spirit of the disciple. By reasoning, conversation and the study of the Vedas the guru leads the disciple to operate a return on himself, to bring peace to his soul, to dispel his darkness and to awaken his discriminative power with regard to the real nature of the self[4].

This does not mean that the function of the guru is always separate from that of the *ācārya;* one can be both and sometimes both the terms are used indifferently to signify the real guru. The teacher is called *ācārya* and the word is explained through three etymologies as one who collects the precepts, puts the students in the proper path and himself practises what he preaches[5]. The Upanishadic text: "He who has a teacher knows" *(ācāryavan puruso veda)* emphasizes that knowledge, particularly spiritual, is efficacious only when one learns it directly from a teacher in person, and not from a book[6]. This

3 See J. Gonda, *A propos d'un sens magico-religieux de skt.guru,* Selected Studies, Vol. II: Sanskrit Word Studies, pp. 297-304, Leiden 1975.

4 See Patrick Lebail, *Les Visages du maître dans le Vedanta,* in: "Le maître spirituel dans les grandes traditions d'Occident et d'Orient", Hermes, n. 4, 1966-67, pp. 146-157.

5 V. Raghavan, *The Indian Heritage,* Bangalore, 1958, p. xxvi, foot-note 3.

6 Chānd. Up. 6.14.2

is true of every school of thought and sect in Hinduism. Thus one finds references to the teacher-pupil successions and the association of particular teachings with certain teachers. The methods of attaining the highest state of spiritual experience are hearing about, reasoning about, and meditating upon the ultimate Reality[7]. One must first hear about it from the Vedas and from the lips of a guru, an illumined teacher. Then one must reflect on and reason about it, and finally one should meditate on it. The guru's function is twofold: he explains the spirit and letter of the Vedas; but what is more important is that he teaches the spiritual doctrine by his life. The guru's daily acts, his casual words, sometimes even his silence transmit spiritual insight and ennoble the character of the one who is near him and lives constantly with him. His presence purifies and enriches the soul of the disciple.

2. The image of the guru in the Upanishads

When the disciple Satyakāma returned to his teacher (ācārya) there took place a dialogue which is significant to convey the meaning and role of a spiritual teacher. The teacher said: "My dear, you are radiant as is a man who knows Brāhman. Now who has been instructing you?" The disciple replied: "Not human beings; but it is you alone whom I should like to teach me, for I have heard from men like you that wisdom learnt from a teacher produces the best results". Then the teacher repeated the very words the others had spoken. Nothing of it was omitted[8]. Saṅkara comments on this passage thus: "One who knows Brāhman is always tranquillized with his senses, wears a smiling face, is free from all anxiety and fully satisfied[9]; hence the teacher remarked that the disciple appeared as if he knew Brāhman". People other than human beings, i.e., deities have taught him: it means that nobody else should dare to teach except his own teacher. What would be the use of anybody else saying anything with regard to truth. The disciple does

7 Brh.Up. 2.4.5: śravana, manana and nididhyāsana.

8 Chānd. Up. 4.9

9 Saṅkara's comment on Chānd.Up. 4.9: prasannendriyaḥ prahasita-vadanaś ca niścintaḥ, kṛtārtho brahma-vid bhavati.

not attach any importance to anybody else except his teacher. Sages like his master have insisted that it is only knowledge learnt from the teacher that becomes best; i.e., acquires its highest character[10].

The teacher is regarded as essential as the remover of a bandage of a blindfolded man who wishes to find his way home. Hence it is said in the Upanishad: "And as, if one released the bandage of a blindfolded man and told him: "in that direction are the Gandharas, go in that direction; thereupon, being informed and capable of judgement, he would by asking his way from village to village arrive at Gandhara; in exactly the same manner does one here who has a teacher to show him the way know that he will remain in this phenomenal world only so long as he is not released; then he will arrive home"[11]. Saṅkara interprets the text thus: our real home is Being (Sat). Our eyes are bandaged with desires for worldly possessions which blind us. When we suddendly meet a person who knows the Self, whose own bonds have been broken, who points out the way, then we are sure that we are not mere creatures of the world but we belong to the ultimate reality. We shall remain in the phenomenal world as long as we are not released from ignorance[12].

The following is a teacher's prayer which is worth citing in order to understand the true nature of the teacher:

Exalted is he in the Vedic hymns[13], possessor of every form[14],
Sprung from the immortal, he surpasses the hymns [themselves].
May he, great Indra, deliver me by wisdom!
May I, O God, become a possessor of immortality!
May my body be robust and vigorous,
My tongue exeeding sweet!
May I hear abundantly with my ears!
Thou art the sheath of Brāhman in wisdom swathed:
Preserve for me what I have heard!

---

10 Cfr. Saṅkara's comment on the same passage.

11 *Chānd.* Up. 6.14

13 *Chandas* is the sacred text of the Veda.

14 Viśva-rūpa: all-formed.

She (Prosperity)[15] it is, who ever and anon
Brings, spreads out, swiftly appropriates to me
Garments and kine and food and drink,
So bring me prosperity
Rich in wool and rich in flocks. All hail!

May students of sacred knowledge (brahmacārin) come to me! All hail!

May students of sacred knowledge come to me from every side! All hail!

May students of sacred knowledge come forward to me! All hail!

May students of sacred knowledge be self-restrained! All hail!
May students of sacred knowledge be at peace! All hail!

May I be glorious among men! All hail!
May I excel the very rich! All hail!
May I enter into thee, O Lord (*Bhaga*)! All hail!
Do thou enter into me, O Lord! All hail!
In thee, possessed of a thousand branches,
In thee, O Lord, I am cleansed! All hail!

As waters follow a downward course, as the months [are merged] in the year, so may students of sacred knowledge, O Ordainer[16], come to me from everywhere! All hail!

Thou art [my] refuge; shine upon me; make me thy home![17]

This is a prayer addressed to the Supreme Being, asking for mental power and physical fitness without which knowledge of Brāhman is impossible. It is in other words a prayer for acquiring intelligence and mental power, especially a tenacious memory, and for physical and moral wealth. According to Saṅkara, the syllable oṁ is preeminent among the Vedic hymns. It is of all forms, as the whole universe is its manifestation. Brāhman means the highest Self *(Paramātman)*. The God addressed is the sheath of Brāhman, as

15 *Śrī*.
16 Dhātri: establisher or creator.
17 Taittiriya Up.1.4.

of a sword, being the seat of his manifestation. One can give also the theistic interpretation by taking the whole formula as a supplication to God; in which case the descriptions are to be taken as those of the attributes of God.

The seeker after the knowledge of Brāhman *(Brahmavidyā)* must be able to concentrate his thought on a given object and keep it uninterruptedly in the field of attention. The study of the Vedas is an auxiliary means to the direct intuition of Reality; concentration is a direct aid to it. The immortal stands for the Vedas which are a means to immortality. Often we need the physical, moral and spiritual strength for the realization of our highest destiny. Oṁ is the sheath or cover of Brāhman. This means that the highest Reality which is the innermost Self of man can be objectified for the purpose of worship only through a symbol.

The teacher prays for getting fortune and students. To the undisciplined wealth is a source of evil; not so to the disciplined. What matters is not the possession or non-possession of wealth but the attitude to it. One may possess wealth and be indifferent to it; or one may not possess wealth and yet be preoccupied to secure it by any means. "All Hail (Svāha)" marks the end of a formula after repeating which one oblation is offered into the sacrificial fire. These prayers offered as oblations express indirectly the eagerness of the true spiritual teacher to transmit wisdom to an increasing group of calm and self-restrained students. His prayers for wealth in cloth and kine, for food and drink are meant to sustain the maintenance of the dependent disciples.

Finally, the master longs for sharing his wisdom among a multitude of worthy candidates. This is expressed in the words: "as water flows downwards, as months go to make up the year, so many numerous students come to me". Only a genuine teacher has the gift to communicate spiritual wisdom widely and effectively. The knowledge and love of God is said to be a penetration of God into the inmost substance of the soul. The teacher longs for the most intimate union and inner completion through participation in the Divine (God or Absolute).

The teacher gives the practical precepts to the student in order to prepare the spiritual aspirant for the intuitive realization of Brāhman by stimulating in him a strong desire for it, accompanied by mental and moral purity.

Once he has given instruction in the Veda, the teacher should proceed to instruct his pupil [as follows]:
Speak the truth.
Do what is right (*dharma).*
Do not neglect study [of the Veda].
After you have given your teacher an acceptable sum, do not let your family line die out.
Do not be careless about truth.
Do not be careless about what is right.
Do not be careless about welfare.
Do not be careless about prosperity.
Do not be negligent in the study and recitation [of the Veda].
Do not neglect your duties to the gods and ancestors.
Let your mother be a god to you.
Let your father be a god to you.
Let your teacher be a god to you.
Let a guest be a god to you.
Perform only deeds to which no blame attaches, no others.
Respect such deeds of ours as have been well done, no others.
Offer the comfort of a seat to whatever Brāhmans may be better than we[18]. Give with faith[19]: do not give without faith. Give plentifully: give modestly; give with awe; give with sympathy[20].
Now if you are in doubt about how to act or how to behave, then behave as Brāmans of good judgement would behave if they were present,
[Brāhmans] who are competent, verserd in these matters, not harsh, devoted to what is right. This is the rule, this the teaching, this the sacred doctrine *(Upanisad)* of the Veda, this the instruction.
And so it should be respected; yes, this should be respected even so[21].

The whole personality of the student must be regenerated through appropriate discipline in one or more lives in order to attain the sacred knowledge of Brāhman. Good work and noble conduct must precede before the illumination is reached. In the above

18 Or 'in their presence not a word should be breathed by you'.
19 *Śraddhā.*
20 *Samvid.*
21 Taitt. Up. 1.11.

passage the ideal of a perfect student are formulated. The injunction to study the Vedas includes also the inquiry into and the understanding of the text so that the disciple may put into practice what he has learnt. *Dharma* has to be undestood in the sense of duty in general, i.e., to oneself, to others, and to God. The necessity of learning is repeatedly stressed, for knowledge in youth is wisdom in age. The Indian sages always held that learning is the eye of the mind. They never allowed to slip away from recollection what has been once studied.

To love our parents is the first law of nature. Let the student do for them daily what is agreeable. A son should be devoted to the service of his parents as long as they live. If they are satisfied with his virtue, he gets the reward of all religious deeds. What is not consistent with reason should not be accepted even if the Brāhmans were to tell it. No human being is absolutely and perpetually blameless. Hence one should take the great men as models only when they perform what is right and noble. A student should not interrupt when the elders full of wisdom and experience assemble to discuss important subjects. They should wait upon them with obedience and eagerness to learn. Faith *(Śraddlbā)* means earnest belief, trust, loyalty, confidence, reverence, composure of mind, and religious zeal. One has faith when one has a firm and active faith in the words of a competent spiritual guide and the revealed scriptures and is earnest about it. Devotion, adoration, oblation, sacrifice and prayer become blemishless only if they are performed with faith. Even if the gift is rich, the giver in true humility should feel as if it were only a small thing in comparison with greater gifts. The soul is softened and consoled by such acts of charity which is the spring of virtue. Intellectual and ethical virtues are absorbed through imitating one's elders, inspired by a genuine admiration for their virtues. Moral character has its basis in the habits formed in the light of the experience of those who are better than oneself; namely, the good Brāhmans. In case of doubts and conflicts one should follow the Brāhmans who have love for all beings; their tenderness of sentiment and enlightened consciousness should be our standards.

So far the word used to signify the teacher has been ācārya. In the following texts the term guru is used to signify the same. The guru is the personal teacher and the spiritual preceptor who has himself gained spiritual knowledge and hence becomes the competent master to impart this knowledge to the disciple. The knowledge of brāhman is to be sought properly from a qualified guru:

> When he surveys the worlds built up by ritual works
> *(Karma)* a Brāhman must despair.
> Between what is made and what is unmade[22] there is no connection: To know [the truth of] this, let him approach a guru with fuel in hand[23], and let [the guru be] versed in the Veda, Brāhman his [only] goal.
> Let him approach him properly, tranquil and at peace,
> His mind at rest, and then this wise [preceptor] *(guru)*
> Will teach him the science of Brāhman in its very essence
> Whereby he may know the Imperishable Real, the Person[24].

In the world of transmigration *(samsāra)* there is nothing which is not made, for all worlds produced by *karma* are transitory. There is nothing eternal in it. The student is a seeker after that which is eternal, immortal, immovable. Hence there is no use in *karma* which is full of trouble and which leads to misery. Thus disgusted, the student should only approach the guru who possesses the qualities such as control of mind, control of senses and mercy, who is versed in the recital of the Vedas and who is centred in the Brāhman. The guru is not only learned in the scriptures but also should be a man of realization.

Having duly approached the guru, let the disciple propitiate him and question him about the true and immortal Person *(Purusha)*. To the disciple whose heart is subdued, who is free from such faults as pride, who has control over his senses and mind, let the teacher communicate the knowledge of Brāhman. Again the same teaching is further emphasized as follows:

> The supreme mystery of the end of the Veda *(Vedānta)*
> Was pronounced in an earlier age;

---

22 The uncreated Brahmā-world, *Chan.*Up.8.13.

23 The token of discipleship.

24 Mund.Up. 1.2.12-13.

> Let it not be told to an unquiet man,
> Or to one who is neither son nor pupil.
> To the great-souled man who loyally
> And greatly loves (*bhakti*) [his] God,
> Who loves his spiritual master (*guru*) even as his God,
> The master of this discourse will shine with clearest light,
> With clearest light will shine[25].

It is declared in the above passage that the entire teaching of the Vedānta will become manifest only to him who has acquired peace of mind and who has the highest love for God and for his guru. This is the first occurrence in Brāhmanic literature of the term *bhakti* in its technical religious sense. Although the verse in which the term *bhakti* occurs is the very last of the Śvetāsvatara Upanishad which is rather late among the Upanishads, still it need not be considered a later addition. For the *bhakti* attitude unmistakably pervades much of this Upanishad, and particularly in chapter six, as above. This attitude consists in trust in the Lord, loving adoration, recourse to his salvific action. Liberation is achieved by renunciation, asceticism, meditation, love of God (*bhakti*) and divine grace (*prasāda*).

One of the minor upanishads which are of more recent date describes the need and qualities of the guru:

> The radiant lustre of the "internal sign" is the self-own [non-dual Absolute]. Through instruction by a superior teacher the "inetrnal sign" becomes the radiant light of the thousand [petalled] lotus [at the crown of the head], or the light of awareness hidden in the cave of the wisdom-faculty *(buddhi)*, or the fourth state of consciousness abiding in the *sodaśānta*[26]. The sight of that [supreme reality] depends on a true teacher.

> [The true] teacher is well-versed in the Veda, a devotee of Vishṇu, free from jealousy, a knower of yoga and intent on yoga, always having the nature of yoga, and pure.

---

25 Svetas.Up. 6.22-23.

26 This term refers to a "spot sixteen digit-lengths over the crest".

He who is equipped with devotion to the teacher, [who is] especially a knower of the Self, possessing such characteristics [as are mentioned above], is designated as a guru.
The syllable gu [means] darkness; the syllable ru the destroyer of this [darkness]. By reason of [the power] to destroy darkness, he is called guru.

The guru alone is the supreme Absolute, the guru alone is the supreme way, the guru alone is the supreme knowledge, the guru alone is the supreme resort.

The guru alone is the supreme limit, the guru alone is the supreme wealth. Because he is the teacher of that [non-dual Being], he is the guru greater [than any other] guru[27].

The *Advaya-tāraka-upanishad* expounds the *tārakayoga*[28] which consists in the practice that saves one from falling into the cycle of rebirth and leads to the realization of the non-dual Absolute; an ascetic who has subdued the senses and is filled with the six virtues such as quiescence, control of self, arrest of vain desires, patience, mental concentration and trust, is fit for this. The Upanishad distinguishes between an "internal sign", an "external sign" and an "intermediate sign". These three signs or visions can be said to constitute different phases of the well-known tantric practice *#āṁbhavī-mudra*. The tāraka-yoga comprises of two distinct phases: the practice and experience of the three "signs" terminating in the resplendant tāraka-state and subsequently the ultimate realization of the non-mental state revealing Being itself. Such a realization is impossible without the guru[29].

27 Advaya-Tāraka-Upanishad 13-18.

28 *Tāraka* literally "a star", it refers in *rāja*-yoga to the light between and in front of the eyebrows which is seen in meditation. The pupil of the eye is also called *"tāraka"*.

29 See GEORG FEUERSTEIN, *The Essence of Yoga,* London, 1974, pp. 207-11. See also JEAN VARENNE, *Sept Upanishads,* Paris, 1981, pp. 99-119 for the French translation and introduction.

3. Respect for the guru in the *Mahābhārata*

The *Śānti Parva* contains many general counsels on morality and good government. In this context it is proposed that the greatest of all virtues is respect for father, mother and guru. One should worship these three persons with great respect and do whatever they command without any hesitation. One should never do what they forbid. What they command should always be done without any doubt. The one who serves his father regularly will easily cross this world. By serving the mother in the same way one will attain to the region of felicity in the next. By serving the preceptor (guru) with regularity one will obtain the region of *Brahmā*. Those who behave properly towards these three will obtain great fame in the three worlds and will be blessed; their merit and reward will be great. One should not transgress them in any act. Respect to them is shown by eating only after they have eaten and by never eating anything that is better than what they eat. We should not impute to them any fault and always serve them with humility. He who honours these three is honoured in all the worlds. On the other hand, he who disregards them fails to obtain any merit from any of his acts.

One ācārya is superior to ten brāhmans learned in the Vedas. One Upādhyāya is again superior to ten ācāryas. The father again is superior to ten upādhyāyas. The mother again is superior to ten fathers, or perhaps the whole world in importance. There is no one that deserves such reverence as the mother. The preceptor (guru) is worthy of greater reverence than the father or even the mother[30]. The father and the mother are authors of one's being. The father and the mother only create the body. The life on the other hand that one obtains from one's preceptor is heavenly. Such a life is subject to no decay and is immortal. One should not punish one's father and mother even if they deserve punishment. He who imparts true instruction to the disciple and communicates the Vedas and gives knowledge which is immortal should be regarded as both a father and a mother. The disciple in grateful recognition of what the guru has done should never do anything that would in-

30 Gurur *garīyām* pitrto *mātṛtaś*ceti me matiḥ.

jure the guru. He who does not reverence the preceptor after receiving instruction from him by obeying him dutifully in thought and deed incurs the sin of killing a foetus (the greatest sin). The guru always shows great affection for his disciples. The latter should show their gurus commensurate reverence. If the gurus are worshipped, the sages (Ri#is), the gods and the fathers (pitris) are all pleased[31].

4. The guru in the law books

Aphorisms relating to dharma, the hindu norm, are the most ancient extant treatises of a juridical character which form part of the hindu tradition (Smriti). They are concerned also with religious observances. There existed a body of domestic priests who are permanently or temporarily attached to a family either as spiritual teachers (guru) or as secular teachers. Here are some of the aphorisms that concern the guru or ācārya (the spiritual master).

The teacher is called Ācārya because the student gathers from him dharmas. Never should a student think ill of the teacher. For the teacher gives him a new birth in knowledge. And that is the highest birth. Mother and Father engender his body only[32].

The student must be gentle, subdued, controlled in senses and shrinking from doing wrong, firm in his fortitude, neither lazy, irascible, nor jealous. He must in private bring to the teacher's notice any inadvertent or deliberate transgression of the rules of conduct on the teacher's part. To such a disciplined student all the meritorious sacrificial and household acts bear fruit in his studentship itself[33].

The teacher must with the same anxiety as he would display toward his son impart learning to his pupil, with the utmost attention and without keeping back anything in the dharmas. Except in unavoidable circumstances the teacher must not so detain the pupil in his private work as to hinder the student's learning. Divided in his devotion, the pupil who finds incompetence in his teacher

31 The Mahābhārata 12.108

32 Apastamba Dharma Sūtra 1.1.14.

33 Ibidem 1.3.17-24; 1.4.25 and 29.

ceases to be a student. And the teacher too who fails to impart knowledge ceases to be a teacher[34].

It is in the context of initiation of the student by a guru that these injunctions were given. The initiation is the consecration in accordance with the texts of the Veda of a male who is desirous of and can make use of sacred knowledge. Coming out of darkness, he enters darkness, whom a man unlearned in the Vedas, initiates, and so does he who, without being learned in the Vedas, performs the rite of initiation. As a performer of this rite of initiation he shall seek to obtain a man, in whose family sacred learning is hereditary, who himself possesses it, and who is devout in following the law. And under him the sacred science must be studied until the end, provided the teacher does not fall off from the ordinances of the law.

The Laws of Manu condense in the form of diversified maxims all of the content of dharma, whether it be the specifically religious rules, institutions, customs and ethical precepts which dominate an individual's life. This work gives some "definitions" of various hindu religious personages among whom are included the *guru* and the *ācārya.*

"The brāhman who having initiated a disciple with the sacred thread teaches him the Veda along with rituals and the treatises of secret knowledge (Upanishad) is by the wise called *ācārya.*

"Again the brāhman who teaches parts of the Veda or the Vedāngas to another for his livelihood is called *upādhyāya* (subteacher)".

The brāhman who performs according to rule the rites on conception and the like, and feeds the child with rice for the first time is called *guru.*

He who, chosen by any one, performs fire-kindling rites called *Agnyādheya pākayajñas* and the sacrifices like *Agniṣṭoma* etc, for another is called the sacrificial priest.

He who by Vedic knowledge fills both ears rightly is to be considered (like one's) father and mother; one should never injure him.

---

34 Ibidem 1.8.25-28,.

An *ācārya* by respectability surpasses ten *upādhyāyas*; a father by respectability surpasses hundred *ācāryas* and a mother by respectability surpasses even a thousand fathers.

Among the natural father and the giver of the Veda, the father who gives the Veda is more revered; the birth of the twice-born man through the Veda is eternal, here and hereafter (after death).

As his father and mother beget him mutually out of sexual union, one should know that (birth to be merely) his cause of existence, when he is born from the womb.

But the birth which the teacher who has completed the Veda, duly brings about for him by the *Gāyātrī*, that is the true (birth), free from old age, eternal.

He who confers the benefit of the Veda *(Śruta)* on any one, be it little or be it much, he should know him to be here his guru, by reason of that benefit through the Veda.

The Brāhman who is the cause of the Vedic birth and the director of one's duty, even though a youth, is legally the father of an old man (whom he teaches)[35]".

It must be remembered that the terms *ācārya* and *guru* are not used in this book with the precision one might expect after this definition; in fact at the end of this section 2 both are used as equivalent.

5. The guru and disciple in the Bhāgavata Purāna

The early chapters of the eleventh book of the *Bhāgavata Purāna* teach what is characteristic of the Bhāgavata religion and its way of salvation. Nimi asked the sages various questions concerning the attainment of salvation *(moksha)*, one of which is: "How can one whose mind is not controlled and who is of dull understanding easi-

35 Manusmṛti 2.140-150.

ly cross over the *māyā*[36] which causes the creation, preservation and dissolution?" The sage Prabuddha replied:

"One desirous of knowing the highest good should resort to the guru who is versed in the Vedas [which embody Brahman in the form of words], who has realized the ultimate Reality and who is free from attachment and hatred. Under the guru whom one should love as one's own self and as the object of one's devotion, one should, by rendering devout service to him, learn the ways of life of the Lord's devotees, by which Sri Harī is pleased, Sri Harī who is the soul of the universe and gives himself away to his devotees. First the disciple should learn detachment of the mind from all objects [body, children, etc.] and attachment to the Lord's devotees.

And he should also learn to cherish in all sincerity compassion, friendliness and humility towards one's inferiors, equals and superiors respectively. He should [further] learn [to acquire] purity [external and internal], devotion to his religious duties, endurance, control over his speech, a habit to study the scriptures, sincerity, continence, non-violence and evenness of mind under the stress of dualities [like pleasure and pain, profit and loss]. He should learn to see the Self [Atman] [as the intelligent substance] and Iśvara [the Ruling Principle] pervading all, live in solitude, without any sense of possession for any dwelling, wear pure clothing or rags and feel satisfied with whatever he could get for food. He should also learn to have faith in the scriptures celebrating the Lord, without disparaging other scriptures, and curb his mind, speech and actions, (through control of breath, tongue and activity respectively), and to be truthful and able to control the senses and mind. He should learn to hear, sing and dwell on the story of the advent, pastimes and excellences of Lord Sri Harī of wonderful deeds and to do everything for [pleasing] him. He should further learn to offer to the supreme Lord all his sacrificial activites, gifts, austerities, repetition of the sacred syllables, righteous conduct, and all that he likes for himself, [nay] his wife, children, house and his very life. He should also learn to love devotedly those persons who have realized Sri Krishna as their own self and as the Lord of their life; to serve the mobile and immobile creatures [as the embodiments of

36 Māyā here means the creative power of God (Bhagavān).

the Lord]; and [especially] to serve human beings and among them more espcially those who adhere to their own duty and are devotees of the Lord. He should [further] learn to expound and discuss among the devotees the sacred glory of the Lord, and in association with others find delight and satisfaction resulting in the freedom of the mind from egoism. [Thus] remembering and reminding one another of Sri Harī, who destroys innumerable sins [in an instant], their devotion turning into divine love, the devotees filled with rapture experience a thrill of joy"[37].

These are the duties of a Bhāgavata disciple who puts himself under the guidance of a guru. Whatever a man does, whether it be the body or speech or mind or the senses or intellect or the sense of Ego-consciousness that acts, let him offer that all up to the Supreme Nārāyana. He who is removed from God, first forgets the Lord; then there is wrong perception such as "I am the body". This is caused by the māyā of Bhagavān. Fear arises from devotion to that which is not self. Therefore wise men worship the Lord only, with unfailing bhakti (love), knowing his guru to be one with God and self. In meditation the guru stands between God and self, and is God to all practical purposes to the devotee.

6. The guru in the non-dualist (Advaita) tradition

In the non-dualist tradition one might say that the identity of the individual self (*Jīva*) and the Absolute (Brāhman) is an established fact and that hence it cannot be acquired afresh as a result of human endeavour. But though such identity is always present, it remains unrealized in the state of ignorance. An example is adduced here. As a man who forgets all about his jewel that he wears on his neck suffers sorrow and grief thinking it is lost, but finds it when somebody points it out to him, so is the condition of the individual self in ignorance. We here choose the teaching of the *Vedāntasāra* as representative of the non-dualist school on the necessity of the guru for the realization of the Absolute.

37 The Bhāgavata Purāṇa 11.3.21-31.

"Just as a man with his head on fire goes to the water, so this qualified person, scorched by the fire of an endless round of birth, death, etc, takes a bundle of firewood in his hands and approaches a spiritual teacher versed in the Vedas and intent upon Brāhman, and becomes his follower. As it is said in the Veda,[38] "In order to know him, he should go with fuel in his hands to a teacher learned in the Vedas and intent on Brāhman.

Such a teacher with great kindness instructs him by the method of illusory attribution (adhyāropa), followed by its withdrawal (apāvada). As it is written in the Veda[39]," "To him on drawing nigh with truly calmed mind and sense subdued, that learned one should so expound in truth the Brāhman lore that he may know the true and undecaying Male"[40].

The qualified disciple is one who possesses due intelligence; i.e., one who by reading the Vedas and Vedāngas according to rule either in this life or in the former one has obtained a general idea of the meaning of the whole; who by performing the constant and occasional rites, the penances, and devotional exercises, and abstaining from things done with desire of reward and from those forbidden has got rid of all sin and so thoroughly cleansed his mind, and who is possessed of the four means of knowledge. The four means (sādhana) of knowledge are: discrimination between eternal and non-eternal substances; indifference to the enjoyment of rewards here and hereafter; the possession of quiescence, self-restraint, etc.; and desire for release. As it is evident, in order to qualify for initiation into the spiritual doctrine the aspirant has to undergo a long preparatory course.

In order to describe the pure Absolute (Brāhman) the teacher attributes to Brāhman or superimposes on it certain qualities which in reality do not belong to him, and then withdrawing them, teaches that the remaing is the undifferentiated Absolute. Superimposition *(adbyāropa)* consists in holding for true that which is false, in accomodation to the intelligence of the uninitiated. At a later stage

38 *Muṇḍaka* Up. 1.2.12.

39 Ibidem 1.2.13.

40 *Vedāntasāra* 30-31.

of training this false imputation is gainsaid, and this gainsaying is termed rescission (*apavāda*). *Apavāda* is the removal of this superimposition.

It is interesting to read the commentary of Śaṅkara on the *Muṇḍaka Upanishad* 1.2.12-13. He says that only the person thoroughly disgusted with the cycle of rebirth which is in the nature of ends and means is entitled to acquire the supreme knowledge (*paravidyā*). The mode of disgust is explained further. In the cycle of rebirth (*saṁsāra*) there is nothing which is not made: for all works produced by karma are tansitory. All that is produced by karma is one of the four kinds: that which is produced, that which is reached, that which is refined and that which is modified. But the seeker after what is eternal, immortal, changeless, permanent is not interested with what is full of misery and trouble. Hence such a seeker should approach a guru who is full of mercy, who has control of his mind and of the external senses; even the one who is versed in the sāstras should not independently by himself seek the knowledge of Brāhman without the help of the guru. The learned preceptor who knows Brāhman should teach the disciple the *Brahmavidyā*, that knowledge of Brāhman as it should be taught and thus make the pupil cross the sea of ignorance.

7. The guru in the tradition of qualified non-dualism

The Pañcarātra school emphasizes on absolute and unconditional surrender to God and on leaving the work of salvation to be done by Him. It also teaches that God can grant salvation irrespective of moral considerations. Hence it is evident that this school considers that the grace of God is all important. Out of love for devotees God assumes five-fold forms and seeks to liberate them from the bonds of the cycle of rebirths. Although God in this way works for individual's salvation, every one has to play his part. He has to approach God through a teacher who initiates the individual in the method of worshipping God. God has to be worshipped through his idols (*arcās*), accompanied by the mantras. The worship of idols, ceremony of initiation into the sect and consequent importance of the guru and the predominance of the tantric element, all of which is very much insisted upon in the *Pañcarātra* school, are absent in Rāmānuja. But Rāmānuja attaches a great importance to the guidance that leads the steps of the aspirant aright. In the efforts of an individual to seek spiritual perfection right guidance plays an important role, for it is the guide who takes upon himself the responsibility of commending his pupil to the Lord. Apart from the advanced souls (the *ācāryas*) who have really gone ahead along the path of surrender to the Lord *(Prapatti)*, who may serve as sign posts , the greatest and real guide is Srī Lakshmī, the consort of Lord Vishnu, who mediates between the suppliant and God and secures His mercy for him. Lakshmī like a loving mother pardons her child for all his lapses and gives grace. According to Rāmānuia Lakshmī's intercession is necessary for acquiring divine grace.

A brief account of the succession of the *ācāryas* is given thus. It is declared that in the case of everyone, the only means of securing *moksha* is to have an *ācārya*. To the man desirous of *moksha*, the line of *ācāryas* is stated in the *Śruti* to extend upward even to the Supreme Bhagavān for purpose of meditation. The Supreme Lord is the foremost of all *ācāryas*. Krishna is the *ācārya*, father and guru[41]. *Ācārya* is one who teaches *Brahma Vidyā* while the guru is one who teaches the Vedas "Nārāyaṇa who is the guru of all the world is also my guru"[42]. It is Nārāyaṇa who at the beginning vouchsafed the Vedas to Brahmā and when they were stolen brought them back to him and through him spread their knowledge in the world. It is he who blessed Brahmā's sons to understand all truths by themselves and to follow the path of renunciation. Through them he revealed the

41 This refers to the Rāmānuja school of Srī Vaishnava tradition. The guru in reality in Śaivism is the manifestation of Śiva himself, even when he comes in human form to souls in the lowest rank. Cfr., MEYKANTA, Śivajñāp±tam 8.3. "The thinking man who has learnt to worship the ideal he lives in spirit and in truth, finds it clothed in the form he thinks, and meeting and greeting him in person, to give him the helping hand that he so much needs and longs after. The guru appears now and here, it may be in vision, or it may be in name and form and flesh as the thinker has been longing after to see, and second his efforts, describing to him the glory of the ideal that he has been vaguely thinking after. Hitherto he has been hazily building only with Hope and Faith. He has yet to learn that love which endures to the end, and transcends time and space and the limits of causation. For this purpose the guru describes to him in the clear light of reason the glory of the Promised land, and prepares him therefore by testing his powers, his constancy, and his moral stamina, by a series of disciplinary exercises". See C.V. SVAMINATHAN, in: *Siddhanta Dipika*, XI.2 (aug. 1910).

42 The Mahābhārata 2.38.3.

means of attaining salvation. It is he who later by the agency of such seers as Nārada maintained in tact the tradition of the upanishads. Further through incarnations he himself stood out and revealed spiritual truths and also the means of attaining *moksha*. Nārāyana assumed a new series of ten incarnations in the form of *ālvārs* like Nammāḻvar, Yamunācārya, Rāmānuja. "The wise man should bring his guru to the light (of renoun) and should guard the sacred mantra with great care: from the omission to bring his guru to light and by revealing the mantra he declines in wealth (of knowledge) and in age (spiritual standing)[43]". It will be useful to refer to one of the statements of the Vaishnava saints on God as Guru. God is the guru in one's heart. In the lecture assembly of Embār the subject of who is the first spiritual preceptor for the soul came to be discussed. "The guru imparts the Scriptures", some said. Others opined: "The first is that godly man who helps to take us to the spiritual Preceptor for acceptance". "Not so", said Embār, the first preceptor is that universal Lord who is seated in our hearts, and who unseen gives us the impulse *not to resist,* but to *yield* to the proposals for good services offered by the visible preceptors or helpers"[44].

With the rise of the *bhakti* movement which stressed love of God, the guru became an important figure. He was not only venerated as the leader of the *bhakti* sect but was considered the living embodiment of the spiritual truth and thus was identified with the Deity. It is the guru who prescribes spiritual disciplines and who at the time of initiation instructs the pupil in the use of mantras and to assit him in his meditation.

The guru chooses for him the chosen Deity (Iṣṭta Devatā), i.e., the form of God best suited to the disciple. And corresponding to each divine form there is a sound symbol (*mantra)* which the guru imparts, which is to be repeated every day with devotion. The pupil also learns how to worship the chosen Deity. Thus learning the entire preparatory course of *bhaktiyoga* from his spiritual guide, without an unflinching devotion to one's own chosen Deity, the aspirant cannot make any progress in the way of love of God.

Modern Bhagavatism lays great stress on the respect to be

---

43 See VEDANTA DESIKA, Śrīmad Rahasyatrayasāra, Introduction, pp. 1-10, tr. by RAJAGOPALA AYYANGAR, Kunbakonam, 1956.

44 Ibidem, p. 15

shown to the guru. The first line of the *Bhaktimālā* which enumerates the essentials of religion which are *bhakti* (love of God), *bhakta* (the God-lover), *bhagavanta* (the adorable) and *guru* (the teacher) brings out the importance of the guru. In classical Hinduism perfect obedience was required from the pupil. He was the pupil's second father, more to be respected and venerated than his own natural father. In moden Hinduism God speaks through the guru; and fullest devotion to him is to be shown in thought, word and action.

8. Śrī Ramana Maharśi, the guru (1879-1950)

After having studied what the Hindu sacred texts teach on the nature and function of the guru, now we shall see how this ideal of the guru is exemplified in the person of Śrī Ramana Maharśi. We shall not treat of his doctrinal teaching so much but consider rather his personality as embodying the ideal of a spiritual master. He was a pure non-dualist (advaitin) and the highest experience of non-duality between the Absolute and the self became quite easy for him right from the days of his youth. His life history is quite simple. At the age of seventeen he left home and reached Arunācala where he spent the rest of his life. Through the experience of death he discovered that the Self is untouched by death and that he is immortal Self. Arunācala is one of the sacred places of pilgrimage for the Hindus; there God is worshipped in the form of Light. During the life of Śrī Ramana spiritual aspirants came to Arunacala from everywhere in order to learn spiritual wisdom from Śrī Ramana.

Sometimes people went to him with the idea that his *dar#ana* (vision) might bring earthly goods and blessings. But they soon discovered that Maharśi who was the personification of the supreme God transformed them to be truly aspirants of spiritual good of liberation from passion, desire and egoism. Some others went to him to find a solution to the problems of poverty, illiteracy, disease, war, etc. They were deeply concerned about social reform. The inevitable question which Śrī Ramana put to them was: "Have you reformed yourself first?" The meaning of this question was that the so-called social service should not turn out to be a self-gratification of the ego. For according to him in much of what passes for altruism, there is a core of egoism. It is only that service which contributes to the reduction of the ego that brings the real good[45].

Śrī Ramana does not impose any disciplinary regulation on the aspirant but recognizes the great value of devotion to God and ethical behaviour as valuable aids to purify and strenthen the mind. It also keeps out attractions of the external world and fixes the mind on God, pure and inspiring. This help is often termed the grace of God *(Iśvara-kripa)*. This leads one also to seek and serve a guru; his grace *(guru-kripa)* is a factor that greatly helps or even accomplishes Self-realization or God-realization. The aspirants have first to accept the teachings of the guru and scripture on trust. Maharśi indicates that it is necessary to approach the guru who knows as guide for the entire journey. The guru knows which path suits the aspirant and what directions should be given and what steps to be taken at each stage[46].

Maharśi, recalling his own experience of death and of the Self, explains for the benefit of the aspirant his experience:

> "The "I' or my "Self" was holding the focus of attention by a powerful fascination, from that time forwards. Fear of death has vanished at once and for ever. Absorption in the Self has continued from that moment right up to this time. Other thoughts may come and go like the various notes of a musician, but the "I" continues like the basic or fundamental sruti note which accompanies and blends with all other notes"[47].

He clearly states that a guru is required for the *sādhana*. The proper guru is one to whom one's mind is attuned. The guru's trait *(svarūpa)* is that he should be endowed with tranquillity, patience, forgiveness and other virtues capable of attracting others even with the bare eye like the magnetic stone, and with a feeling of equality towards all. In order to know the true guru one ought to know

---

45 See T.M.P. MAHADEVAN, *Outlines of Hinduism*, Bombay, 1960, pp. 240 ff.

46 *Upadesa Sāram* of Sri Ramana Maharśi tr., Tiruvannamalai, 1960, pp. 18-22.

47 B.V. NARASIMHASWAMY, *Self realization*, Tiruvannamalai, 1953, p. 22.

the form of God as seen in the whole universe and know the form of his own Self. The world contains many great men. But the one in whom you have faith is your guru[48].

From the standpoint of the path of knowledge it is the supreme state of the Self, which is the Sad-guru. It is different from the ego-self, which is called one's self. The ego-self is the Jīva. It is different from the Lord of all (*Sarveśvara*). When through disinterested devotion the *jīva* approaches the Lord, He graciously assumes name and form and takes the *jīva* into himself. Therefore they say that the guru is none other than the Lord. He is a human embodiment of the Divine Grace. The real guru is God himself. To some great souls God reveals himself as the Light of their light from within. The spirit of service is really supreme devotion and the true devotee sees the supreme Being as the Lord immanent in everything. Worship of him by name and form leads one beyond all name and form. Complete devotion culminates in supreme knowledge[49].

The power of Śrī Ramana's presence was extremely effective on the disciples who were with him. Paul Brunton describes thus the impact on him of the silent presence of the Master.

> "I cannot turn my gaze away from him. My initial bewilderment, my perplexity at being totally ignored, slowly fade away as this strange fascination begins to grip me more firmly. But it is not till the second hour of the uncommon scene that I become aware of a silent, resistless change which is taking place within my mind. One by one, the questions which I prepared in the train with such meticulous accuracy drop away. For it does not now seem to matter whether I solve the problems which have hitherto troubled me. I know only that a steady river of quietness seems to be flowing near me, that a great peace is penetrating the inner reaches of my being, and that my thought-tortured brain is beginning to arrive at some rest"[50].

48 D.S. SASTRI, *Letters from SriRamanasramam* Tiruvannamalai, tr., 1962, pp.
49 *Sat-Darshana Bhāsya and talks with Maharśi,* Tiruvannamalai, 1970, v-vii.
50 K. SWAMINATHAN, *Ramana Maharśi,* New Delhi, 1975, PP. 52-53.

The primacy of living personality over doctrine and the experience of the spiritually ennobling presence are part of the Hindu tradition of the guru. Though Ramana Maharśi was a *jīvan-mukta* (a liberated while living in his body), he took interest in things that happened around him and recognized people who were his disciples and sometimes talked to them. He used to lend a helping hand even in the kitchen by helping the cook. But all these modes of action were performed without the least attachment to them. He radiated spiritual light around him.

9. Conclusion

From what we have been saying in the foregoing pages, we can gather that there are three conditions to be an effective guru. First, the guru ought to have a certain knowledge of the Hindu sacred texts, especially the Veda in order to be able to teach the Hindu spiritual doctrine to his disciples. There is a certain charism in the guru who communicates the Veda in a personal and direct manner to the disciple in as far as he himself is convinced of the truth of what he teaches. The guru himself must possess some illumination in the experiential and practical sphere in order to radiate the light of truth which he possesses. He lives the truth in a visible way as intensely as possible. He is the living embodiment of the truth that he teaches. Hence it is easy to understand why the Hindu texts insist on the fact that the guru is a manifestation of God. Śrī Vaishnavas consider him as the visible partial "incarnation" of God, for the guru is more than a teacher and even more than a mediator between God and man.

Secondly, the choice of the guru and of the disciple is important. Not every one is meant for every one else. The guru and the disciple should have a mutual attraction on the personal plane. It is not enough to have an aspiration for learning or doctrine alone. There should be communication of souls through modesty, respect and friendship. The guru ought to inspire the disciple and animate the desire to make progress in spiritual life. And the disciple should show a spirit of docility and commitment to advance in the spiritual knowledge.

Thirdly, the disciple should be capable of assimilating the doctrine. That is to say, he should be "appropriate" *(adhikārin)*. There are three requirements necessary to make a disciple appropriate or suited: he should be attracted to the doctrine by faith *(śraddhā)* in it and in the guru; he should be free from passion, cares, anxieties, troubles, in order to be ready to follow the way prescribed. Spiritual maturity *(adhikāra)* consists in the transformation of the disciple by the illumination and insight which he receives from the guru. Mere intellingence and culture do not guarantee spiritual maturity.

Finally, the characteristics of the Hindu guru are illustrated in an eminent way by the life and teaching of Śrī Ramana Maharśi.

CHAPTER FOUR

THE SĀDHU IDEAL AS REALIZED BY HINDU SAINTS

Introduction

The study of Hindu hagiography presents many difficulties for various reasons. The number of personages venerated by the Hindus is enormous. The cycle of legends that have been collected around them is innumerable. Since the Hindu society is broken up into numerous groups, each caste and sect has credited its own holy men with miraculous powers which have led to their veneration and even to their worship. Over and above this there is no authority or organization in the Hindu society to verify the objective merit of its saints or to control the popular acclamation of holiness of its heroes. Actually there is no effective institution to confer the honour of sainthood on any worthy member.

The fact is that from the beginning of the eighth century A.D., though there were some before that period, there appeared in different parts of India a line of saints and mystics who brought the ancient spiritual wisdom of India to the reach of the common people. They adopted the vernacular language and used the medium of hymns and songs to convey their spiritual message. They belonged to different castes and strata of society and taught the universality and basic oneness of all men. They were pilgrims of God, seeking him and experiencing him wherever they went; irrespective of their belonging to a particular religious sect and school of philosophy, they emphasized the fundamental truths and the eternal values of religion in a remarkably experiential manner. They were strong critics of hypocracy and corruption in the practice of religion, of empty forms and meaningless rituals; they pleaded for sincerity of faith and fellowship of beings and integration of the whole man. They were deeply convinced of the superiority of spiritual values over worldly pursuits and witnessed to their conviction in a powerful, even at times heroic, way. In what follows we shall try to bring out the implications of the term *sādhu* which renders the meaning of the saint in the Hindu context; we shall point out the characteristics of the Hindu saint, as is evident in the Hindu tradition so that the figure of a *sādhu* may become clearer and finally we shall illustrate this *sādhu* ideal as lived and experienced in the bhakti tradition by Rāmakrishna.

1. The Sanskrit Term: Sādhu

The word *sādhu* has a vast range of meanings that are very significant in the study of the ideal of Saints. First, it means "leading straight to a goal", "hitting the mark, unerring"; it also signifies "right, straight, not entangled". Secondly, it means "well-disposed, kind, willing, obedient". Thirdly, it implies "effective, efficient, successful, powerful, good, excellent". Fourthly, it says "good, virtuous, honourable, righteous, honest? Finally, it means "a holy man, saint, sage, seer"[1]. The term *sādhu* is etymologically connected with the word *sādhana*, both having the same root *sadh-*, which again means "directing to the goal, accomplishing one's aim". We know that *sādhana* is the classical term for spiritual endeavour and aim. Its literal meaning is "that by which something is performed"; or "means to an end". In the context of religion, it is always used to indicate the essential preliminary discipline that leads to the attainment of the spiritual experience[2]. *Sādhana* is that by which perfection *(siddhi)* is attained; i.e., instrument of perfection[3].

---

1 M. Monier-Williams, *A Sanskrit-English Dictionary*, Oxford.

2 For the Hindus the essence of religion lies in the *immediate* experience of the divine. This experience presupposes various kinds of discipline which gradually develop from the outer husk to the kernel of religion.

3 However the relation between the *sādhana* and perfection in religion should not be considered mechanical and deterministic, for in the theist current of Hinduism the final perfection is achieved through the grace of God, while in the non-dualist current, grace is admitted at the lower level of religion, and the ultimate realization of Brahman itself is not achieved by the instrument of *sādhana* of knowledge but it only prepares for the immediate illumination of the intellect. On Hindu Saints, see J.C. Oman, *The Mystics, Ascetics, and Saints of India*, London 1903; on Sadhus, see G.S. Ghurye, *Indian Sadhus*, Bombay, 1953.

Sādhana includes all the religious practices which are helpful to the realization of spiritual perfection and thus belongs to the practical side of religion which is the most important aspect of it, distinct from the various theories of relation of man to the ultimate Reality. In modern India the term *sādhu* is commonly applied, as an equivalent to "saintly", to any respected Hindu saint or devotee.

Going beyond etymology and the real sense of the term *sādhu*, we have to note that there is a Hindu religious sect which has appropriated the term as its own proper name. Its followers do not have any temples but declare that the true shrine is the meeting of the faithful, at which they read the writings of their leaders, sing songs and eat a common meal. Final emancipation from the cycle of rebirth is their great hope. They speak of God as the true name (*Satnāma*). They differ little from the sect of Satnamis which was originally founded by Rāidās, a pupil of Rāmānanda; he is known as Rohidas and revered in the Marātha country[4]. Its followers are to be found in the caste of Camārs (leather workers). While they profess to worship the one true God many also worship the Hindu deities. They abstain from meat of all kinds, intoxicating drinks and tobacco[5].

Again, the chief Hindu saint is called Gorakhnāth[6] who is described as flitting round the earth with a train of nine lords *(nāths)* and eighty four *siddhas* ("perfected"), sanctified by penance and austerities. The *siddhas* are properly speaking saints of exceptional purity of life who have attained a semidivine existence. Another class of Hindu saints are called Bhagats who are said to be leaders of sects such as Kabīr and his followers, Rāmānand, Nāmdev, etc.

One finds Sādhus in India, clothed in salmon-coloured robes with clean-shaven heads and faces or with long beards, conspicuous in centres of pilgrimage and public festivities. They belong to one or

---

4 See R.G. Bhandarkar, *Vaiṣṇavism, Saivism and minor religious systems* Strassburg, 1913, pp. 67 and 74.

5 See W.J. Wilkins, *Modem Hinduism,* London, 1975, pp. 351 ff.

6 Of Gorakhnāth nothing authentic is known, though his name is associated with legends dating from a remote past to comparatively modern times. We can mention a modern deified Hindu teacher or sage, named Gorakhnāth who is said to have gone from India into Nepal, and is worshipped there as well as at Gorakpur and Punjab. His followers are called Kanphatas. See Georges W. Briggs *Gorakhnath and the Kanpatha Yogis,* London, 1938, pp. 228ff.

other religious sect, order or fraternity. They come from all ranks of life and from all castes of the Hindu society. Again, we find amongst them all shades of religious belief and philosophical speculation and diatary habits. They certainly command the respect and even the veneration of vast multitudes of the Indian people who credit them with special supernatural power for good or evil. They are believed to possess divine knowledge and wisdom and can guide the ordinary person to reach his ultimate destiny. The glory of Hinduism will be lost if you remove these sādhus who lead a life of renunciation and meditation. It is the sādhus who give encouragement and solace to the householders (ordinary lay people) when they are in religious doubt and distress.

There are certain qualities that are characteristic of the Indian Sādhuism or holiness which will be studied in greater detail in the following pages so that what is of typically Hindu spirituality can become evident and understood. These are asceticism and renunciation; yoga and meditation; realization of the Absolute through knowledge *(jñāna);* love of God *(bhakti);* and social obligation. Although traits of these properties can be found in every good, practising Hindu, yet they are present in a notable way and in some cases to a heroic degree in the sadhus. Besides, these traits are to be grasped better in order to penetrate deeply into the personality of the concrete individual sādhus.

2. Characteristics of Hindu Sādhus

As Carlyle said: "The manner of men's hero-worship, verily it is the innermost fact of their existence and determines all the rest". The qualities which we are going to expose, so to say, form the soul of Indian holiness, which are preeminent in the esteem of the Indian people from the early stages of the development of Hinduism; a fact which speaks volumes for the national character of the Hindus.

1) Asceticism and renunciation

That the mark of a holy life involves asceticism and renunciation of the world which has been for ages a deeply rooted idea in India is beyond question. The term *tapas* is charged with rich signification in the early Vedic literature. The word goes through successive meanings, although earlier connotations are never lost sight of. We can summarise the various meanings as follows: heat, effort, austerity referring to mainly physical austerity; later, it signifies internal asceticism and ascetical introversion. In the mythological cosmogonies it plays an important part. Creation itself had its rise in *tapas*.

> "Darkness there was at first by darkness hidden;
> without distinctive marks, this all was water.
> That which, becoming, by the void was covered,
> That One by force of heat *(tapas)* came into being"[7].

In the *Brāhmaṇas* Prajāpati practises *tapas* in order to acquire creative power. In these writings the efficacy of asceticism is also recognized in the pursuit of knowledge.

> "Heaven is established on the air, the air on the earth, the earth on the waters, the waters on truth, the truth on the mystic love (of the sacrifice) and that on *tapas*"[8].

Tapas is a force which is efficacious by itself, though it does not exclude prayer. In itself *tapas* is not considered moral; hence it is ambivalent by itself; that is to say, it works for good or evil ends, and is often associated with magic. One can resort to *tapas* in order to acquire magical powers, to attain ecstatic states, to obtain divine inspiration, and to attain union with God. Though the earlier *Upanishads* express doubts on the efficacy of austerity *(tapas)*, the later ones recognize its value for the attainment of knowledge and insist on its efficacy. The secret doctrine *(upanisad)* concerning Brahman is this: Its basis is ascetic practice, self-restraint, and works *(karma)*, the Vedas and all the treatises that depend on them *(vedānga)*. Truth is (its) dwelling-place"[9].

---

7 R.V. 10.129, 3: in this cosmogonic poem the origin of the world is explained as the evolution of the existent *(sat)* from the non-existent *(asat)*. Water thus came into being first; from it was evolved intelligence by heat *(tapas)*. See also Śatapatha. Brāhmaṇa 2.2.4.

8 See Ait. Brāhmaṇa 11.6.4.

9 Kena Upanishad 4.8. Cfr. also Prāsna Upanishad 1.10; Muṇḍ. Up. 1.2.11.

In the epics (The *Mahābhārata* and the *Rāmāyana*) the austerities have become longer and more arduous and self-mortification has become a permanent idea and practice in the religious life of India. We shall cite one significant passage in praise of austerities:

"They that are possessed of knowledge say that everything has penance for its root. That foolish person who has not undergone penances does not meet with the rewards of even his own acts. The puissant Creator created all this universe with the aid of penances. After the same manner the sages *(rishis)* acquired the Vedas through the power of penances... It is by penances that persons crowned with ascetic success behold the three worlds with rapt souls... The accomplishment of all purposes depends upon penance. Whatever things there are that are apparently unattainable are sure to be won by the aid of penance... Without doubt, through penance the very status of godhead may be acquired"[10]. Of all the virtues the greatest is self-control *(dama)*. The self-controlled person lays up no merit calling for rebirth, but goes straight to the eternal region of Brahmā. Self-control is obtained by self-mortification *(tapas)*, on which Brahmā and all the world depend.[11]

2) Yoga and meditation

Yogi is a general descriptive term, applied to many who do not belong to any particular religious sect. It has many shades of meaning, from that of a saint to that of sorcerer or charlatan. It is also a general term for ascetics, particularly for those who endeavour by restraint and discipline of body and mind to secure union with the Absolute or with God. They are met with separately as mendicants and as hermits, and in groups. They are not supposed to live alone or to wander about but to abide in monasteries, or in temples, and to dedicate themselves to meditation. Yogis also go on pilgrimages, visiting shrines and holy places, though they make their monasteries their headquarters. Some do live alone in the jun-

---

10 The Mahābhārata 12.161. Unless otherwise noted, all the references from the Mahābhārata are to the Bombay edition.

11 The Madhābhārata 12.160-61.

gles, practising yoga; but hermits of this kind are extremely rare.

The yogis are respected everywhere by people who touch their feet with fingers dipped in holy water and receive flowers, fruits or pieces of coconut, as charms and talisman. Their touch may work wonders on the sick and the unfortunate. Their curse is feared and this becomes an incentive to do homage to them. The yogis do not undertake any employment nor engage in trade and business. Usually they beg for their food; but in case of abundance of offerings at shrines or monasteries they do not go out to beg at all. Very often the devotees bring what is necessary for the sustenance of the yogis. They also beg to feed the hungry and the sick; the income of monasteries is used for this purpose; namely, to practise charity towards the needy and the suffering. They also receive guests of all castes and treat them well.

In this context, we have to speak of the important concept of sacrifice *(yajna)* which commonly means offering of gifts, fruits and grains and sometimes also animal victims to the gods. In the *Bhagavad-gita*[12] it has a wider meaning of the spirit of renunciation *(tyāga)*. The self-centred action *(ātmakāranāt)* is opposed to *yajna* which is used for self-less or God-centred action. Action done for the good of others, actions which imply denial of the bodily self and realization of the higher self, actions which involve renunciation *(tyāgātmaka)* not only do not bind the doer but positively help the agent to attain liberation. *Yajna* in the wider sense is the essence of all *dharma* (morality and religion) and forms the soul of *karmayoga* (the discipline of action).

The reason for renunciation in the Hindu spirituality is evident. One who runs after pleasure suffers; one who renounces desires becomes happy. Desire is the cause of suffering; renunciation of worldly pleasures is the highest kind of purity. It is the best austerity *(tapas)*. Renunciation of desires brings on happiness. Egoism is the root of love and hatred, of pleasure and pain. Complete renunciation of desires for pleasure is the condition of intuition of the self[13].

The word *yoga* is primarily a technical term which significies a method or a way of disciplined activity whereby an end is achie-

12 See 3.9; 3.13; 4.31.

13 The Mahābhārata 12.174.18-51.

ved. It is not the end itself that is meant by *yoga* but the disciplined activity which leads to the desired end[14]. This is its use in the *Bhagavad-gītā* and the Mokṣadharma of the *Mahābhārata*. In these texts Saṁkhya and Yoga are proposed as two methods of reaching final liberation *(mukti)*. They respectively signify the way of salvation by pure knowledge and the way of the disciplined self-less action. The first is an intellectual method, understood as implying quietism, renunciation of action *(sannyāsa, vairāgya)*. The second, i.e., yoga is the method of unselfish disciplined activity, with indifference to results. This yoga is synonymous with *karma-yoga*, a method of salvation characterized by participation in action without interest in the fruits thereof. One cannot avoid action in life; but it must be brought under a rule of conduct *(dharma)*, suitable to one's situation in life.

Yoga as a system of physical and mental discipline, as a code of disciplinary practice plays an important part in asceticism and in all the acquisition of knowledge. Professor S.N. Dasgupta explains the need of yoga even when knowledge is insisted upon thus: "When the mind is once purged of all impurities, truths arrived at by philosophical discussions carry whole-hearted conviction. Yoga holds that discussions are not enough for the purpose, for in order to be assured that our minds would not be attracted by worldly temptations, certain psychological exercises should be undertaken in order to move the mind in a direction, the reverse of ordinary experience. The (Yogi) looks to the yoga practice for gaining a complete mastery over his mind"[15]. Interest in the yogi was not only in his knowledge but also in his superior powers. Again S.N. Dasgupta observes: "Throughout all the epoch of Indian culture we find the highest reverence paid to the (yogis) who were believed not only to possess a superior sense, by which they could know the highest truth beyond the ken of ordinary vision, but also to wield the most wonderful miraculous powers which Patañjali has described as the *vibhutis* of Yoga, by which the (yogi) showed his control not only over his mind and the minds of others, but also over inert external objects"[16].

---

14 See F. Edgerton, The meaning of Saṁkhya and Yoga, in: American Journal of Philology, XLV (1924), pp. 1ff.

15 See his *Yoga Philosophy*, (In relation to other systems of Indian Thought) Calcutta, 1930, p. 330.

16 Ibid., p. 347

The powers of asceticism *(tapas)* and meditation which arise from putting one's self in rapport with creative force are declared to be supernatural. It was believed that by ascetical practices men could come into intimate relations with the spirit-world and obtain power to change the natural course of events and things. This led to the origin of yoga, for yoga is associated closely with the control of the physical sense and of the mind of man. Bodily discipline becomes a means to further mental control. As the *Kena Upaniṣad* (2, 3) says:

> "The self cannot be known by him who has knowledge, but only by him who has no knowledge. Hence comes the effort to subdue all the activity of the senses and the mind to empty the intellect and thus to make it ready for a new apprehension".

The aims of yoga in Patañjali are explained as controls of vaious kinds, a graded series of disciplines, directed to steadying the mind; gradually advancing stages of rigid control of body and mind the stoppage of all movement and all thought, so that the soul be absorbed in itself, losing the sense of duality, of subject and object; immediate perception of the self in the self by the self.[17] The practice of *yama* and *niyama* favours the acquisition of passionlessness *(vairāgye);* i.e., freedom from desire, either of the things of the world or the pleasures of heaven.

Patañjali defines meditation as a current of unified thought.[18] Vyāsa explains this as a continuum of mental effort[19] to assimilate the object of meditation, free from any effort to assimilate other objects. It is by meditation that the meditator penetrates into the object of thought and grasps its inner reality. This penetration into the essence of things is achieved not by lateral enrichment by uncontrolled associations, analogies, and symbols, but by taking possession of the real through assimilation. God can be chosen as object of meditation only to develop the power of concentration

17 See J.H. Woods, *The Yoga system of Patañjali,* Cambridge (USA), 1914, p.

18 Yoga-sūtra 3.2.

19 Pratyayasyāikatānatā.

and not to achieve union with him as the ultimate goal which, for the Yoga system, is the realization of the spiritual nature of oneself. The *Bhagavad-gītā*[20] teaches meditation not only for the purpose of attaining peace, equanimity, and detachment, and for the control of the sense, mind, soul, and egoism, but above all for the vision of the Supreme Self abiding in all things. More profoundly meditation is proposed in order to concentrate on Krishṇa, the Supreme Lord of all, and to contemplate his "incarnate" form and thus to participate more intimately in his divine mode of being and acting and to enter into Krishna himself through love and surrender.

There is not the slightest doubt that meditation in the Indian cultural and religious tradition has been considered as essential to any spiritual life and much more so to the ascetical and mystical life of a sādhu. It does not signify a mere reflection or deliberation or even profound and sustained thinking although these intellectual exercises may have their role in the life of a saint. When we speak of meditation it implies the spiritual and existential sense, i.e., a personal living in a meditative or contemplative way which becomes gradually one with the object of meditation through assimilation and absorption. Hence no Hindu saint can dispense with meditative practice. A saintly man is a meditative and contemplative man who lives the divine life in union with the Absolute or with God.

3) Moral perfection

A Hindu saint is looked upon as a morally perfect man. It is well known that Hindus make a distinction between morality and spirituality and extol spirituality more than morality which is just a preparation for, and transcended by, the spiritual perfection. But moral perfection is so necessary that without it any higher experience of love of God or of knowledge of God or of the Absolute is impossible. Hence every saint is supposed to possess to an eminent degree the moral qualities that the Hindus think as a necessary part of any holy person.

---

20 13.24-25; see M. DHAVAMONY, *Hindu Meditation;*, in: «Studia Missionalia», XXV (1976), pp. 115-116; especially on the Bhagavad-gītā, pp. 132-39.

The general term for morality is *dharma*. We shall outline the meaning and relevance of *dharma* for holiness. The source and fountain of all morality is God. God is the author of morality *(dharmakartā)*, the protector of morality *(dharmagoptā)*, and the possessor of morality (dharmin). He is the creator of the Vedas which prescribe certain actions and prohibit others. What are prescribed by them are right; what are forbidden by them are wrong. God is the promulgator of moral law *(pravṛttavedakriya)*. He is the embodiment of holiness *(mahātmyasarīra)*. The divine law is the moral standard. But it is not arbitrary. What is right is commanded by him; what is wrong is forbidden by him. Moral perfection constitutes his nature[21].

Good conduct is the foundation of morality[22]; virtuous persons are characterized by it[23]. Morality is what is approved by one's own conscience.[24] The Vedic prescriptions, cusṭomary conduct, good conduct of the virtuous, and one's own conscience are the sources of morality that have to be followed in one's life. The good of mankind or social solidarity is the highest *dharma;* the conduct of the virtuous for the good of mankind is considered the best[25] *Dharma* is of two kinds: that which is prompted by desire for fruits (*sakāma*) and that which is free from desire for fruits *(niskāma*). The former leads to happiness in heaven which is not eternal, while the latter leads to final liberation (*mokṣa*).[26]

Dharma as a moral principle has a personal and inner character. As the *Mahabharata* says:

> "Thou thinkest that thou hast knowledge of thy deed. But knowest thou not that the ancient, omniscient One (Nārāyana) liveth in thy heart? He knoweth all thy sins and thou sinnest in his presence. He that sins thinks that none observes him. But he is observed by the gods and by Him alone who is in every heart"[27].

---

21 See the Mahābhārata 12.338.

22 Ibid. 12.259.6: Dharmasya niṣṭhātvācārah.

23 Ibid. 12.260.4: Sadācāro mato dharmaḥ santaś cācāralakṣaṇāḥ.

24 Ibid. 12.132.19: Sa dharmaḥ satkṛtaḥ sadbhir bhūtipravarakāraṇaiḥ. Hṛdayenābhyan{jñāto yo dharmas taṁ vyavas}ati.

25 Ibid. 12.259.26: Lokasaṃgrahasaṁyuktaṁ vidhātrā vihitaṁ purā. Sūks madharmārthamyataṁ satāṁ caritam uttamam.

26 Ibid. 12.16.13.

27 1.74.28-29

A person who wanted to realize God, i.e., a saint, is supposed to develop the highly moral qualities of compassion, forbearence, peace, non-violence, truth, fidelity, modesty, curiosity and control of anger.[28] *Dharma* itself is described as consisting of ten highest moral qualities; namely, learnedness, austerity, self-sacrifice, faith, sacrificial ceremony, forbearance, purity of emotions and pity, truth, control of self. "Fix your mind on these and try to acquire them because these are the roots of *dharma*."[29] But the essence of *dharma* is declared to consist in not doing to others what is disagreeable to oneself.

> "Do not do to others what is disagreeable to yourself; that is *dharma* in brief; the other proceeds from desire"[30].
> "Listen to the essence of *dharma* and after having heard it, take it to heartl What is disagreeable to you, do not do to others"[31].
> "What for many words, in short the *dharma* says, oh men! to help others is a virtue; to injure them is a sin"[32].
> "Listen to the essence of *dharma* which is proclaimed in millions of books; to help others is a virtue; to injure them is a sin"[33].

What is conducive to non-injury is *dharma*. "*Dharma* was declared for restraining creatures from injuring one another. Therefore that is *dharma* which prevents injury to creatures[34]. *Dharma* was declared for the advancement and growth of all creatures. Therefore that which leads to advancement and growth is righteousness.[35]

---

28 The Mahābhārata 12.262.37-38.

29 Ibid., 12. 161.5-6.

30 Ibid., 5.39.57 Cr.ed.: Na tat parasya saṁdadhyāt pratikūlaṁ yad ātmanaḥ saṁgraheṇaiṣa dharmaḥ syāt kāmād anyaḥ pravartate.

31 Pañcatantra 3.103.

32 Pañcatantra 3.102.

33 Vikramacarita 13.2.

34 The Mahābhārata 13.109.12. It is interesting to know the three passages from this chapter (109), verses 10-12: Prabhavārthāya bhūtānāṁ dharmapravacanani kṛtam / yaḥ syād prabhava saṁyuktah sa dharma iti niścayaḥ.

Dhāranād dharmam ityāhur dharmeṇa vidhṛtāh prajāḥ
Yaḥ syād dhāraṇasaṁyuktaḥ sa dharma iti niścayaḥ.
Ahiṁsārthāya bhūtānāṁ dharmapravacanaṁ kṛtam
Yaḥ syād ahiṁsāsaṁyuktaḥ sa dharmaḥ.

35 Mahābhārata 12.109.10, cfr. the foot-note 34.

Among the five virtues such as austerity, generosity, rectitude, non-injury and truthfulness, non-injury *(ahi£sa)* is the first and foremost. A wide definition of *ahi£sa* is given thus: abstension from a desire to harm any creature, in any circumstance and in any manner by action, speech and thought.[36] More positively, *ahi£sa* signifies universal love, compassion. One should practise compassion, self-control and giving.[37] Compassion is better than giving *(dayā dānād viśiṣyate)*[38]. The three injunctions are necessary to go about doing good even though we find ourselves in a world of evil. Self-control is necessary for we must not be elated by success or deterred by failure. Compassion is more than sympathy or intellectual or emotional feeling. It is love in action, fellowship in suffering. It is feeling as one's own the circumstances and aspirations of others for self-perfection.

The moral ideals that are set forth before the Hindu saints are non-injury, truth, non-stealing, purity, and control of the senses.[39] They are sometimes observed as vows, especially in the case of monks and hermits. It is these ideals that have given the people of India a common idea of a saintly life. Purity means both ceremonial and moral purity, the former being considered as preliminary to the latter. All the purificatory baths and ceremonials and all the regulations regarding food and drink are meant to lead to the purity of mind and body. Control of the senses implies control of the mind and of the body. When this is practised to a higher degree it becomes asceticism. The higher phase of self-control is detachment. The saint has not only to overcome what is evil but also to become detached from worldly ties and goods. Final liberation from the cycle of rebirth is not possible so long as one clings to the things of the world. Detachment implies also non-appropriation of what belongs to another. Truth as a cardinal virtue in Hinduism means far more than mere truthfulness; it means eternal reality. The pursuit of truth wherever it may lead and whatever sacrifices it may involve is indispensable to the spiritual progress of man. The basis of these

---

36 Sarvathā sarvadā sarvesām anabhidrohah.

37 Bṛhadāraṇyaka Up. 5.2.3.

38 Vasiṣṭha Dharma Sāstra 10.5.

39 Manu 10.63: ahiṁsā satyaṁ asteyaṁ śaucam indriyanigrahaḥ / etaṁ sāmāsikaṁ dharmaṁ cāturvarnye' bravīn manuḥ.

virtues is non-violence which, as we have explained before, means positively universal love towards all living beings. In the words of the *Mahābhārata* we can summarize the path of moral perfection of the Hindu holy men and women thus:

> Those that betake themselves to a life of celibacy and *brahmacarya*, that perform penances, and that are cleansed by learning, Vedic knowledge, and proper vows, succeed in overcoming all difficulties. They that have checked all the qualities that appertain to passion *(rajas)* and darkness *(tamas)*, that are possessed of high souls, and that practise the qualities that are called good *(sattva)* succeed in overcoming all difficulties"[40].

4) Pursuit after sacred knowledge

Saints and sages (sādhus) are the repositories of divine wisdom and knowledge who guide the destiny of the world.

They are the messengers of *Brahma-Vidyā* and divine peace.

They disseminate divine wisdom and revealed truth among men so that they may believe in them. Their testimony to the divine wisdom is all the more powerful because they live their wisdom and become shining examples of truth and non-violence. In fact, all the efforts made to practise asceticism and renunciation, moral purification and detachment, self-control over mind and body, the practice of yoga and meditation: all these are directed to prepare the ground for the acquisition of sacred knowledge and divine love. First we shall deal with the obtaining of the *Brahma-Vidyā* and in the following section we shall expose the ideal of love of God *(bhakti)*.

Sanatsujāta expounds the *Brahma-Vidyā* thus: "It is for attaining to that Supreme Self that asceticism and sacrifices are ordained, and it is by these two that the man of learning earneth virtue. Destroying sin by virtue, his soul is enlightened by knowledge. The man of knowledge by the aid of knowledge attaineth to the Supreme Self. Otherwise he that coveteth the four objects of hu-

40 Mahābhārata 12.110.

man pursuit taking with him all that he doth here, enjoyeth their fruits hereafter, and (as these fruits) are not everlasting cometh back to the region of action (when the enjoyment is over). Indeed the fruits of ascetic practices performed in this world have to be enjoyed in the other world... That asceticism which is not stained by (destire and other) faults is said to be capable of procuring emancipation... It is by asceticism that they that are learned know Brahman and win immortality"[41]. Again, Vyāsa instructs his son on the paramount importance of concentration on the highest of all objects, the knowledge of the all-pervading Self thus: "One possessed of those Six attributes, viz., contentment, grieflessness, freedom from attachment, peacefulness, cheerfulness, and freedom from envy, is sure to become full or complete. They that, transcending all consciousness of body, know the Self which resides within the body and which is understood by only persons of wisdom with the aid of the six entities (already mentioned, viz., the Vedas, truth, control of the senses, charity, penance, renunciation) when endowed with only the attribute of *sattva,* and also with the aid of the other three (instruction, meditation, and yoga) succeed in attaining to emancipation. The man of wisdom, by understanding the Self which presides within the body, which is divested of the attributes of birth and death, which exists in its own nature, which being uninvested with attributes requires no act of purification, and which is identical with Brahman, enjoys beatitude that knows no termination"[42].

In this connection arises a problem as to whether knowledge or cognition is indeterminate *(nirvikalpa)* or determinate *(savikalpa),* whether it excludes or includes relations. Śaṅkara has distinguished between knowledge as it is in itself *(svarūpacaitanya)* and knowledge as a product of the relation of the individual self to some object *(vṛtti caitanya).* Being identical with Brahman, the differenceless, attributeless pure consciousness, the former cannot be conceived as entering into any relation and is therefore regarded as indeterminate whereas the latter because of its origin in time and dependance on the relation of an individual self to a particular

41 Ibid., 5.43.
42 Ibid., 12.251 (Ganguli).

object is said to be determinate. But since according to Śaṅkara all distinctions including that of the subject and the object are only empirically true, the latter cannot be called normal from the ultimate point of view. For Śaṅkarites knowledge in itself is non-relational and indeterminate in character. The subject and the object of empirical knowledge necessarily point to a basic reality of which they are but apparent aspects. This basic reality is the real Self or Brahman. According to Rāmānuja, on the other hand, knowledge, however simple and pure it may be, always involves the discrimination of a substantive, an attributive, and a relation between them. Knowledge necessarily implies a relation between the subject and the object and all knowledge is relational and therefore determinate in character. The usual distinction between the determinate and indeterminate knowledge is explained to mean the difference between the first cognition and a subsequent cognition of an object, both of which involve judgement. Since both are cognitions of objects qualified in some way, the difference between the determinate and indeterminate cognition is one of degree and not one of kind. Indeterminate cognition is the apprehension for the first time of an object of a certain character. It implicitly involves a system of relations which is gradually unfolded in the determinate cognition.

This whole discussion has its importance with respect to the knowledge of the ultimate Reality, God or the Absolute, in the spiritual experience of the saint. While the school of Śaṅkara sees the indeterminate perception as an approximation of the pure, absolutely indeterminate intuition of the Absolute, all differentiation being illusorily superimposed to this fundamental and necessary apperception, Rāmānuja holds that the indeterminate perception is only relatively such, since no reality is purely undifferentiated.[43]

5) Love of God (htakti)

The *Bhagavad-gītā* is the crowning of Hindu theism. God is creator, sustainer and destroyer of the universe, its begining, middle and end; transcendent as the highest Person as well as immanent

43 See N.K. Brahma, *Philosophy of Hindu Sādhana,* London, 1932, pp. 141-42.

and dwells in the hearts of men as the foundation and ultimate principle of things that exist. All creatures subsist in Krishna but he is not established in them. The message of the *Gītā* is that God is not an impersonal Absolute but the lover of men. He is declared to be father, comrade, and beloved. The relationship between God and man is one of grace and love. "With strong desire I have desired thee; therefore shall I tell thee thy salvation. Think of me; worship me, sacrifice to me; pay me homage; so shall thou come to me. I promise thee truly, for I love thee well... turn to me as thy refuge; I shall deliver thee from all evil"[44].

The discipline of action *(karmayoga)* consists in performing action with complete detachment which alone can cease to bind oneself to rebirth. Right action leads to detachment which in turn leads to a higher state of spiritual perfection and liberation. As ignorance and delusion are the cause of attachment to the world, right knowledge or intuitive vision of the true nature of the reality both of the Absolute and of the self is essential for salvation. In non-dualist current it is intuitive realization of one's identity with the Absolute (Brahman) that is the goal of all spiritual striving. In theist current the intuitive knowledge of the individual self's dependance on God is the goal, and this is attained by means of love of God *(bhakti)*. *Bhakti* is an affective participation of the devotee in the divine Being. The God of *bhakti* is gracious to men and has compassion for all; but he is specially benevolent to those who love him. For saints like Tukārām, *bhakti* consists in surrendering all actions to God and feeling the greatest misery in forgetting God, and in clinging affection of the heart for a personal God[45]. Tulsī Dās considers Rāma as absolute knowledge and love and advocates utter self-surrender to and loving confidence in Rāma's power to save men from the world of rebirth.[46] Mānikkavācakar expresses this love in deeply mystical terms: "The Light supreme deep plunged me in love's sea! How sweet his mercy is, sing ye, and beat

44 Bhagavad- gītā 18.64-66.

45 Tukārām sings thus: A beggar at Thy door, Pleading I stand; Give me an alms, O God, Love from Thy loving hand. Spare me the barren task, To come, and come for nought, A gift poor Tukā craves, Unmerited, unbought. (*Temple Bells*, ed. A.J. Appasamy, Calcutta, no date, p. 91).

46 *The Vinaya Patrika* (Letter of Request) is full of poems addressed to Rāma whom the poet Tulsīdas considers the true incarnation of God, where he asks for grace, prays for mercy, and entreats for help.

47 Tiruvācakam 11.12.

Te%o%o l nam."[47]

There are four kinds of those who love God; of these those of wisdom are alone the best.

> "Fourfold are the good people who love and worship me; the afflicted, the man who seeks knowledge, the man who strives for gain, and the possessor of knowledge.
> Of these the possessor of knowledge, ever integrated, who worships and loves One alone excels;
> to such a man I am exceedingly dear and he is dear to me. All these are noble; but the man of knowledge is my very self, so I hold; for he with disciplined self has resorted to me alone as the highest goal.
> At the end of many births the man of knowledge resorts to me; Who thinks "Vāsudeva (Krishna) is all that noble soul is hard to find"[48].

The four kinds of *bhaktas* (lovers of God) are those who implore God to alleviate their sufferings; those who seek but have not yet found knowledge of him; those who pray to him for material benefits; and the "knowers" or possessors of knowledge. All these are good people; but the possessors of knowledge alone are the best. The *Mahābhārata* also speaks of the four kinds of lovers of God: "I have heard that there are four kinds of worshippers (viz., those who are eager for a religious life, those who are enquirers, those who strive to comprehend what they learn and those who are wise). Among them all, they that are devoted to realizing the self and do not adore any other deity, are the foremost. I am the end they seek, and though engaged in acts, they never seek the fruits thereof. The three remaining classes of my worshippers are those that are desirous of the fruits of their acts. They attain to regions of great felicity, but then they have to fall down therefrom upon the exhaustion of their merits. Those amongst my worshippers, therefore, that are fully awakened (and, as such, that know that all happiness is terminable except what is attainable by persons that become identified with me) obtain what is foremost (and invaluable). Those that are awakened and

48 Bhagavad-gītā 7.16-19.

whose conduct displays such enlightenment, may be engaged in adoring Brahman or Mahādeva or the other deities that occur in heaven but they succeed at least in attaining to myself"[49].

The goal of *bhakti* is union with the personal God; this goal is to be reached by successive steps: the discharging of one's ordinary duties of life in a selfless manner, having faith in God and without attachment to the fruits of actions; devoted service to God and his cause; the practice of concentration of the mind on God and meditation on him. The seers of truth, who are single-minded, and in constant union with God in love, are the best of lovers of God. The grace of God is the response to the *bhakti* of man. It may sometimes seem arbitrary but every true devotee knows that it depends upon God who freely responds to love; he is easy of access to those who constantly think of him and seek him. The *sādhanas* merely help to purify the mind *(citta)* of the God-lover so that it might become a suitable mirror for the reflecting of *bhakti* which is eternal and unconditioned. The highest *bhakti* is beyond the chain of causes and effects. Grace, very important in Hindu theism, is also admitted at the lower stage of spiritual perfection in the non-dualist school. In the theist spirituality the realization of God cannot be claimed as a matter of right, nor does it necessarily follow as a consequence of good deeds, or of austerities, or of sacrifice or of profound learning. It is exclusively the award of divine mercy.

6) Social reform

The sādhus have been time and again insistent that religion essentially consists in the inward form, i.e., in the thought and ideas which determine the outward form and that the reform consists in the change of the ideas which one has of men and of society. The ideas in Hinduism that have created discrimination based on caste, sex, status of high or low rank, rich or poor have been outright rejected by saints of different religious sects. Perception of factitious difference between men and men, due to heredity and birth, submission to outward force or power more than to the voice of

---

49 The Mahābhārata 12.342.33ff.

conscience, passive acquiescence in evil or wrong doing, and a general indifference to social well-being of one's fellowmen have been repudiated by holy men, as we constantly read in their writings. Tukārām insists on the need of helping others for God's sake:

> "Are you in need of God?
> This is an easy means of attaining Him.
> Utter such words as will keep you at peace,
> Much or little; do good to others, says Tukā"[50].
> God's mercy is universal and does not make difference with regard to high or low qualities of men.
> Again Tukārām says:
>
> "Let my purpose now be firm, to think on Thee without ceasing.
> None who did this ever fell into despair; none despaired of mercy to beggars such as he.
> With Thee, says Tukā, there are no distinctions: king and clown are equal at the feet of God"[51].

Tulsīdās gives a portrait of the nature of holiness. The saint is simple in his words but they are full of meaning. One recognizes the holy man by his simplicity. Unimpassioned, he gives happiness to all. Just and self-restrained, ever singing the praise of God, ever enlightening the ignorant, he wanders from place to place for this purpose. Ever devoted to helping others and ever devoted to the supreme goal, he works out his life in love. He is discreet in speaking the truth or in keeping silence. He is sweet in his relation to others and speaks words which never give pain to others. He shows neither enmity nor over-friendship in relation to others. His thoughts dwell on the One Lord, for he knows well that this world is a mirage. He longs for God; he has abandoned desire and betaken himself to humility and content. Gentle are the words of the holy man, falling like nectar on the ear. They beget the happiness of comprehending the Supreme; they lift and carry away the errors and sins of the world.[52]

---

50 *Temple Bells,* op. cit., p. 111.

51 Ibid., p. 36.

52 G. Grierson, *Vairāgya Sandipini,* Indian Antiquary, as cited by A.J. Appasamy in his *Temple Bells,* op. cit., pp. 112-13.

3. The Sādhu ideal as lived by Rāmakrishṇa

We shall single out Rāmakrishṇa, a *bhakta* who has by word and example shown that the Hindu ideals of holiness are realizable in the concrete way in day to day life, as witnessed by other men who came into contact with him and to know him more closely. We do not deal with his biography but with the main ideal of *bhakti* as lived and experienced by him.

Rāmakrishṇa (1836-1886) declared that love of God *(bhakti)* was his sole reason for being. He really had such a profound sense of love of God that he sang divine praise all through his day. Rāmakrishṇa practised the love of God which Krishṇa put in these words in the *Bhagavad-gītā:*

> "Who sees me in all and who sees all in me, for him I am not lost, nor is he lost for me. Who loves and worships me, embracing unity, as abiding in all beings, in whatever state he be, that man of yoga abides in me"[53].

Among the different kinds of yoga Rāmakrishṇa chose as his favourite yoga the path of love of God *(bhakti);* but this did not prevent him from practising *jñāna-yoga* which led him to gain the supreme knowledge of God. In fact one of the striking aspects of Rāmakrishṇa's spirituality was the plurality of his experiences and the rapidity of the results that he obtained from the spiritual point of view.

As a young priest, Rāmakrishṇa began to experience the love of God, considering himself as servant and God as master, seeking to emulate Hanuman in his devotion to Rāma. Hanuman is the deification of the ideal servant of God, Rāma. With his marvelous gift for imitating others, Rāmakrishṇa identified himself with Hanuman, and began to feel his love for Rāma in such a way that he soon began to live on fruits and roots, and his behaviour resembled that of a monkey. His protectors were frightened at this attitude; but a miraculous vision of Sītā released him completely from his experiment as a monkey. This and similar experience in which others would have lost their sanity was a terrible ordeal for him. He came

---

53 6.30-31.

through all this and faced new spiritual experiences of love of God. In fact many thought that Rāmakrishṇa had become mad but his female guru, Bairavi Brahmani, said to him: "My son, in this world everyone is mad. Some are mad for money, some are mad for creatures, some are mad for luxury or fame. You are mad for God"[54]. Rāmakrishṇa had passed through various higher states of spiritual discipline *(sādhana)* that are described in the *Bhakti-Śāstras;* he is said to have attained at this stage the state of *Mahābhāva,* the supreme rapture that crowns all other states of love of God. Sri Caitanya alone was known to have reached such a sublime state of exaltation in recent centuries.

The *bhakta* chooses a particular God or an aspect of God *(Iṣṭadevatā)* and dedicates his attention to experience this aspect in successive stages of worship and meditation. As a result of this he succeeds in attaining his ideal, seeing it, conversing with it, feeling it and experiencing it more and more profoundly. Thereafter, the presence of God becomes living and constant because an act of concentration will be enough to make God appear. The *Iṣṭadevatā* of Rāmakrishṇa was the Divine Mother Kāli who filled his life. She had become for him all forms and penetrated all forms. *Bhakti* is love for God without limit. Now the heart of Rāmakrishṇa was made for the limitless love for God.

This love develops in various ways in the *bhakta's* heart, experiencing God who can be regarded and loved as a master, a friend, a parent and a spouse. At each of these stages there is a greater and greater divinization of the *bhakta* and more deeper union and communion with God himself. For the *bhakta* God is not the impersonal Absolute but the Supreme Person. Rāmakrishṇa explained to Keshub Chandra Sen that he had realized God as Pure Spirit and Pure Consciousness and believed that God could assume all forms: "It is absolutely true that God takes a human form to manifest Himself on earth, as in the case of Krishṇa, and it is also true that God can manifest Himself to his believers in varied forms. But it is equally true as well that God is without form. He is the indivisible Saccitānanda: Existence, knowledge, Absolute Felicity. He has been described in the Vedas as being at the same time without form and

54 *The Gospel of Śrī Ramakrishna,* Tr. by *Swami Nikhilananda,* Madras, 1947 Introduction, p. 18.

able to assume forms. He is also described with and without attributes. Do you know what I mean? Saccitānanda is like an infinite ocean. Intense cold changes the water into ice, which floats on the water in blocks of various shapes. In the same fashion, under the influence of *bhakti* (love), one can apprehend the forms of God in the ocean of the Absolute, These forms have meaning for those who are impassioned of God. But when the sun of knowledge rises, the ice melts and becomes water again, as it was before. The water above and the water below are everywhere the same water. That is why a priest in the *Bhagavad-gītā* says: "O Lord, you have a form and you are also without form. You walk before us, O Lord, in the form of a man, and yet you are described in the Vedas as being beyond the words of thought."[55]

The awareness of one's being distinct from God makes it possible to rejoice in the Presence of God and to love Him. Rāmakrishṇa says: "O Lord, when I am conscious of my body, my relation with you is that of the servant toward his master"[56]. The ideal of the *bhakta* consists in the adoration and love of the personal God, the omnipotent and gracious Lord. The world for the *bhakta* is the real manifestation of the power and glory of God who is present in everything. Rāmakrishṇa clearly asserted that the attitude of *bhakti* was not only dear to him but that it was in his nature to see the form of God and love him. He said: "Who will ever be able to know God through reasoning? Even the reading of the six *darśanas* would not suffice. One must sing the Name of God and His glory. One can be set free of this life when one believes that God is the author of everything that is. The Will of God is exercised in everything, even in the little movement of a leaf."[57]. Instead of saying: "I am He", Rāmakrishṇa preferred to describe his mystical experience in terms as follows: "The waves belong to the Ganges, not the Ganges to the waves"[58]. His prayer was: "O God, you are the Master, and I am your servant... You are the Mother, I am your child. You are my Father, my Mother. You are All, and I am a fragment of you"[59].

55 Ibid., p. 191; see also p. 859.
56 Ibid., p. 782.
57 Ibid., p. 94.
58 Ibid., p. 103 and 812.
59 Ibid., p. 134.

We shall analyse the idea of *bhakti* according to Rāmakrishṇa more systematically and expose its various aspects and stages of development.

Bhakti means "intense and single-minded love of God". Says Rāmakrishṇa: "The other day I told you the meaning of *bhakti.* It is to adore God with body, mind, and words. "With body" means to serve and worship God with one's hands, go to holy places with one's feet, hear the chanting of the name and glories of God with one's ears, and behold the divine image with one's eyes. "With mind" means to contemplate and meditate on God constantly and to remember and think of his līlā; "with words" means to sing hymns to him and chant his name and glories"[60]. The import of this statement is that a man should yearn for God with all his might, at all cost, in all manner. He who yearns after God cannot bestow any thought on such trifles of life as food, drink, and progeny, and riches[61]. This yearning after God is similar to that of a miser after gold, to that of a drowing man for breath, to that of a worldly man for the things of the world, to that of a devoted wife for her beloved husband[62].

As in photography you cannot impress anything on smooth glass unless it is coated with proper chemicals, so also in the human heart there should be chemicals of *bhakti* in order to impress on it the image of the divinity[63]. In other words through *bhakti* the mind and soul must be absorbed in God. *Bhakti* can arise only when there is wholehearted devotion to God as that of a chaste wife to her husband.[64] The more a man becomes detached from the objects of the senses, the more he becomes devoted to God and grows in the love of God[65]. *Bhakti* is given only to pure souls who are uncontaminated by the world so that they might be able to love God and to have a single aim, namely, to have the mind entirely fixed upon the Lord[66].

There are three kinds of *bhakti:* the selfish, mutual, and unselfish. The selfish love makes a man only care for his own happiness

---

60 Ibid., p. 652.
61 *Sayings of Śrī Ramakrisima,* Madras, 1965, nn. 615-18.
62 Ibid., nn. 619-23.
63 Ibid., n, 747
64 Ibid., n. 748
65 Ibid., n. 749
66 Ibid., n. 750

without caring for the weal and woe of the beloved. Mutual love is that in which the lover desires not only the happiness of the beloved but also his own. The unselfish love consists in seeking only the welfare of the beloved and is not interested whether he himself suffers pain and hardship thereby.[67]

There are also three aspects of *bhakti: sattvic, rajasic* and *tamasic*. The *sattvic bhakti* partakes of humility. It is performed in secret and in meditation. He does not perform acts of *bhakti* by any kind of ostentation in his food or dress or manner of life. The *rajasic* devotee shows of his love of God in exterior manifestations by sectarian marks and worships with pomp and splendour. The *tamasic* devotee applies force to God like a robber seizing things by force.[68]

There are different stages of *bhakti* as proposed by Rāmakrishṇa himself: the company of holy men *(Sādhusaṅgha),* faith in and devotion to the things of the spirit *(srāddhā),* single-minded devotion to one's ideal *(nishta),* intense love of God *(bhakti),* the state of speechless absorption in the thought of God *(bhava),* and this speechless absorption in God when intensified *(mahābhava);* this stage is only attained by great souls *(mahāpurushas)* and incarnations of God *(avatāras).* Finally there is the stage of the most intense love of God *(prema).* This last stage includes the forgetfulness of the world and of the self, including one's own body. This last stage brings the God-lover face to face to God and he attains to the supreme goal of life.[69]

In brief, all kinds of *bhakti* can be divided into two: the lower and the higher. The lower bhakti means devotion as enjoined by the scriptures *(vaîdhi-bhakti)* and the higher which is the supreme love of God, i.e., love is the one thing that is necessary in life; this love springs from within as in the case of divine incarnations like Caitanya. The supreme *bhakti* is also called *prema bhakti* in which the devotee contemplates God as his dearest and nearest relative. It involves the forgetfulness of the exterior world and the forgetfulness of one's own body. There are also two elements in this kind of love of God: God is entirely mine *(mine-ness)* and I am entirely his *(I-ness).*[70]

---

67 Ibid., n. 767.
68 Ibid., n. 768
69 Ibid., n. 770
70 Ibid., nn. 772-82.

CHAPTER FIVE

THE MYSTERY OF GOD ACCORDING TO THE BHAKTI MYSTICS OF MODERN HINDUISM

In the line of succession of those religious leaders who preached the religion of *bhakti* (love of God) during the period of the Mughul Empire in India, Kabīr, Tulsī Dās and Tukārām are the most prominent mystics whose writings have had great influence on the religious life and ideas of the people of North and West India. Today their religious lyrics are recited in homes and temples and are the inspiration of vast masses of people. These three mystics were ardent devotees of Vishṇu[1] in one or other of his manifestations as Rāma[2] or Viṭhobā[3]; the outstanding characteristic of their theology is love and self-abandonment to a personal God. Their conception of God has a unique place in the religious history of India[4], for it often rises to a sublime level, freed from the crude representations of the Deity as found in some sects of Hinduism. We shall study the idea of God in the writings of these mystics with particular attention to their structure and signification.

---

1 Vishṇu is the second god of the Hindu Triad with Brahmā and Śiva. Vaishṇavites worship him as the Supreme God, other gods being subordinate to Him.

2 Rāma, originally the name of the hero of the Epic *Rāmāyaṇa* first composed by Valmiki, is the chief incarnation *(avatār)* of the God Vishṇu.

3 The popular Vaishṇavism of the Marāṭha country is centred around the shrine of Vithoba at Pandharpur, a city situated on the banks of the Bhima. The full name of the God is Viṭṭhal, probably a corruption of the Sanskrit name, Vishṇu.

4 Vaishnavite theism has a glorious history beginning from the pre-Christian sect of the Bhagavatas who worshipped Vasudeva, later identified with Vishṇu and Krishṇa. These Bhagavatas were theists and stressed the importance of devotion to a personal God, in contrast to the sacrificial and ritual religion of the *Brahmanas*. Their theistic religion finds a clear and definite expression in the *Bhagavad-gītā*. In this text Krishṇa reveals himself as the Supreme Person and discloses his transcendent form.

1. Kabir's idea of God

Whether by upbringing Kabīr[5] was a Hindu or a Mohammadan, there can be little doubt that his theology of God was basically Hindu although it was subject to Islamic influences. Hence, his teaching about God was characterized by boldness and independence, for under the sway of Islamic thought he ruthlessly cleared the ground of much that was defective in Hindu conceptions.

It is not surprising then that Kabīr taught and emphasized strict monotheism. He speaks of the unity of God thus: "He is one: there is no second"[6]. "In heaven, the realms below, in earth and waters, one alone, Rāma, watches over all"[7]. "[Then shall man know] that one God is everywhere contained, and that there is no second"[8]. The fact that Kabīr uses many names in speaking of God should not lead us to consider him a polytheist. He calls God Rāma, Hari, Govinda, Nārāyana, Brahmā, Allah, etc., and teaches that though people might use several names for Him, there is but One God. "Rāma, Khudā, Śakti, Śiva, are one: tell me, pray, how will you distinguish them?"[9] "By the One name I hold fast: this Kabīr proclaims aloud"[10]. Kabīr in fact introduces Hindu gods in his verses and illustrates some moral or religious truth by means of Hindu mythologies; but he never recognizes their independent existence:

> "Dead is Brahmā, Vishṇu, Maheśa; dead is Geneśa, the son of [Pārvatī.
> Dead is the Moon, the Sun, the Serpent-god:
> Hanumān is dead who built the bridge.

---

5 Kabīr lived between 1440-1513. His work is in popular Hindī and was transmitted orally. The sources from which the extracts from Kabīr's teaching have been taken are:

1) Ahmad Shah's translation of the *Bījak*, Cawnpore, 1917;

2) Macauliffe's translation of the *Ādi-Granth*, in his *Sikh Religion*, Vol. VI, 1909.

An excellent selection of these translations is to be found in: F. E. Keay, *Kabīr and His Followers*, Galcutta, 1931.

6 *Bījak, Śabda* 43.

7 *Bījak, Ramaiṇī* 59.

8 *Ādi-Granth, Prabhātī* 2.

9 *Bījak, Śabda* 48.

10 *Ibid.* 62.

Dead is Krishṇa, dead is the Maker. One only did not die- the [Creator.
Kabīr says, He alone dies not who is not held in coming and [going"[11].

Here, an interesting problem arises. Does Kabīr understand the idea of God in the non-dualist or panentheistic sense ? Mr Ahmad Shah maintains the idea was non-dualist[12]; and indeed some of the verses seem to bear this out. There are also some passages which appear to imply qualified non-dualism in Rāmānuja's sense. For example, see the following passage:

"The great (God) reacheth from the lower to the upper regions [of the firmament;
He illumineth the silent realm....
Know that He pervadeth the body as well as the universe;
He batheth in Mansarowar (the lake of the heart);
His pass-word is "Soham" *("I am He")*[13].

On the other hand, Kabīr leaves no doubt about his teaching on the nature of God. The Absolute (Brahman) of non-dualism is a pure abstraction, for no man can worship a God who is without attributes and wherever people are religious it has been found necessary to recognize God as possessing attributes. But this does not mean that God's nature is accessible to every kind of knowledge. Kabīr holds that the mystery of God can be reached only by mystical knowledge that can be possessed through and in love of God *(bhakti)*.

"Tat tvam asi[14] is the preaching of the Upanishads; that is their [message.
Great is their reliance upon this; but how can they, however mighty, describe Him?"[15].
How can I explain His form or outline? there is no second who [has seen Him.

---

11 *Bījak, Śabda* 45.

12 See F E. Keay, *Kabīr and his Followers, op. cit.* p. 71.

13 *Ādi-Granth, Bhairau* 1.

14 «That thou art»: That (the Absolute Self) is thou (the individual self).

15 *Bījak, Ramaiṇī* 8.

How can I describe the condition of the unconditioned...?"[16].

The eyes of love *(bhakti)* alone can get a glimpse of the mystery of God's nature.

"Kabīr says: Listen to me, friend: he understands who loves. If you feel not love's longing for your Beloved One, it is vain to adorn your body, vain to put unguent on your eyelids"[17].

Kabīr gave up the worship of Hindu gods and believed in Rāma alone as the Supreme God who is in no way an incarnation of Vishṇu. The God whom Kabīr worshipped is a concrete Person, the Saviour of mankind, who is merciful, joyous, bountiful, happy, perfect, and often spoken of as Father.

"By my Father I have been comforted.
. . . .
How shall I forget that Father from my mind?....
My Father is the great Lord.
How shall I go to that Father?[18]

God is omnipresent and omnipotent. In this contex we have to make a precision. While stressing the immanence of God in creatures, Kabīr would have nothing to do with idolatry, for he reasoned that if God is One, the whole basis of idolatry vanishes.

"If God dwell only in the mosque, to whom belongeth the rest of the country. They who are called Hindus say that God dwelleth in an idol: I see not the truth in either sect"[19].

Finally, Kabīr's conception of God could be better focused if we examine the way he experiences his own relationship to God. He makes use of the idea of husband and wife as an illustration of

---

16 *Ibid.* 6-7.

17 Tagore's translation, *One Hundred Poems of Kabīr,* quoted from *North Indian Saints.* (Madras, no date), pp. 27-28.

18 *Ādi-Granth, Āsā* 3.

19 *Ādi-Granth, Prabhātī* 2.

the relationship between God and the bhakta (devotee); God is the husband to whom the religious soul surrenders entirely with loving trust and with whom it is united by the closest of ties. Kabīr also frequently refers to his "drinking the elixir of Rāma", which is another way of expressing the deep satisfaction that he finds in ecstatic union with God.

> "Such knowledge of the Supreme Being hath manifested itself: I am imbued with it *(literally,* I am steeped in His colour). All the rest of the world is led astray in error, but my mind is intoxicated with the elixir of Rāma"[20],
> "Kabīr, if I cast down mine eyes and take the friend into my heart, I enjoy every pleasure with my Beloved, and I disclose this to no one"[21], All are wives of Rāma: unmovable Purusha[22] is the Husband"[23].

Kabīr having turned away from Hindu mythology and polytheism proposes a double path to find the One God and to know Him mystically; namely, a moral path and the path of love. God is present in the heart of hearts and it is in one's heart that he has to be sought after. "Search in thy heart, search in thy heart of hearts; there is his place and abode"[23a]. This immanent presence can be consciously possessed only on condition that the heart is pure and humble. "Unless you remove evil from your hearts; how shall you find [God] by dwelling in the forest? ... I have met God who dwelleth in the heart"[23b]. "When I was proud", says Kabīr, "Thou [wert] not [in me]; now that thou art [in me] I am not proud. Now thou and I have become one; seeing that we are both one, my mind is satisfied"[23c.] Mere knowledge of the Śāstras only puffs up the mind of the pundits and this is an obstacle to the knowledge of God. "All read *Smṛti* and *Vedas* and *Purāṇa,* none have vision of the Inward Light",[23d]. Having

20 *Ādi-Granth; Śri* 2.
21 *Ādi-Granth, Ślok* 234.
22 Purusha, the Male, i. e., God.
23 *Bījah, Ramaiṇī* 27.
23a *Ādi-Granth, Prabhātī* 2.
23b *Aidi Granth, Mārū 2.*
23c *Ādi-Granth, Gaurī* 72.
23d Bījak, Śabda, 14.

removed from the heart sin which is the obstacle to the knowledge of God, the devotee of God should love him, for love alone makes the mind penetrate into the Essence of God. "Saith Kabīr, By love I have obtained [The Lord]. By becoming simple [in heart] I have met God,[23e]. Kabīr's frequent reference to the divine unknowableness is met with side by side with his insistence on the need of loving meditation on God's name *(Satnām)*, so that He may be brought within the reach of men. *Śabda* is the mysterious utterance of Speech which gives the devotee the knowledge of the unknown, makes him wise and thus leads him to the mystical experience of God. Kabīr proclaims with deep conviction "I am a lover of the Word which has shown me the unseen (God)".

2. God in the theology of Tulsī Dās[24].

Tulsī Dās accepts the traditional threefold manifestation *(Trimūrti)* of the Supreme: Brahmā the creator, Vishṇu the preserver, and Śiva the destroyer. Taken separately, they appear and act in accordance with their distinctive functions. Brahmā creates all things[25] and is also considered as the helper and delegate of the gods[26]. He carves out everyman's destiny on the forehead[27] and dispenses the fruit of good and evil works[28]; mortals blame him when things go wrong[29]. But, unmistakably Tulsī subordinates him to Vishṇu. The following passage indicates how when Brahmā was approached by the gods and sages for help, he proclaimed his dependance on Vishṇu.

> "When Brahmā learnt the whole matter, he pondered and said: I can do nought; but the immortal Lord, whose servant you are, will help both you and me"[30].

23e *Ādi-Granth, Gaurī* 6.

24 The name of Tulsī Dās (1543-1623) dominates the religious poetry of modern India. His main work in Hindī is the *Rāmacaritmānas* («Sacred Lake of the Aets of Rāma»). Abbreviated references in our text refer to this work, translated into English by Douglas P. Hill, Oxford, 1952. A = Ayodhyākāṇḍa; Ar = Araṇyakānda; B = Bālakāṇḍa; C = Caupāī; Ch = (Chanda; D = Dohā; K = Kiṣkindhākāṇḍa; L = Laṅkākāṇḍa; S = Sundarakāṇḍa; U = Uttarakāṇḍa.

25 B.C. 6.

26 B. C. 82ff; B. Ch. 19ff.

27 B. C. 32; B. D. 68; B. C. 97; L. C. 29.

28 A. C. 282.

29 A. C. 47; 49.

30 B. Ch. 19.

Śiva is the god of dissolution, archetype of the perfect Yogi, immersed in deep meditation and contemplation. He now and then receives the most exalted titles which we expect a Vaishṇava mystic like Tulsī to reserve for Vishṇu alone. Thus, Śiva is called *Bhagavan* (the Lord)[31], *Jagadātma* (the soul of the world)[32]. This could be explained partly by his syncretistic tendency to effect a reconciliation between the Saiva and Vaishṇava rivals and partly by his henotheistic tendency that is sometimes noticeable in Hindu worship. However even Śiva like Brahmā is subordinate to the incarnate God Rāma[33]. "... he (Rāma) by whose power Brahmā creates, Hari preserves and Śiva destroys..."[34].

It is Rāma, the chief incarnation of Vishṇu, who is held to be infinitely superior to Brahmā's and Śiva's worship[35]. Śiva and Brahmā long for his grace[36] and address hymns of praise to Him as their Lord[37].

Rāma, according to Tulsī Dās, is identified with the Absolute (Brahman). He is the Absolute made personal. "There are two forms of the Absolute made impersonal and personal; unutterable, fathomless, without beginning and unique"[38]. Rāma is regarded as the manifestation of Brahman.

"Even in their hearts was a yearning to see with their own eyes the Supreme Lord, impersonal, indivisible, without end or beginning, whom mystics contemplate, whom the Veda defines as "Not thus, not thus", pure delight, without attribute or equal, from a part of whom are born many a Śaṁbhu, Brahmā and Vishṇu, the Blessed Lord"[39].

Tulsī constantly refers to the negative description of the Absolute found in the *Upanishads: neti, neti* (not thus, not thus)[40] and ascribes to Rāma the following negative epithets: unbounded,

31 B. C. 46.
32 B. C. 64.
33 A. C. 127, 254.
34 S. C. 21.
35 K.D. 25; L.C. 22; U.Ch. 5.
36 Ar. C. 5.
37 B. Ch. 20; U. Ch. 6.
38 B. C. 23.
39 B. C. 144.
40 This is repeated 12 times in Tulsī's work. Cfr. B. D. 12; A. C. 93; Ar. C. 25; K. Ch. 1; L. D. 117; U.C. 110.

stainless, guileless, without ego, unslayable, without second, without desires, unnamed, without form, etc.

Tulsī Dās considers Rāma, the Supreme Being, under two aspects: *nirguṇa* (without qualities) and *saguṇa* (with qualities). In the former aspect he is the Absolute of which the earlier *Upanishads* speak and in the second, this Absolute is endowed with a personal form, especially *Saccidānanda:* Being, consciousness and bliss. In this personal aspect the Supreme Being is Vishṇu in his many incarnations and particularly he is Rāma. When Tulsī speaks of the two aspects of the Supreme Being, he does not mean any difference between the *saguṇa* and the *nirguṇa* aspects of Brahman.

> "There is no difference between the personal and the impersonal; so say the sages, the Purāṇas, wise men and the Vedās. The impersonal, formless, invisible and unborn becomes personal for love of the faithful. How does the impersonal become the personal? Just as water is not different from snow and ice"[41].

Tulsī Dās explains these two aspects thus. Rāma in as far as he is the Absolute (Brahman) is immanent in all beings as the ground of all souls and of all material realities. This indwelling form of Rāma is referred to as without qualities or *nirguṇa,* and this property of immanence is expressed by the Hindī word *antarajāmï* (in Sanskrit: *antaryāmī*)[42]. "0ne-who-lives-in-All *(Ramaiyā)*: literally, the one-who-sports-in-all, the one-who-delights-all, is a title of Rāma[43]. On the other hand, the externalized form of Rāma, i. e., the Supreme God in as far as He takes up the manifest form, is referred to as with qualities *(saguṇa),* in contrast to the immanent, indwelling form; this is expressed by the Hindī word *baherajāmī* (in Sanskrit: *baharyāmī).*

41 B. C. 116.

42 Tulsī's *Kavitāvalī,* VIII. 129, in Raymond Allchin's translation, London, 1964, p. 181.

43 See *Kavitāvalī,* VII. 53, in the seme trans. p. 151.

"By his taking a Name is the externalized form
Of Rām yet greater than the immanent,
And as the new-calved cow with dripping udders
Hastens when she hears her young, *so hastens he to his devotees*[44].

We cannot deny the influence of the *Adhyātma Rāmāyaṇa*[45] on the non-dualist flavour of Tulsī's writings, for this work combines the non-dualist system of Śaṅkara with the devotion of Rāmājuna's followers; yet in many ways Tulsī differs from this source also[46]. Of course, one can select statements from Tulsī's writings to prove his adherence either to the non-dualist position or to the qualified non-dualism of Rāmānuja or even to the dualist position of Madhva. It must be said that Tulsī himself was an independent thinker who tried to harmonize divergent theological systems. We can legitimately draw a distinction between his theoretical stand-point and that of religious experience. Though he does teach the ' "attributeless" aspect of Rāma, the essential unity of the individual self with the Supreme Self, and the illusory nature of the world, yet he affrms the superiority of the saguṅa form of Rāma over the unmanifest, «qualityless" *(nirguṅa)* form and thus departs strikingly from the strictly non-dualist position[47].

In other words, Tulsī clearly indicates where his preferences lie. «Though you are the Absolute, indivisible and eternal, comprehensible only by intuition, though I know and speak of that form of yours, yet I constantly turn back therefrom and spend my love on

---

44 *Kavitāvalī*, VII. 129, Trans. p. 181.

45 This work is a short Sanskrit text of some 4000 verses (15th Cent.) For the whole question of Tulsī's dependence on earlier works, see Ch. Vaudeville, *Études sur les sources et la composition du Rāmāyaṇa de Tulsī Dās*, Paris, 1955.

46 It was the non-dualism of Śaṅkara which formed the base from which the great predecessors of Tulsī Dās departed. Although Śaṅkara himself is the reputed author of several devotional hymns, stili in his system the idea of a personal loving God is relegated to the status of a popular religion. On the other hand, for Rāmānuja, God is perfect personality, dependent on nothing external, the Supreme Spirit endowed with qualities, identified with Vishṇu; this truth is proved by religious experience and confirmed by reason.

47 See Purshottamdās Agravāl, *Tulsī's Philosophical Thought*, in: "Nāgari-Pracārinī Patrikā", 1959, pp. 251-62. Scholars discuss the basic theological position of Tulsī Dās. See Giridhār Sharmā Caturvedī, *Gosvāmī's Philosophical Thought* in: "Tulsī Granthāvalī", Benares, 1923, vol. 3, pp. 63-130; and Rājpati Dīkshit, *Tulsī Dās and his Age*, Benares, 1952, Ch. 7. For these references I am indebted to R. Allchin's book above cited, p. 54.

the Absolute made man»[48]. "Some there are who contemplate the impersonal Absolute, but I delight in the King of Kosala, the Lord Rāma himself in personal form"[49].

In a significant passage Tulsī speaks of Kākabhuśuṇḍi's encounter with an advaitic mystic as follows:

"... being himself (the advaitin) a mystic, devoted to the knowledge of the Absolute, and thinking that I was fully qualified to hear it, he began to give me instruction in the nature of the Absolute, uncreated, one without a second, impersonal, dwelling as sovereign in the heart, having no parts, desires, names or forms, comprehensible only by intuition, indivisible, incomparable, transcending mind and sense, stainless, imperishable, immutable, limitless, sum of all bliss. He said: the Vedās declare that thou art It, and that there is no more difference between It and Thee than between water and its waves. With all manners of comparisons the sage instructed me, but the doctrine of the impersonal laid no hold upon my heart... I would have nothing of the impersonal doctrine and persisted in expounding the personal" [50].

"Now all the sages whom I questioned told me that God is present in all creation; but this doctrine of the impersonal did not satisfy me; I became ever more attached to the Absolute made personal»[51].

These passages imply that while some seek release in the way of contemplation of the impersonal, the true lover of God *(bhakta)* turns from such soulless worship of the abstract to devote himself in intense love and self-abandonment to the personal Lord.

Rāma is the beloved God incarnate, chosen as the object of Tulsī's devotion and love. He is not only the Absolute made personal, the first cause of all things, but also the sole means of salvation. He becomes incarnate and the precise reasons for the act of incarnation cannot be truly grasped. However, Tulsī indicates some reasons for incarnation; one is that whenever virtue declines and iniquity is in the ascendency, God becomes incarnate to relieve the

48 Ar. C. 12.
49 L. Ch. 35.
50 U. C. 106.
51 U. C. 106.

distress of the virtuous; another is that for the sake of saints and devotees he takes on man's form so that by knowing and reciting his deeds they may be freed from the world of transmigration.

> "Whenever Rāma assumes human form and plays his many parts for his worshipper's sake, I go to the city of Avadh and take delight in watching his childish pranks. I go there and witness his birthday celebrations and stay there for five very pleasant years. For the boy Rāma is my patron deity, his form as beauteous as a myriad Loves. I gaze and gaze at the face of my Lord and satisfy the desire of my eyes" [52].
>
> "As a bridge for religion, for the sake of the world's wellbeing, and to lighten the load of earth did he take incarnation as a man. lt is the Master's way to care for order, faith and affection. And it is Raghuvira's vow to uphold the world and the Vedas"[53].

Here we have to note that Tulsī Dās, in contrast to what other Hindus say, shows his anxiety to explain that Rāma's humanity is not real but merely a conscious appearance of divine activity. When Tulsī has occasion to say that Rāma felt weary, he adds immediately that he was using a mere conventional phrase[54]. Rāma's grief over his wounded brother Lakshman is explained by saying that the God was merely playing the part of a mortal man[55].

The mystery of God can be approached and attained by love *(bhakti),* though not excluding knowledge *(jñāna).* Sutīkṣṇa who was devoted to God and showed constant, all-absorbing, unwavering love to Him was granted the vision of God. He proclaimed in ecstacy, "Then shall my eyes today be blessed with the vision of his lotus face who frees us from rebirth" [55a]. In a significant passage of Tulsī Dās, the Supreme God says: "In the hearts of those who in thought and word and deed make me their place of refuge and

52 U. G. 73, 109.
53 *Kavitāvalī* VII. 122, Trans. p. 178.
54 A.C. 87
55 L.C. 61.
55a Ar. C. 9.

worship me without desire I dwell eternally"[55b]. It is love alone which opens the mystics' spiritual eyes to the true nature of the supreme Being who is personal or rather, in Tulsī's words, the Absolute made personal, whereas mere knowledge at most would grant only the vision of the impersonal aspect of the Absolute[55c].

3. Tukārām's conception of God

Tukārām [56], the best known and best loved poet-mystic of Maharāṣtra, composed numerous poems (about 4500 are attributed to him) and these reveal depths of theistic experience and a wide range of religious vision. They contain spiritual wisdom for people in every walk of life, portraying various levels of spiritual experience from the initial, elementary piety of a simple Hindu to the sublime mystical experience of the personal God in union of love and surrender. Tukārām's life-long devotion to Viṭhobā (Incarnation of Vishṇu) testifies to his intense personal religion and his verses appear to be the natural expression of a mind holding constant communion with God; they certainly entitle him to a high place in the history of Indian theism. His predecessor in the *bhakti* tradition, Nāmdev [57] was an inspiring example to him. Nāmdev's religious experience can be illustrated by the following poem of his.

55b A. C. 128ff.

55c Ar. C. 12; L. Ch. 35.

56 (1598-1650) The original verses of Tukārām have been published in several editions; the most important ones are: the critical edition called *Indū Prakāsh*, published in Bombay, 1873 and the edition of V. N. Joag, Poona, 1909 with the commentary. A complete English translation by J. N. Fraser and K. B. Marathe is available under the title: *The Poems of Tukārām*, 3 vols., Madras 1909-15.

Our sources unless otherwise indicated are 1) W. S. Deming, *Selections from Tukārām*, Madras, 1932. (This translation follows the above English translation but slightly revised); 2) R. G. Bhandarkar's Translation in his *Vaiṣṇavism, Śaivism and minor religious systems*, «Grundriss der Indo-Arischen Philologie und Altertumskunde», III Band, 6 Heft. Strassburg, 1913 pp. 94ff. 3) The above mentioned Fraser-Marathe Translation.

For a good introduction to the religious background of Tukārām's teaching, see G. A. Deleury, *Psaumes du Pèlerin*, 2e edit., Paris, 1956, pp. 9-34.

57 Tradition places him between the 13th and 14th century.

Now all my days with joy I'll fill
Full to the brim,
With all my heart to Viṭṭhal cling And only to him.
He will sweep utterly away
All dole and care;
And all in sunder shall I rend illusion's snare.
O altogether dear is he
And he alone,
For all my burden he will take to be his own.
Lo, all the sorrow of the world
Will straightway cease,
And all unending now shall be
The reign of peace.
For all the bondage he will break of worldly care,
And all in sunder will he rend
Illusion's snare.
From all my foolish fancies now
Let me be free,
In Viṭṭhal, Viṭṭhal only is
Tranquillity[58].

There is not the slightest doubt whether Tukārām was a theist or not. His deep and sincere faith in God is amply testified in a hundred of his abhaṅgs. Just one telling poem is sufficient to show this.

"What manner of faith shall we offer; what single thing is fit to
[present you?
You fill all and lie beyond all; you are present in our bodily form,
[whether we speak, eat, taste or smell.
How shall we control our organs and sort out merit and guilt?
[What ceremonies or deeds shall we perform?
Where is the scene where you are not present?
What do I gain by closing my eyes?
What spell or charm shall I utter?
Where shall we place our faith?

58 See N. Macnicol, *Psalms of Marāṭha Saints,* Calcutta, 1919, p. 47.

Where is the spot in which you are not?
Whither shall we turn? Where shall we set our feet?
There is no spot known to us that is void of thee; how can I
[search for such a place?[59]

Tukārām believes in the immanence of God in the whole of "creation" and this belief of his should not lead us to think that he favoured idolatry. The passage which seems to savour of idolatry is this: "Brahmā dwells in all things; there is no place void of him; then, how can you say an image is not God?"[60] Although Tukārām believed that God was actually present in the image, it is equally evident that he did not think that God was confined or limited to the idol. The following passage bears this out.

"Thy feet are everywhere to me; let me trust in thee alone. I see thy feet everywhere: the three worlds are pervaded by Viṭṭhal. Discussions of thy nature are a maze of error; let me refuse to enter into them. Tukā says, There is no particle without thee, yet I see thou art greater than space itself"[61].

That God is greater than space itself is an impressive argument to counteract any trace of idolatry and, I should dare say, any crude type of pantheism. The fact that he was greatly impressed by the divine immanence probably explains why he stressed the presence of God in the idol. In order to understand the significance in Tukārām's life of image-worship, we have to consider his notion of God's indwelling in all things, and especially, among saints and sacred objects. God pervades all things and his presence and influence are felt everywhere[61a]. Through God the whole world is related to us and hence the world is not worthless or an object of scorn; each life is blended with the life of all.[61b] The special presence of God is realized in sacred objects; hence, the image carries the

59 Abhaṅg 214 (Fraser-Marathe trans.). *Abhaṅg* is a particular form of poetic composition; the popular metre used by many poet-mystics.

60 Abhaṅg 1146 (Fraser-Marathe transl.).

61 Abhaṅg 217 (Fraser-Marathe transl.).

61a Deming's selec. no. 305-6.

61b *Ibid.* no. 369.

divine presence as much as saints. Tukārām makes his mind clear on the subject of image-worship by teaching that God is separate from the world and from all taint of pollution,[61c] that he does not consider the image, in as far as it is a created thing, to be God. Certainly he recognizes the image as the abode of God, the symbol of God, but not as God Himself in the sense that a created reality as created is worshipped.

The divine immanence thus vividly presented, Tukārām equally brings to light the divine transcendence.

> "Thy greatness is unsearchable. Even the Vedās became silent and the power of the mind becomes stunted. What possibility is there of my mental power reaching him whose light it is that the sun and the moon display? Even the thousand tongued (the great serpent) is unable to expound thy greatness. How then shall I be able to do so? Says Tukā, we are thy children, thou art my mother, place us under the shadow (protection) of thy grace"[62].
> "All the world says that there is not a space so minute as a sesamum seed without thee. The old Rsis, sages, pious and holy men said that thou art in the heart of all these things... Thou hast filled up numberless universe and also a residue still remained. But to me thou hast become inaccessible"[63].

That Tukārām was a theist is evident beyond doubt from what has been said so far. But was he a strict monotheist? Some scholars[64] seem to think he was not and adduce the reason that he venerated more than one deity. Given the fact that he was not always speaking of his religious experience in strictly theological terms and that though he venerated lesser deities as is customary among Hindus, the outstanding fact of his life was his whole-hearted love to the one Deity of his predilection, namely Viṭhobā, we can legitimately conclude to his certain profession of monotheism. This is what he explicitly states with respect to this point:

61c *Ibid.* no. 323.

62 Bhandarkar's trans. 1st coll. no. 4361.

63, *Ibid.* 1st coll. no. 4419.

64 See W. S. Deming, *op. cit.*, p. 15.

> "If I praise any other but thee, let my tongue rot away. If I care for any other but thee, let my head be crushed. If I find pleasure in others, surely it is sinful that very instant. If the ears drink no nectar of God's glory, what use are they? Tukā says, If I forget thee for one moment, what purpose will life serve?"[65]

Further, while emphasizing the unicity of the Supreme Being, did he adhere to non-dualism as proposed by the followers of Śaṅkara? In this connection we can point out Mahīpaṭi's story of Tukārām sitting under a blanket with his fingers in his ears as a protest against a Vedāntin who was reading to him a non-dualist treatise.[66] Whether this story is authentic or not, we have Tukārām's own clear pronouncements indicating his rejection of non-dualism. "The fool hath said in his heart", not, "there is no God", but, "I am God". In a good many *abhaṅgs* Tukārām condemns non-dualism.

> "When monism is expounded without faith and love, the expounder as well as the hearer is troubled and afflicted. He who calls himself Brahman goes on in his usual way, should not be spoken to and is a buffoon. The shameless one who speaks heresy in opposition to the Vedas is an object of scorn among holy men. Even an outcaste is superior to him who cuts off the relation between God and his devotee (by asserting them to be identical), so says Tukā"[67].
> " For me there is no satisfaction in the doctrine of monism. Sweet to me is the service of thy feet. Confer this gift upon me making it fit (to be given by thee). Thy name and singing of it are dear to me. The relation between God and his devotee is a source of elevated joy. Make me feel this, keeping me distinct from thee. All this belongs to thee. Confer it upon me some day"[68].

65 Abhaṅg 151 (Fraser-Marathe trans.).

66 See W. S. Deming, *op. cit,* p. 15

67 Bhandarkar's tran., 1st coll. no. 1471. See R. D. Ranade, *Indian Mysticism: Mysticism in Maharashtra,* Poona 1933, pp. 327-336, where Tukārām's theism is discussed.

68 *Ibid.* 1st coll. no. 3753.

When in fifty or more *abhaṅgs* Tukārām describes the soul's union with God, his expressions imply loss of individuality on the part of the devotee and seem to imply identity between God and the God-lover.

"I am melted, I am lost in thee; when fire and camphor mingle, is blackness of any sort left behind? My flame and thy flame, says Tukā, are become one»[69].

" A sugar crystal and sugar powder differ only in the name. There is no difference when sweetness is to be judged. Tell me, oh Pāṇḍurang, how thou and I are distinct. Thou has moved the world and me and mine are the results. Gold in the form of ornaments is worn on the foot, the hands, nose and the head. When all these are thrown into the crucible, where remains the distinction? Profit and loss are real in a dream when one goes to sleep; both vanish when one is awakened, so says Tukā"[70].

"When salt is dissolved in water, what is it that remains distinct? I have thus become one in joy with thee and have lost myself in thee. When fire and camphor are brought together, is there any thing remnant? Tukā says, thou and I were one light"[71].

The meaning of these texts seems to refer to the losing of self-consciousness in moments of ecstacy and not to the ontological identity between God and the devotee. Far from implying the disapperance of the self into the Absolute, liberation for *bhakti* mystics means release from the bonds of the body and the attainment of a state in which the self enjoys the presence of the Beloved. To describe it more deeply, the freed self attains to the nature of God in union of love but not to strict identity with him *(Brahmaṇo bhāvaḥ na tu svarūpaikyam).*

Tukārām's description in strongly personal terms of the relationship between the Supreme Being and the devotee shows that God for him is the Supreme Person who loves men, who shows them kindness and mercy, and who protects them.

---

69 *Abhaṅg* 1679 (Fraser-Marathe trans.).

70 Bhandarkar's trans. 1st coll. no. 1992.

71 *Ibid.* 1st coll. no. 2482.

> "God is ours, certainly ours, and is the soul of all souls. God is near to us, certainly near, outside and inside. God is benignant, and fulfills every longing even of a longing nature. God protects us, certainly protects us, and subdues strife and death. God is merciful, certainly merciful, and protects Tukā"[72].
> "No deeds I've done nor thoughts I've thought;
> Save as thy servant, I am nought.
> Guard me, O God, and O, control
> The tumult of my restless soul.
> Ah, do not, do not cast on me
> The guilt of mine iniquity.
> My countless sins, I, Tukā, say,
> Upon thy loving heart I lay"[73].

God is not only the Master whom Tukārām serves faithfully but the Supreme Lover who loves all men and demands love in return. His love is compared to that of a mother, father, brother and bosom friend.

> "Thou art to me mother, father, brother and bosom friend; treasure, family and beloved of the soul. Now I need no other grounds of assurance. I have placed on thy head all my burden of gaining and keeping... Thus says T'uka's brother, O God, who doest and makest man to do, in thee is fulness of faith, devotion, worship and attendance on God»[74].

God's love is more generous than the mother's for her child. Tukārām delicately describes this love in touching terms. "When her child is sick the mother spends her life for him; yet there is no common generosity like that of Nārāyaṇ. Assuredly my own experience has taught me this. Tukā says, you must be truthful, for no assumption will achieve your object"[75]. More tellingly is God's generosity viewed as being beyond measure. "A beggar like me has but two hands, while the giver's treasure is inexhaustible. What shall I fill it

72 *Ibid.* 1st coll. no. 1870.
73 N. Macnicol, *Psalms of Marāṭha Saints, op. cit.* p. 76.
74 Deming's selec. no. 272
75 *Ibid.* no. 274

with? I have but one storehouse. His loving acts are pouring into it; my tongue is weary with counting his gifts. Tukā says, Now let me rest where I am, in humble obedience at his feet"[76]. God hears every petition and fulfils all our desires, giving to each what he finds sweet. He never allows anything to prevent us from meeting him[77].

His mercy is also sung in wonderful terms by Tukārām: "Thou art a mine of mercy and a sea of compassion"[78]. "In that hour (i. e., of peril) thy heart was moved with pity ... Lo, I have saved my servants from death. How else could they have lived through the battle? Such mercy dost thou show to thy worshippers; thou art indeed our mother, says Tukā"[79]. In his merciful love He takes the initiative of coming to his devotees to abide in them. "What wonder is it that he comes when you call him; he runs to his worshipper even when he does not remember him. Tukā says, To him will I lift up my song"[80]. God's condescending love will even risk his own life. This idea is something quite unique in Hinduism and it justifies quoting the verse in full.

> "In love for his son, the father lays aside a stone, although he goes hungry for that purpose. He places a burden upon his own arms and shoulders, and soon he makes his son master of an estate. He gladdens his eyes by putting ornaments upon him and he displays the greatness of the store he has made. Tukā says, He will not let any one else vex him; he will risk his own life for him"[81].

This infinite and merciful love is far removed from being a kind of blind love devoid of knowledge. His omniscience penetrates into the intimate abyss of our hearts. "Thou knowest our hearts, though we tell thee nothing. Thou doest pervade the world; there is no need to tell thee aught"[82]. "God knows, God knows; he pro-

76 *Ibid.* no 275.
77 *Ibid.* no 277.
78 *Ibid.* no 279.
79 *Ibid.*
80 Deming's selec. no. 280.
81 *Ibid.* no. 283.
82 *Ibid.* no. 273.

vides what the mind longs for... he hides in the innermost recesses of the mind"[83].

In spite of the many shortcomings and failings of his devotees, God loves them. Tukā's God is not a God of revenge but of forgiveness and loving kindness.

"However badly a child speaks, his mother loves to hear him. It is sweet to her because she loves her child and satisfies his childish longings. She willingly bears the blows he gives her as he nestles in her bosom. Tukā prays to Pāṇḍurang; his case is like that of the child»[84].
"A child may be unkind to his mother, yet she still loves him. Forgetting that she is weary, she lifts him to her lap and presses his body against hers. He weeps at his distress and is ever ready to give up her life for him. She jumps up when he calls her name; she flings away her life, says Tukā"[85].

God's love especially goes out towards those who are helpless and he feels his chief delight in bringing succour to them; he bears their burdens on his head; he suffers them not to stray from the path but takes them by the hand and leads them[86]. He seeks to win over sinners. " That thou art the saviour of the sinful is deeply printed on the three worlds"[87].

Finally, God's love towards his devotees is considered to be so intimate that he is said to cling to their person and not to let them go. "All other gods come and go but this God (Viṭhobā) keeps with one all through life. His inspiration fills all my limbs; ... whatever I do he will not leave me. This deity has devoured my life, with all the five elements of my body[88].

In short, "Where pardon, peace and purity dwell, there God abides"[89]. To sum up, what God meant to Tukārām, what expe-

83 *Ibid.* no. 276.
84 *Ibid.* no. 284.
85 *Ibid.* no. 287.
86 *Ibid.* no. 290.
87 *Ibid.* no. 296.
88 Ibid. no. 307.
89 Abhaṅg 706 (Fraser-Marathe trans.).

rience of God he possessed in his so intensely deep spiritual life, can be seen from his memorable words, comparable to Henry Newman's *Lead Kindly Light* and Francis Thomson's *Hound Of Heaven:*

"Holding my hands thou leadest me,
My comrade everywhere.
As I go on and lean on thee
My burden thou dost bear.
If as I go, in my distress
I frantic words should say,
Thou settest right my foolishness
And tak'est my shame away.
Thus thou to me new hope dost send,
A new world bringest in,
Now know I every man a friend,
And all I meet my kin.
So like a happy child I play
In thy dear world, O God,
And everywhere I, Tukā, say
Thy bliss is spread abroad[90].

4. Critical conclusion

We have endeavoured to outline the teaching of these mystics on the idea of God. We have presented the evidence by means of direct citations from their writings in order to show what sublime ideas they had of God. Let us now attempt a résumé of these conceptions.

God is conceived as perfectly spiritual and absolutely transcendent. He is the Supreme Spirit, the only Lord of the whole universe, invisible, incomprehensible, of infinite understanding, omniscient, omnipotent, omnipresent, immanent in nature and in man, yet transcending all things. The God of these mystics is then as truly transcendent, spiritual and absolute as the Brahman of the *Upanishads*.

90 N. Macnicol, *Op. cit.*, p. 71,

This God is also morally most perfect. He is perfectly righteous in Himself, morally stainless and pure. He rules over the universe, comes into closest personal contact with the needs and sorrows of men, listens to their praise and prayer, speaks in each man's conscience, approving or disapproving his actions and comforting the penitent with His pardon and sweet presence. Intimately involved in the world of men and of nature, and full of loving kindness, He nonetheless remains the universal, the perfect, the unchangeable God.

God is thus conceived not only as the Absolute Being but as the Supreme Person, the universal personal Spirit who sustains relationships at once personal and perfectly moral[91] with every human person. He bears the closest possible religious relation to men for He receives their worship and responds to their prayers not for His own sake but for their good. He knows all about us and sympathizes with us. He "incarnates" himself to reveal Himself and His plan of saving men from evil. He guards and helps the poor, the oppressed, the sinful. In brief, He loves men and in turn He asks for our love, worship and service.

Such sublime conceptions, though they have been justly praised by many foreign Orientalists, have been attributed by them to Christian influence on these mystics. In the case of Kabīr we are sure that he knew the *Qur'an* and was acquainted with its contents, for he often mentions this sacred book and even refers to Adam and Eve. Besides, many of the ideas of the Sufis appear in the teaching of Kabīr[92]. The other two mystics are supposed to have undergone the influence of Christianity. For example, Sir G. A. Grierson remarks: "Tulsī Dās was the first Hindu to teach that God was δυνάμενος συμπαῦῆσαι ταῖς ἀσῦευεῖχις ἡμῶν ("able to sympathize with our infirmities"; cfr. Heb 4, 15), a belief which is commonly conside-

91 We are aware that the worship of Krishṇa is sometimes vitiated by its erotic nature. The relation of the soul to God in this worship is that of a passionate woman to her lover. Such a religion inevitably leads to a deep sensualism both of the spirit and of the body. But the worship of Krishṇa as proposed by these mystics is pure and high-minded. G. Bhandarkar remarks that in the religious literature of the worship of Viṭhobā, Krishṇa is conceived not as the lover of Rādhā, his mistress, but as the husband of Rukmiṇī, his lawful wife, and thus «the Vaiṣṇavism of the Marāṭha country is more sober and purer». See Bhandharkar, *op. cit.*, p 89.

92 See Keay, *Kabīr and his Followers, op. cit.*, p 90-92.

red to be peculiar to Christianity". However, he ascribes this to Nestorian influence[93], J N. Fraser and J. F. Edwards[94] have pointed out at least forty-three verbal parallels between Tukārām's verses and the New Testament. Some of these are as follows:

1) "We know the fact, O God, that thy elusive ways cannot be fathomed" (Abhaṅg 1656).
"How unfathomable his decisions are, and how untraceable his ways!" (Romans 11. 33).
2) "It is worship that Nārāyaṇ desires; God is a spirit" (Abhaṅg 17).
"God is Spirit, and his worshippers must worship Him in spirit and sincerity" (John 4.24).
3) "The soul has first to perish and then to live" (Abhaṅg 2041). "Whoever gains his life will lose it, and whoever loses his life for my sake will gain it" (Math. 10.39).
4) "Worldly life and life with the highest - he who acts both parts together, in the end he achieves neither. If a man seeks to lay his hands on two grain-pits at once, he will end by destroying himself" (Abhaṅg 3465).
"No slave can belong to two masters, for he will either hate one and love the other, or stand by one and make light of the other. You cannot serve God and money" (Math. 6.24).

On account of such parallels these scholars think that Tukārām may have come into contact with Christianity.

However, we seem to lack evidence to prove or disprove this hypothesis. Besides, we should not forget that the sublime conceptions of these mystics could very well be, and indeed are, the spontaneous expressions of an intensely religious mind holding constant communion with God, poured out in their genuinely religious moods. At any rate, the similarity is truly remarkable and the poems of these mystics should very well serve as an excellent bridge to Christ. *Bhakti* which means love and surrender to God involves the idea of God as the Supreme Person. Of all Hindu religious

---

93 *The Imperial Gazetteer,* vol. II, Oxford 1909, p. 418.

94 *Life and Teaching of Tukārām,* Madras, no date, p. 178.

experience, *bhakti* experience comes nearest to Christian experience, for in this experience we come across the necessity of repentence and of a purified heart before God's grace can become effective, the need of realizing fellowship with God in union with Him, and the profound sense of dependance on Him alone and of loyal service and surrender to Him.

Very often some of the present-day Hindu theologians argue that the *bhakti* experience of the supreme Being is not the best in Hinduism and that the non-dualist experience of the impersonal Absolute, as Śaṅkara and his followers propose it, should be considered the best form of religious experience and that Christianity in so far as it is a way of *bhakti* is necessarily an inferior religion, however sublime and noble it may appear to be. If non-dualism were true, and if creatures were to be considered both ontologically and experientially as things of mere illusion, they would lack true significance and the argument of these theologians would be valid. But this view should be rejected as wanting in true religious significance and meaning. True enough, the mystics we have studied have sometimes made use of ambiguous, non-dualist expressions. But it seems to us that they were struggling hard to express the mystery of the Supreme Being and that they perhaps thought that the non-dualist way of expressing the transcendence of the Absolute could be better preserved as being in conformity with the Upanishadic non-dualist teaching; or perhaps they indulged in syncretism in an attempt to please everybody. Not being themselves professional theologians, for they detested theoretical speculations, they attempted to translate into words what they personally experienced as religious truths and in this attempt they were not rigorously consistent nor did they avoid all ambiguity. But they never left any doubt with regard to their preference and seemed to think that non-dualist experience left the religious soul cold and abstract and advocated a higher experience of faith in and love to God as the Supreme Person. The oft-repeated statement that *bhakti* belongs to an inferior form of religious experience presupposes that *bhakti* is necessarily always imperfect. This view runs counter to the Hindu doctrine of higher bhakti which means total participation of the religious soul in the nature of a Personal God, in perfect union with Him and in the experience of most perfect love for and surrender to Him. For an experience of the total loss of the self or of complete absorption into the Absolute Self the mystics we have studied testify by their experience they have neither need nor taste. Underneath the questionable beliefs of *Karma and Samsāra*[95] and the hardly tenable doctrine of emanation, which are basic to the Hindu religion to which they adhered, lies their authentic religious experience, their intense spiritual and mystical life, which expresses itself in their need for God, their search for God, their embrace of God insofar as they have found Him.

95 *Saṁsāra* means rebirth as the result of a man's action *(Karma)* in previous birth.

CHAPTER SIX

TĀYUMĀNAVAR, A MYSTIC OF DIVINE UNION

Introduction

Tāyumānavar (ca. 1704-1742) was a sage, saint, mystic, siddha, yogin and a scholar, all combined in a unique way. His scholarship and saintliness reached the ears of Vijayaraṅga Cokkanātar, the King of Tiruchirappalli, who made him the steward and manager of the royal estates. He was well-versed in the knowledge of the Hindu sacred books and continued his studies along with his official duties. He found a guru who was a man of great learning and piety whose name was "the teacher of silence" (Maunamuni). Tāyumānavar wanted to leave his secular work but his guru told him "to be still". He was impressed by this advice and carried on his royal service with undisturbed mind "like the waveless sea". When the king died in 1731, the queen Mīnākṣi became enamoured of the young man but he escaped from her advances and fled to Ramanatapuram and continued his intense religious life and practised higher yoga of concentration and meditation. Then he settled at Vedaraniyam and was happily married. His married life did not deter him from his mystical life, and after the death of his wife he totally dedicated himself to the service of God and his fellowmen[1].

1. "The Revel in Bliss" (Ānantaka‰ippu)

Tāyumānavar's love for his Guru and Lord Śiva, combined with his profound scholarship both in Sanskrit and in Tamil religious literature, flowered into religious and mystical lyrics which

1 For the life of Tāyumānavar, see S.V. SUBRAMANIAM *Tāyumānavar*, Annamalai University, Annamalai Nagar, 1977, pp. 1-25 and 118 (in Tamil).

are noted for deep religious feeling, beauty of expression, and sweetness of rhythm. In fact his writings unquestionably formed the greatest Śaiva production of the eighteenth century.[2] They gave new impetus to the *bhakti* religion of Tamilnadu. Tāyumānavar's Śaivism is a religion of harmony which synthesizes the Vedānta and the Siddhānta without conflict. He teaches that God is greater and more important than religion. He says:

> "The creeds in conflict know in common
> One only God, almighty Thee
> To each according to this need Thou hast chosen
> To appear distinct without a difference.
> All creeds roll, as rivers to the sea,
> To Thee, O Ocean of vast Silence."[3]

Ānantakka%oippu (The revel in Bliss)[4] which can be said to contain the cream of his teachings is cast in the form of a love song to express the soul's relationship to God, like a maiden relating to her most intimate lady friend "secrets unsayable". In ballad form the soul discloses the visit of her divine lover. I give my own translation[5] of the original Tamil text and comment[6] on each of the thirty verses.

Verse 1:

The Light which is the beginning and has no beginning, which shines in me as Bliss and Knowledge, appeared as the Silent One. He said to me a word not to be said.

---

2 See J.N. Farquhar, *An outline of the religious literature of India,* Oxford, 1920, p. 351.

3 The translation is by K. Ramachandra; see his *The Message of Saint Tāyumānavar, in: X Internationales Kongress für Religonsgeschichte,* Marburg, 1961 Sektion V A: Indien, p. 162.

4 The text of *Ānantakka%oippu* is taken from the edition of the South India Śaiva Siddhānta Works Publishing Society: *Tāyumānavatikal Tiruppāṭalkal,* Tinnevelly, 1996, pp. 678-688.

5 Some of the existing English translations are either too literal or too liberal;, I have consulted the following ones: L.D. Barnett, *The Heart of India,* London 1924, pp. 85-88, which contains only 20 verses; Shuddhananda Bharati, *Voice of Tayumanar,* Madras, 1963, pp. 130-133, which is more a spiritual interpretation than an exact translation. A good selection of Tāyumānavar's writing has been well translated by T. Isaac Tambyah; see his *Psalms of a Śaiva Saint,* London, 1925. This work does not contain any interpretation of the theology and mysticism of Tāyumānavar.

6 My commentary is based on the teaching of Śaiva Siddhānta theologians as found in the Meyhanta Śāstras. See also my *Love of God according to Śaiva Siddhānta,* A Study in

Commentary

Śiva is the cause of the origin and the end of everything; but he has no beginning and no end. The soul is also eternal; but God stands in inseparable relation to it, develops it, dwells in it and yet transcends it. But God alone creates its body, organs and spheres of activity and experience and objects. *Ānava,* the original impurity of darkness, is one in all beings and is eternal. The difference between the three eternals which have no beginning and no end is that God alone is independent of anything else whereas the other two, namely, the soul and *ānava*, are dependent on God for their being and activity. Karma is the cause of all birhs and deaths. *Māyā* is the material cause from which all things are evolved and into which all things are dissolved. God's *śakti* is the instrumental cause and God is the efficient cause. God is beyond the fettered souls and fetters.

God Śiva is Saccidānanda: Existence (Truth), Knowledge and Bliss. In other words he is Life, Light and Love. He shines as Knowledge and Love (Bliss) in the soul. Mauni, the silent One, is an epithet of Śiva, as being absorbed in millennial meditation. Mauna guru is also the name of the poet's teacher. Śiva teaches the mystic Truth by a silent sign and symbol of hand. No one can reveal that mystic Truth by word of mouth. *Nāda* is the primary sound from which all other *tattvas* emerge. The form of the word *(corparapanca)* is responsible for the elements which form concepts or the energy which enables the soul to discriminate, group and classify. It represents speech. *Vaikāri* is differentiated sound or the spoken word which is used to explain one's ideas to others.

Verse 2

How can I tell what that spoken word is? Beguilingly he seated me all alone, with nothing before me. Making me happy, friend, he grasped me and clung to me.

Commentary

I cannot explain the experience that is effected by the unspoken word. He made me seated all alone, silent, without any determination of the objects of senses. He bestowed on me bliss and possessed me by his grace. The mystical state is a state of union with God in love. The mystic speaks of the complete stripping of his soul when he is united with God. He becomes stripped of all relations to rebirth and fetters. His mind and heart become Śiva. the Lord takes possession of him.

Verse 3

He bade me put all attachments away and cling to him within. How can I say what it is that I got as I clung to him? He spoke of things never spoken, lady friend.

Commentary

Detachment from worldly goods and attachment to God as the refuge residing in the soul are the characteristics of this experience. This vision of the Lord produces immense bliss which cannot be expressed in words. *Śivānubhuti* (perception or apprehension of Śiva) is realized in oneself and cannot be communicated to others. When the soul is attached to God alone, ever remembering him and praising him with love, it attains to his sacred feet. This love of God brings supreme bliss of being united with him. Once the soul manifests its all absorbing love to God by the help of divine grace, realizing that its true nature is to be most intimately united with God, God causes the soul to enter into the mystical experience of blissful union with him.

Verse 4

Speaking of untold miseries, I had roamed about baffling as a mere devil-ridden body. But the Lord drove away the devil of desire and held me down to his feet.

Commentary

The mystic confesses that in his search for God he was wasting his life with words which brought sorrow. He was saved from the demon of desire and brought to the sacred feet of the Lord. The mystical union is lived and possessed in deep love of God, the soul being completely divested of any desire or passion for anything else. Those who dwell in the feet of the Lord will never lose their mystical union on account of their steadfast and continuous love. Blissful union with the Lord is itself rendered possible if they love him in humble submission. As they are united with God in love, all their impurity will disappear.

Verse 5

Controlling (the mind) and withdrawing the senses, I grew in love for his form. He enfolded me unto himself, lady, and blended with me so that I could not speak at all.

Commentary

The three expressions of *bhakti, caryā, kriyā* and *yoga,* are the means of receiving Śiva's grace. *Caryā* consists in the external service to God. It creates in the mind a yearning for spiritual progress. *Kriyā* consists in the external and internal worship of God with rites and ceremonies prescribed in the Āgamas. It helps the aspirant to perform his religious actions in the presence of God. *Yoga* consists in meditation on God in his subtler form. To achieve this meditation one has to control the five senses and concentrate the mind on the form of God. Thus *yoga* leads to the imprint of divine wisdom, for only when the soul reaches this stage it becomes rid of the "I" and "mine", and becomes fit to receive the knowledge of God. The descent of the divine grace is the distinctive mark of the path of *yoga.*

Verse 6

He broke the custom and I lost my (ancestral) line. If I were to tell this by word of mouth I will lose my life. He is not my false husband (paramour). He is my Saviour, the Supreme God, O my friend!

Commentary

God breaks the habit in the soul of empirical experience of the world and of the self and separates the soul from such a connatural experience due to *māyā.* If I were to speak of it, I will lose the life of supreme bliss. God is acknowledged as the true Lord and Saviour of the soul. He is the true husband of the soul, for he is inseparable from the *bhaktas* even for a moment. The soul (the mystic bride) through grace is united in love with God (the mystic bridegroom). The Lord gives bliss to those who love him, for his nature is perfect

Verse 7

He continued to make my eyes shed tears of bliss like the undammed ocean; hairs in my body stand erect; and to melt my heart, lady friend.

Commentary

The *bhakta* melts in love for God. God is accessible only to those whose heart dissolves into love. Out of intense joy in the possession of the supreme love into which he melts, the mystic weeps, wails, praises God; his hairs stand erect.

Verse 8

My Lord told me: "Cast off whatever your mind had hitherto looked upon in your perception as real and unreal"; behold his skill in making me his (or "himself").

Commentary

The Siddhāntin's doctrine of *Satkāryavāda* distinguishes clearly between the existing thing *(u‰‰atu)* and the non-existing thing *(illātu)*. When a thing is in the state of cause it has no form *(illātu)*; when it exists in the state of effect, it has form *(u‰‰atu)*. It is the theory of causation according to which an effect is held to exist in its cause. The world process is operated according to this causation. The mystic is asked to cast off all that is seen in the effect or is unseen in the cause from the mind. Thus purified from attachment to mundane things the soul becomes God's. The mystical state is one of complete renunciation of worldly things and of total surrender to God in the spirit of absolute love.

Verse 9

"You are not the earth and other elements; reflect, you are not the organs of action and sense. You are pondering consciousness." So he said. Blissful are the words that the Lord spoke in love, friend.

Commentary

In the state of union the soul is liberated from bonds, from births and deaths. For the true nature of the soul is not to identify itself with the environment. When associated with master or organs of action and senses it loses its inherent consciousness. The soul realizes its inseparable union with God through ceaseless love. This love comes to the soul as soon as it knows that it is Śiva who makes it possible for the soul to see in the same way as the soul makes it possible to the eye to see.

Verse 10

To those who love him, he is love; he is faithful, my Lord, the blissful silent One. The gracious master laid his feet on my head; lo, I realized my self and died to my (empirical) thought.

Commentary

If without forgetting God, the *bhakta* praises him through love, he will join the blessed feet of God. The mystic disposes himself to receive the imprint of God's grace through love *(bhakti).* God is not merely one who loves souls but one whose very essence is love. The ignorant, i.e., those who are not enlightened by *bhakti,* think that God and love are different. But the true *bhaktas* perceive that God and love are one. God manifests himself as love in his *bhaktas* by entering into their inmost self and communing with them.

Verse 11

As I considered how death and birth come to me, they grew from the treacherous illusory mind which is alike oblivion and remembrance, friend.

Commentary

In the *sakala* state the soul is embodied and clothed with various organs and internal and external senses. The soul desiring to experience sense objects undergoes as a result of this experience the chain of rebirths in accordance with its *karma.* The empirical knowledge of the soul is determined by the internal and external organs of knowledge and hence the soul forgets what it has already known and remembers certain experiences. In the *k l vala* state the soul is devoid of body and of any quality; it lacks activity and has no experience of the world. This happens during dissolution. The products of *māyā* are the perceptive faculties by means of which *prarabdha karma* is experienced and *āgamiya karma* is stored up, and the objects of empirical experience.

Verse 12

My mind is the stone-banyan tree under which God as silent Teacher appeared; (or, My mind is the banyan tree of wisdom where the divine silent Master appeared). And with a (mystic) sign of hand he removed the bondage of my works and set me in the flood of his benign grace, O friend.

Commentary

God by his grace takes his abode in the mind not merely as the sustainer and ruler but as the lover in union with the beloved. God comes and abides in the mystic's mind to relieve him of the pangs of love. The five organs of sense make possible knowledge about the phenomenal world *(pāśajñana)*. The *antakkāranas* make possible knowledge about the soul and its true nature *(pāśajñana)*. But the imprint of grace is necessary for God-realization *(patijñāna)*. The previous two kinds of knowledge cannot contribute this, although together they may lead up to it. *Śiva* appears to the ripened soul as a Guru to confer *jñāna* by means of which the soul takes an attitude of perfect equanimity with the impurities all removed.

Verse 13

"See everything with grace", he said. Without realizing its truth, I beheld with my understanding in my own determinate conceptions; I saw nothing but the darkness (of the worldly things); I saw not even myself the seer of the worldly things; what is this, o lady friend?

Commentary

In the ripened soul divine grace settles down; it is otherwise called "the imprint of God's *jñāna*". The darkness of *ānava* is dispelled by divine and mystic wisdom imparted in the shape of grace *(arul)*. Souls unconscious of the sea of grace in which they are plunged seek the sea of bewilderment and go after the mean enjoyments of worldly pleasures, disregarding spiritual delights and divine communion. Like the five senses which are not aware of the soul whose instruments of perception they are, the soul does not know the grace that is its guide and illuminator.

Verse 14

He taught me by the single word: Do not think in your mind of me as other than you. Be without the second. How can I tell you the joy which resulted from that word?

Commentary

The mystical experience of God's immanence is not of such a nature that the soul and God become identified and lose each his individuality. If the soul were to know God in an objective manner, opposing the knower to the known, such a knowledge would be imperfect and empirical. In mystical knowledge the soul in union with God through his immanent grace knows God and itself. The supreme love effects union with God and hence the soul is said to be one with God in advaitic relationship. *Advaita* for the Siddhāntin means that as the true nature of the soul is to be united with God through his *Śakti,* so in the liberated state this ontological relationship of union is consciously and mystically realized. *Advaita* here simply means experience of oneness in union and not of identity. The mystical experience of God's immanence is not of such a nature that the soul and God become identified and lose their individuality.

Verse 15

The field where grows the bliss of Śiva; drawing near to that open space and weeding out the weeds of darkness, I then beheld. I perceived nothing but the beauty of my Lord, lady friend!

Commentary

When Śivajñānam in the form of grace descends on the self, the self puts off the fetters of impurity and realizes the Lord within its being. As God illumines the soul, the soul acquires the divine wisdom and intuits the true nature ot the three fundamental realities, namely, bondage, the soul, and God's immanence. They are not successive insights but three aspects of the divine wisdom itself experienced by the soul. The liberating wisdom is God's gift to his *bhaktas.* Śiva manifests himself to the soul and enables it to perceive mystically his own true form. He imparts knowledge by illuminating the *bhakta's* understanding from within, revealing his true nature by means of grace. This is recognized in Śaivism as the descent of divine grace in varying degrees.

Verse 16

Life, the laughing-stock of those who see it, we with both eyes see it depart. It passes away as in sleep. Say, what good, what advantage is there in it, O lady friend!

Commentary

For the Siddhāntin, the phenomenal world is before the all-knowing Śiva so insignificant that it does not appear to exist. However the phenomenal world is real; but it loses its glamour and appears to be non-existent in the presence of Śiva, even as darkness appears to be non-existent to one who gazes at the rays of the sun. Evolution (birth), existence and involution (death) are the result of the *malas.*

Verse 17

I know not anything good; granting me the vision of the pure state of stillness that is beyond the *nāda tattva,* he removed my unrest, the all-powerfull One, by resting his feet upon my head, O my friend.

Commentary

Nāda is the primal sound, born of Śiva and his grace, from which all the other *tattvas* emerge. It is activated by the *jñāna-śakti.* This is the energy of the Lord and is symbolized by the drum in the hand of the Nataraja which represent the cosmic dance. Above the *nāda* in the state of *Parā-Śvam,* i.e., supreme Bliss, a state in which God is without name, form or function. It is this form of *Parā-Śvam* which perfected souls experience.

Verse 18

His dynamic blessed light of bliss transformed me, who am less than an atom, by his grace into perfect fulness without moving hither or thither. What a wonder this is, friend.

Commentary

The *Parā-śakti* is the supreme energy of Śiva, which is pure intelligence. Its only function is the performance of grace for the sake of soul. It is that which knows and which makes known. God is gracious intelligence *(aru‰-cit)* while the soul only partakes of it. They are alike but do not become one or identical. Śiva is the gracious intelligence while the soul is an intelligent being having destiny in the grace of Śiva. God is the intelligence which is self-luminous while the soul receives such light and knowledge from God.

Verse 19

Creating, conserving and dissolving: all these works are the ingenious Lord's and yet they do not affect him, not so much as a grain of sesame. On this true witness it is worth reflecting, lady friend.

Commentary

God is the prime mover of all, the first cause of creation, conservation and dissolution. God gives to souls through his śakti the results of good and bad deeds through which the soul experiences births and deaths. The world evolves in order that the *ānava* of souls may be worn away. The *aru‰o-śakti* or *turodhana-śakti* is responsible for evolution, conservation and dissolution and concealment. All things are activated by God who nevertheless remains unaffected and there is no change in him whatever.

Verse 20

There thought is born; there thought dies and is purified; there all states exist and there I who see stand without the second.

Commentary

As long as the soul is joined with *ānava mala* alone it cannot know anything. When it is joined with inner organs it receives knowledge and experience. The type of knowledge that comes to the soul depends on the number of tattvas to which the soul is attached. The inner organs *(manas, citta, buddhi, ahamkara)* are capable of perception; but they are non-perceptive with respect to the soul because they can do nothing without the activation of the soul. In the *kevala* state the soul is bound by *ānava* alone; in the *sakala* state it is bound by *ānava, māyā,* and *karma*; in the *śuddha* state the soul is free from all the three *malas.* Due to the imprint of God's grace the soul acquires the true knowledge of the Lord. God can be known only through grace-wisdom. In the state of mystical experience the soul stands most intimately united with God and becomes one with him as explained above.

Verse 21

Is there a "there" and a "here", when the light of the Being-Knowledge-Bliss has seen arising and spreading as an undivided form? Can we speak then of one or two?

Commentary

God's true form is Being, Knowledge and Bliss; or Life, Light and Love. We cannot perceive him as "This is God"; "That is God". He can be perceived only through his grace. Śiva is always the transcendent Being and cannot be limited to this or that form, though he manifests himself to his *bhaktas* according to their stage of spiritual progress. To the mystics he manifests himself as not having any form or attribute.

Verse 22

This body must die one day. O worldlings, why hold it as true? Don't you know anything of this? What is your answer to the summon of Yama (god of death)?

Commentary

The Siddhāntin postulates three types of bodies which the soul inhabits. The gross body *(sthūla)* perishes at death. The subtle body *(sūksma)* is the immediate organ of the soul which accompanies it in various rebirths until the final release. The causal body *(kārana)* is the body which encases the soul in its original state which is bound by *ānava* alone. Death is the event in which the soul leaves the gross body behind.

Verse 23

Are there deceivers like us? We who live with the belief that foul fleeting body is the true reality. Should we not believe as real the light of grace?

Commentary

One of the characteristics of the soul is that it assumes the nature of the reality with which it is associated; the soul affected by the three impurities loses sight of its true identity; i.e., its Śiva-form, and identifies itself with egoism, *karma* and *māyā*. *Māyā* does not mean illusion as in the Advaita Vedānta.

Verse 24

Away with likes and dislikes. those entanglements result in rebirth. As the Lord taught, O heart, be still, becoming intelligence.

Commentary

In the higher spiritual experience the soul comes to have a new way of looking at its experiences in the world. Previously it felt likes and dislikes for pleasure and pain respectively; but now it is above these desires and aversions; it acquires a new sense of detachment. The restlessness involved in pursuing pleasure and evading pain has given way to a calm mind that is undisturbed by pleasure or pain. Desires and aversions result in pleasant and unpleasant experiences. They play a major part in bringing about *karma.*

Verse 25

Are there not any who realize who I am? In this land of body which does not realize who I am, worthlessly caught in the flame of lust, did I come here to lose the heavenly wealth (true wisdom)?

Commentary

In conjunction with various *tattvas,* the soul attains the stage of experiencing the world. But it should not be reckoned as one of the *tattvas* as it is an intelligent being. Endowed with divine wisdom *(Śiva-jñāna),* realizing its true nature, the soul becomes a *jīvanmukta. Pasujñāna* is the knowledge that comes out of cogitation and results in the awareness that there is a soul distinct from the *antaḥkāranas. Pati-jñāna* is the knowledge that comes from the final imprint of grace, by which the soul realizes its inseparable union with God.

Verse 26

My Father gave me the shining sword of true wisdom in order to sever this bewildering delusion which plunges people in the snares of women, gold, land, forgetful of the purpose of their life.

Commentary

The *pāsa-jñāna* gives the soul the knowledge that the world with all its attractions in the form of women, gold and land, is the non-intelligent delusive *māyā,* whose joys fleet away, leaving sorrow behind. The soul frees itself from this bondage by the help of the divine wisdom.

Verse 27

The desire of women with eyes like sword is what feeds the flame of our sorrow. Knowing this even the god of love gave up his body. If so, is it not the rule that the holy ones renounce this desire, O lady friend!.

Commentary

Rāga is an evolute that actuates the *icchā-śakti* of the soul and creates in it a desire for things. In conjunction with matter the soul is subject to five kinds of afflictions; it is subject to delusive knowledge of mistaking the transient for the eternal; it feels the pride of agency and of ownership of things of this world; it is the victim of desire for objects; it feels impelled to pursue these objects; it mistakenly identifies itself with the non-self.

Verse 28

Lady, this world created (by Brahmā) shall fade away like suffron in sunlight. So say the Vedas and Āgamas. Those who do not heed this follow the path that is evil; can it be the right path, O lady friend?

Commentary

The created world in course of time passes away into the state of dissolution; so too the bodies of souls. One cannot spend one's life in pursuing the things of the world and of the body.

Verse 29

The charms of evil women have no sway over the pure in mind. Janaka's realization of true knowledge in his own domestic life is an example. He was ever happy in this bliss, O friend.

Commentary

Even the state of domestic life can lead one to acquire true knowledge and realize God; for what is essential is purity of mind and the loving contemplation of God, which gives b1iss and happiness.

Verse 30

Is there a "no" and a "yes" (with regard to the desirables)? If you want to have bliss, you will know it by abiding a while as knowledge (of Śiva). This is the mystic rule that our Lord spoke, O lady friend!

Commentary

The knowledge of God consists in the realization of God in one's own self; this consciousness merges into mystical contemplation of God in love and bliss. While every knowledge is graciously imparted to souls by God, the supreme knowledge is the unmediated gift of God, whereas the lower knowledge is the gift of God mediated by organs of perception, sensations, products of *māyā*. Śiva imparts the mystical knowledge by illuminating the *bhaktas'* understanding from within, revealing his true nature by means of grace.

2. Conclusion

In Tāyumānavar's mysticism it is stressed that the intuitive higher knowledge is not capable of verbal expression and communication at least to those who have not attained it. The indefinable does not mean that which is presented as having no understood meaning but whose meaning is directly understood. "Not by speech, not by mind, not by sight can he be comprehended. How can he be comprehended otherwise than by saying, "He is"[7]. This comprehension is an awakening which cannot be conveyed or communicated. Communication is possible by other means than verbal expression: by silence and by the living together of the guru and the disciple. The self is silence *(upaśānto 'yam ātma)*. The teacher Pipplada tells his pupils: "Dwell with me a year with austerity, chastity, and faith. Then ask what questions you will[8]. Two kinds of knowledge are admitted: for example, that which is seen by the eye; and that by which the eye sees. One is empirical and the other is mystical. The mystical knowledge is not that which is known by the soul but that by which the soul is known through Śiva's grace; namely, the *patijñānam*. The revel in bliss in the mystical experience is not just a rapture or ecstasy, a transient state, an intellectual

7 Katha Upanishad 6.12.
8 Prasna Upanishad 1.2.

perception but a dynamic delight in the possession of God. This delight *(ānanda)* is expressed in the capacity to experience things in a spirit of perfect equanimity: *sama dukha sukham:* an equality in pain and pleasure; it is expressed in the experience of love and union with God; and finally it is expressed in the joyful giving up of worldly goods or in the sacrifice which means a self-giving.

CHAPTER SEVEN

HINDU HOSPITALITY AND TOLERANCE
(Hindu attitude to foreigners, strangers and immigrants)

Introduction

Indian society has always been noted for an infinite variety of races and languages combined with widely different religious customs, cultural traditions and caste systems and psychological tempers resulting not only from different geographical settings and climates but also from fluctuating populations and invasions from outside. Their amalgamation has not destroyed their intrinsic freedom and self-identity; there has not been an infringement on their freedom of worship and thought and no annihilation of their distinctive social personalities. Each caste fulfilled a vital function and was part of the social organism as individual cells are part of a living body. Hinduism dispensed with any particular dogma and instilled respect in all its adherents for a variety of other forms of worship and belief. It allowed ample freedom to different groups to secede and form their own religious sects. Hindus respected differences in beliefs and ways of thinking and living without enforcing any kind of uniformity; this allowed them to have a flexibility not only with Indian society but also without. All foreign invaders eventually became incorporated into the social fabric of India as distinct castes within their system. This incorporation did not prevent them from retaining their own individual character and personality. It is in this general perspective of the Hindu society that we have to understand its attitude to people of different caste, foreigners, strangers and immigrants. We shall divide the subject into four parts: Hindu hospitality, Hindu tolerance, Neo-Hindu attitude to human family, and finally Hindus' fight against communalism.

1. Hindu hospitality

Already in the Rig Veda there are indications as to how one should behave towards foreigners or strangers. The moral God Varuna punishes those who offend against his eternal ordinances and binds them with calamity, sickness and death. This just God is also a merciful one who hears the prayers of the sinner and forgives his sins.

> "If we to any dear and loved companion
> Have evil done, to brother or to neighbour,
> To a member of our own clan or to a stranger,
> That sin do thou, O Varuna, forgive us.
> If ever we deceived like cheating players,
> If consciously we've erred, or all unconscious,
> According to our sin do not thou punish;
> Be thou the singer's guardian in thy wisdom"[1].

The singer Vaśiṣṭha is filled with pious grief for his offences which he committed, consciously or unconsciously, willingly or unwillingly against Varuna. The above passage is significant in that it makes it clear that the God bestows attention upon the conduct of men towards their fellowmen and explicitly mentions the misdeeds committed towards human beings along with the offences against gods themselves. "Whatever sins we might have committed against the gods or against a friend, or against the father of the family, may this prayer efface them! Heaven and Earth, preserve us from evil"[2]. The passage Rig Veda 5.85.7, cited above, goes beyond the members of one's own family or friends and extends to strangers. It is interesting to note that the Vedic singers in some hymns have given the front rank among the sins committed against *men* to offences against themselves as priests. Again, it is also said, somewhat in anticipation of later teaching, that by being hospitable, the host has his sins (eaten up) and has purified himself of all evil[3]. In the Upanishad, a guru counsels his departing student thus: speak the truth; practise virtue... Let there be no neglect of the du-

---

1 Rig Veda 5.85.7-8.

2 Rig Veda 1.185.8.

3 See E. WASHBURN HOPKINS, *Ethics of India*, New Haven, 1924, p. 49.

ties to the gods and the fathers. Be one to whom the mother is a god. Be one to whom the father is a god. Be one to whom the teacher is a god. Be one to whom the guest is a god"[4]. People are exhorted to be hospitable; it is said that a guest who is disappointed with his host takes along with him as he goes his host's merit and leaves behind his own evil, even as a king who fails to do justice takes upon himself the criminal's sin. If one has nothing else to give his guest, he should give him at least 'water and a welcome', as the saying is[5]. As the great Epic says: "If a guest turns away from a house with expectations unfulfilled, he is supposed to take away the merits of the householder and leave the latter all his misdeeds"[6].

In the Hindu Law Books we find a clearer formulation of the ways of conducting oneself with respect to the guests. The householders and wives win great merit if they act thus. To a brāhman who has not studied the Veda a seat, water, and food must be offered without rising to honour the guest, unless he is worthy of such a salutation for other reasons. A brāhman shall not rise to receive a kshatriya or Vaisya, though they may be learned. In the case of a Sudra as a guest the brāhman shall give him some work to do and may feed him afterwards. Or the slaves of the Brāhman may bring rice from the royal stores and honour the Sudra as a guest[7]. The reward for honouring a guest is immunity from misfortunes, and heavenly bliss. The host shall meet the guest, honour him according to his age by the prescribed formulas of salutation, and offer a seat to him. He shall wash the guest's feet. He shall converse kindly with the guests and make him happy with milk or other drinks, with eatables or at least with water. He shall offer the guest a room, a bed, a mattress, a pillow with a cover, and ointment and whatever may be necessary. If the guest comes around the time of the dinner, he shall feed him. If the guest is in enmity with the host who hates him or accuses him of a crime or who is suspected of a crime he shall not eat his food. For it is said in the Vedas that he who eats the food of such a person eats his guilt[8]. The

4 Taittirīya Upanishad 1.11.
5 Vaśishta Dharmaśāstra 13.61; Āpastamba Dharmasūtra 2.2.4.14.
6 The Mahābhārata 12.191.12.
7 See Āpastamba Dharmasūtra 2.2.4.15-20.
8 *Ibidem* 2.3.6.14-20.

reception of guests has been compared to an everlasting Vedic sacrifice. One of the chief characteristics of the Vedic sacrifice is the use of the three sacred fires *(vitāna)*. Hence Apastamba shows that three fires also are used in offering hospitality to guests[9]. Numerous rules are prescribed about the manner in which one should receive and treat the guests according to their caste and the moment in which they come, for hospitality is a veritable religious duty and the host procures heaven, whether welcome or indifferent [10].

Among the Hindus eating is a sacramental act, not a mere physical indulgence prompted by desire. He who cooks for selfish motives or eats alone has been condemned in the Rig Veda[11]. The Vaisvadeva is a rite which precedes eating, in which an offering *(bali)* is made to all kinds of beings. At this moment one has to look out for any guest to be fed before he actually sits down to eat. Food is first offered to the Lord, and what is taken is his prasāda; i.e., what the Lord has been gracious to give us; it is his leavings[12].

"Before a householder eats, he shall feed his guests, the infants, the sick people, the pregnant women, the females under his protection, the very old people, and those of low condition such as servants, slaves and the like who may be in his house[13]. It is interesting to note the definition given of a guest: "He is called a guest who, belonging to a different village and intending to stay for one night only, arrives when the sun's beams pass over the trees. According to his caste a guest must be asked about his well-being, about his being free from hurt, or about his health. A brāhman shall feed people of other castes with his servants for mercy's sake"[14]. "If a brāhman who has come for shelter to the house of a householder receives no food, on departure he will take with him all the spiritual merit of that host"[15]. Speaking of the duties of the householder it is said:

9 *Ibidem* 2.3.7ff.

10 *Ibidem* 2.3.7.1-10.

11 Rig Veda 10.117.

12 See Taittirīya Āraṇyaka 10.32-35; Chāndogya Upanishad 4.17; 5.1.2.19-23.

13 Gautama Dharmaśāstra 5.25.

14 *Ibidem* 5.40-45.

15 Vaśishta Dharmaśāstra 8.6.

"Let him honour visitors who come to his house by rising to meet them, by offering them seats, by speaking to them kindly and extolling their virtues, and all creatures by giving them food according to his ability.
A householder alone performs sacrifices, a householder alone performs austerities, and therefore the order of householders is the most distinguished among the four.
As all rivers, both great and small, find a resting-place in the ocean, even so men of all orders find protection with householders.
As all creatures exist through the protection afforded by their mothers, even so all mendicants subsist through the protection afforded by householder"[16].

Even the hermits have to obesrve the regulations which concern the reception of the guests. A hermit has to feed his guests in due order, the worthiest first; afterwards the maidens, the infants, the aged, the half-grown members of his family; then the other members of his family; finally the outcastes and Sudras. The master of the house and his wife may eat what remains[17]. In the Ordinances of Manu it is said that the householders should perform five sacrifices every day: "Teaching the Veda is the Veda sacrifice; offering cakes and water is the sacrifice to the manes; an offering to fire is the sacrifice to the gods; offering of food is the sacrifice to all beings; honour to guests is the sacrifice to men... Whoever presents not food to those five: the gods, guests, dependents, the manes, and himself, though he breathes, lives not"[18]. Further it is said:

"To a guest that has arrived one should give a seat and water, and food also as he best can, having reverenced him first duly. A brāhman guest not reverenced takes away all the good deeds of even one who always gleans ears of grain for his support, or even sacrifices in five fires.

16 *Ibidem* 8.12-16
17 *Ibidem* 11.6-11
18 *The Ordinances of Manu,* Tr. Arthur Coke Burnell, New Delhi, 1971 (reprint), 3.70,72.

Grass, earth, water, and kindly speech as a fourth; ever these are never wanting in the house of the good...
Now a Kshatriya is not called a guest in a brāhman's house, nor a Vaisya, nor a Sudra; neither is a friend. the kinsmen, nor a guru of the householder"[19].

The undercastes are inferior; friends and kinsmen are the same as one's self; the guru is superior; the same holds for each caste towards the lower. But whoever comes to the house should be received with welcome words and given food, resting place, as far as one can. When the author of the Laws of Manu was compiling the ordinances, the Hindus accepted the legal fiction that foreign outsiders should be regarded as fallen Kshatriyas; it seemed quite natural to treat the Persians, Dards, and certain other foreign nations as kshatriyas who had sunk to the condition of Sudras by reason of their neglect of sacred rites and their failure to consult or respect the brāhmans[20].

The sense of hospitality was so keen among the ancient Hindus that the reception of the guest was raised to the status of a religious rite, called *Ātithiyajña* (the offering of food to a guest), in the *Grihyasūtras.* These religious sayings are noteworthy: "A guest arriving at the right time burns him up who neglects him"; "A brāhman guest who stays unhonoured in the house of a man who daily performs the Agnihotra takes way all his merit". The rites of hospitality are described thus. When the guest arrives at the main entrance of the house, the host goes to meet him and greets him in an appropriate manner. The kind of salutation depends on the relationship between the two parties. An inferior bows his head before his superior but in the case of venerable persons such as teacher, mother or father he touches their feet respectfully. The guest responds by reciting a formula of blessing. In practice a guest is generally considered as a superior and is honoured accordingly. Then the guest is led into the house and the cushion or chair is offered to him. A servant brings water to wash his feet. He is offered water to drink. Finally he is presented with a bowl containing a special beverage *(madhuparka)* composed of sugar, ghee, curds

19 *Ibidem* 3.99-101,110.
20 *Ibidem* 10.44

and honey. He has to accept it with both hands and place it by his side on the "ground without drinking it. He stirs the drink three times in succession and consumes it in one or three mouthfuls. And then he drinks a little water. In the case of a brāhman or a king as guest, the rite is completed with the offering of a cow as a present to the guest. In the Vedic times the cow was slaughtered in his honour, as the scapegoat for his sins in order to achieve ritual purification. In later times the sacrifice became entirely symbolic. The whole ceremony ended with a meal[21].

In the *Mahābhārata* a parable is narrated to illustrate the principle of gradual rise in social rank and ultimately to salvation. A small insect was passing on the road in the track marked by the wheels of a bullock cart. When it heard the cart coming it tried to run away from it. The sage Vyasa who was travelling in the cart saw the insect running away from the cart and asked the reason for doing so. The insect replied that it heard the noise of the cart coming close to it and that it was because of the fear of being crushed by it that it was running away from it. Vyasa said: "You are a member of the insect category of creation, and so you cannot enjoy the joys brought in by the senses. Is it not better for you to die?" The insect replied: "Everybody loves life. May he be an insect or a brāhman. I was a sudra in my former birth. But since I did not respect the brāhmans and guests and possessed many bad qualities like anger, cruelty, cunningness, greed, jealousy, etc., I was born as an insect. But because I honoured my old mother regularly and once served a brāhman guest well, I remember my previous birth". Vyasa then said that he himself was the brāhman guest and had visited the insect sudra and wished him further welfare. On the same day he explained also to the insect the theory of karma and counseled the insect to accept death in order to acquire a higher birth. The insect followed the advice of the sage and was born successively as a porcupine, a pig, a deer, a bird, and then a human being in the different classes of a cāṇḍāla (low caste), vaisya, ordinary kshatriya and a king. As a king the insect left the kingdom and started to perform a severe penance. Again Vyasa visited it in its wel-

21 See JEANNINE AUBOYER, *Daily Life in Ancient India,* London, 1965 pp 197ff; V.M. APTE, *Social and Religious Life in the Gṛihya Sūtras,* Bombay, 1954, pp. 81-86.

fare and advised it, saying, "O insect, protection is the divine duty of the kings and you will obtain brahmanhood, only if you perform your duty well. Hence protect well your subjects and control your senses. And then you will achieve brahmanhood. "The insect who was then a king did so as told and was reborn as a brāhman. Finally, after performing many sacrifices as a brāhman and acquiring the knowledge of Brahman (the Absolute) it achieved final deliverance *(moksha)*[22]. Here the doctrine of gradual higher births in consecutive higher classes (varnas) as a result of the proper performance of the duties of one's own class *(svadharma)* is taught together with the theory of the law of action (karma). The summit of the caste system is the brāhman class who were considered sacred because of their being the authoritative interpreters and transmitters of the Veda and the principal ministers of the religious sacraments. The hierarchy of castes is based on how close a caste comes in its life-style to the pattern set by the brāhmans who are themselves arranged in hierarchy on the basis of spiritual learning, adherence to the Sacred Law, and birth. As regards the duties of the class *(varna)* the Epic lays down the following ethical behavior as essential to all the classes. "Absence of wickedness, pity towards all creatures, non-violence, non-indifference (activeness), performance of *śrāddha,* and entertainment of guests, truth, peace, fidelity to one's wife, contentment, purity, non-jealousy, knowledge of the self and curiosity: these are the common dharmas of all classes"[23]

The sub-castes are formed along many factors that are not strictly traditional. There are many sectarian castes organized along religious lines, as for instance, the Lingāyat caste in Bombay and South India, the Baishtams of Bengal. There are other castes formed by race mixtures; such are the khas of Nepal, who are the offspring of mixed marriages between Rajput immigrants and native yellow-skinned and slanted-eyed women; the Shagirdpeshas of Orissa who descend from high caste men and maid-servants; the Rajbansi Baruas of Chittagong who are the descendants of Bengali women and Burmese men. Another type of caste arises from migration and change of occupation; the Babhans of Bihar and Uttar

22 The Mahābhārata 13.117ff.

23 *Ibidem* 12.285.23-24.

Pradesh are former brāhmans who lost their caste status by becoming farmers. Most castes, especially the occupational ones, are governed by the panchāyats, the council of headmen who rule with a stern hand.

It should be remarked that originally caste was not as rigid an institution as it became after the invasion of the Muslims in the eleventh century A.D. Endogamy, commensality and craft-exclusiveness were not rigidly enforced. The process of Muslim conquest in India made the caste system more rigid, for the Hindus, ineffective to resist the Muslims, protected themselves by close caste associations. It appears that the change in the Hindu attitude to foreigners seems to be mainly due to Muslim conquest; from the 12th century until today the caste system, with some modifications, has substantially subsisted in its modern forms.

The caste system did not allow the Hindus to be freely associated with foreigners. This created the difficulty in the mutual comprehension between them. The touch of the foreigners' hands is deemed polluting by the high caste Hindus. The foreigners find it difficult to draw aside the veil which hides the inmost feelings of the caste Hindus. Willing and active co-operation in the social, political and religious sphere was hindered by the rigid caste system. An individual's personal liberty of action is checked in many ways that are unknown to foreigners. Moreover caste restrictions continually collide with the conditions of modern life. True, the system favours an intense class pride which is not conducive to solidarity among man and man. Finally, on the spiritual plane on which Indian culture is based, there was no inequality between castes since any man is free and able to reach the supreme salvation through religious wisdom and love of God. Hence, it is understandable that the bhakti mystics and saints reacted strongly against caste discriminations on any count. The Telugu poet Vamana writes:

> "If we look through all the earth,
> Men, we see, have equal birth,
> Made in one great brotherhood,
> equal in the sight of God.
> Food or caste or place of birth
> Cannot alter human worth.
> Why let caste be so supreme?

'Tis but folly's passing stream...

Empty is a caste dispute:
All the castes have but one roof,
Who on earth can ever decide
Whom to praise and whom deride?

Why should we the Parias scorn,
When his flesh and blood were born
Like to ours? What caste is He
Who doth dwell in all we see[24]?

Brahmanism offered salvation only to the people of Aryan birth. The Theravāda Buddhism and Jainism restricted salvation only to the monks and nuns. The new theist movements (the bhakti religion) within Hinduism offered an easy path to salvation to all people, whether of low caste or of higher caste, the path of loving devotion to God, without the need to forsake life in society. All devotees of God are equal before God and are equally dear to God, to whichever caste they might belong. Thus Hinduism itself offered a strong religious bond, transcending class or caste distinctions to a society threatened with disintegration by foreign invasions.

Not only the religion of bhakti (love of God) which tried to do away the caste system in the Hindu society, but also the essence of dharma as propounded and defended in their Scriptures contributed to the practice of universal love for all beings. Already in the great Epic statements to this effect are to be found". "I know the secret of ancient dharma which enunciates the good of all beings in the world and friendship with all"[25]. "He verily knows the substance of dharma who is always the friend of all and who is interested in the welfare of all in thought, word and action"[26]. These two verses declare that compassion to all persons and interest in the welfare of all is *dharma*. Even more emphatically dharma was propounded as follows. "Dharma was declared by Brahman for the advancement and growth of all creatures. Therefore that which leads

24 Gover, *The Folk Songs of Southern India*, London, 1872, p. 275.
25 The Mahābhārata 12.262.5.
26 *Ibidem* 12.262.9.

to advancement and growth is righteousness. Righteousness was declared for restraining creatures from injuring one another. Therefore that is righteousness which prevents injury to creatures. Righteousness *(dharma)* is so-called because it upholds all creatures. In fact all creatures are upheld by righteousness"[27]. He who perceives the unity of existence and sees all things as his own self (*sarvātmabhava* attitude) promotes the welfare and well-being of all human beings and of all living beings in the universe. The *sādhārana dharma* are the universal principles that govern all actions like truth, compassion and non-violence; among them all the most comprehensive dharma is stated to be this: what is harmful to oneself, one should not do to others. This is the quintessence of *dharma*[28]. Compassion and abstension from injury regard all creatures as equal in thought, word and action; kindness and benevolence are the eternal duties of all humanity.

The Brahmo Samāj and Ārya Samāj (the Hindu reform movements) condemned the caste system in general. But Vivekananda justified it as good but interpreted it in a way that brought it into harmony with the western ideals of social and religious equality. He says: Caste is a natural order. I can perform one duty in social life, and you another; you can govern a country, and I can mend a pair of old shoes, but there is no reason why you are greater than I, for can you mend my shoes? Can I govern the country? I am clever in mending shoes, you are clever in reading Vedas, but there is no reason why you should trample on my head; why if one commits murder should he be praised, and if another steals an apple why should he be hanged? This will have to go. Caste is good. That is the only natural way of solving life. Men must form themselves into groups, and you cannot get rid of that. Wherever you go there will be caste. But that does not mean that there should be these privileges. They should be knocked on the head. If you teach Vedānta to the fisherman, he will say, I am a fisherman, you are a philosopher, but I have the same God in me as you have in you. And that is what we want, no privileges for any one, equal chances for all; let everyone be taught that the Divine is within, and every

27 *Ibidem* 12.109.10ff.
28 *Ibidem* 13.113.8.

one will work out his own salvation[29]. Gandhi defended the dharma of class and stages of life *(varnāśrama dharma)* but did not support untouchability. He merely affirmed that the division of society on hereditary lines into four classes made for a more ordered society. Does untouchability in the case of a cobbler or scavenger attach to birth or to occupation? If it attaches to birth, it is hideous and must be rooted out; if it attaches to occupation, it may be sanitary rule of great importance. It is of universal application. The fault does not consist in recognizing the law of heredity and transmission of qualities from generation to generation but it lies with the faulty conception of inequality[30].

2. Hindu Tolerance

Let us now consider the Hindu, and particularly the neo-Hindu, attitude to other religions, which can be described as an all-embracing manifestation of hospitality and which the Hindus themselves love to call tolerance. The problem of relation of Hinduism to other religions is more focused in the modern context of encounter with world religions. The neo-Hindus are never tired of saying that "all religions are the same". This statement is interpreted in various ways. Some would say that all the great religions are the same in the sense that they are one and the same in their essence but expressed each in its own particular idiom due largely to the accidental historical and cultural differences. Others would say that all religions are the same in as far as they all have the same end or goal; all religions are expressions of man's hunger for the Absolute, although the content of each religion is different. On the other hand each man should be faithful to his own religious tradition in which he was born. It is wrong to persuade a man to give up his own faith which is that of his ancestors and to be converted to another faith. Proselytism is not only unnecessary but morally wrong, and usually discreditable both in method and in intention.

---

29 The Complete Works of Swami Vivekananda, Vol. III, Almora, pp. 245-6.

30 See M. K. GANDHI, *Hindu Dharma* (The Glory and The Abuses), Ahmedabad, 1978, pp. 80-82.

Some Hindus even say that since the all-embracing tolerance is essential to Hinduism itself, it is 'superior' to other religions . Hinduism as eternal religion *(sanātana dharma)* is interpreted by some as meaning that its origin is lost in antiquity and will persist for ever; by others that Hinduism in its essence is also the essence of true religion, the universal religion which lies behind all particular religions . As Gandhi said: "Hinduism tells everyone to worship God according to his own faith or dharma, and so it lives at peace with all the religions"[31]. All religions , being dharmas, are true but imperfect; because they are imperfect, they must aim at perfecting themselves rather than at converting individuals from a dharma that is theirs to one that is alien to them. As S. Radhakrishnan asserts: "When the Hindu found that different people aimed at and achieved God-realization in different ways, he generously recognized them all and justified their place in the course of history.. The Vedānta is not a religion, but religion itself in its most universal and deepest significance. Thus the different sects of Hinduism are reconciled with a common standard, and are sometimes regarded as the distorted expressions of the one true canon"[32]. He justifies the Hindu tolerance thus; "Hinduism does not distinguish ideas of God as true or false, adopting one particular idea as the standard for the whole human race. It accepts the obvious fact that mankind seeks its goal of God at various levels and in various directions, and feels sympathy with every stage of the search. The bewildering polytheism of the masses and the uncompromising monotheism of the classes are for the Hindu the expression of one and the same force at different levels... Hinduism developed an attitude of comprehensive charity instead of a fanatic faith in an inflexible creed... Hinduism does not mistake tolerance for indifference. It affirms that while all revelations refer to reality, they are not equally true to it. Hinduism requires every man to think steadily on life's mystery until he reaches the highest revelation"[33]. He finally concludes his plea for tolerance with the religious pluralism as the future of mankind. "We are slowly realizing that the world is a single cooperative group... I see no hope for the religious future of the world,

31 *Young India,* Oct. 6,1921.

32 *The Hindu View of Life,* London, 1927, ch. 1.

33 *Ibidem* ch. 2.

if this ideal is not extended to the religious sphere also... To obliterate every religion other than one's own is a sort of bolshevism in religion which we must try to prevent. The world would be a much poorer thing if one creed absorbed the rest. God wills a rich harmony and not a colourless uniformity... That the Hindu solution of the problem of the conflict of religions is likely to be accepted in the future seems to me to be fairly certain... The more religious we grow the more tolerant of diversity shall we become"[34].

In this context of Hindu tolerance we have to face also the challenge of Hindu communalism. India consists of the Hindus, the Muslims, the Jains, the Christians, as religious "communities". The term "communal" can be used simply as the neutral adjectival form, as, for example, 'communal representation'. But the term generally refers to a narrow, selfish, divisive, and aggressive attitude on the part of a religious group. Communalism in India refers to the functioning of religious communities, or organizations which claim to represent them, in a way which is considered detrimental to the interests of other groups or of the nation as a whole. It implies some kind of political involvement. One should not confuse the many organizations which are solely concerned with the religious and cultural affairs of particular sections of the population with communalism. By definition all forms of communalism are contrary to the principles of the secular state.

The Hindu communalism today finds its expression in the Hindu Mahāsabha, the Rāshtrīya Swayamsevak Sangh, the Rām Rājya Parishad, and the Jana Sangh, all of which have roots in the Hindu nationalism of Swami Dayananda Sarasvati, the founder of the Ārya Samāj. He was not only a religious reformer who worked to eradicate caste and idol worship but also a creator of a spirit of Hindu unity and militant opposition to any kind of anti-Hindu influence. His attempt to restore Hinduism to the purity of Vedic times was accompanied by aggressive denunciations of Islam, Christianity and the West. He attributed India's sufferings and troubles to the "meat-eating and wine-drinking foreigners, the slaughterer of the kine". Tilak and the Extremists in as far as they blended Hinduism with nationalism, provided much of the direct inspirations

34 *Ibidem.*

for the Hindu communal parties. The Rāshtrīya Swayamsevak (RSS), the Hindustan National Guard, and the Hindu Rāshtra Dāl provided troops to fight the Hindu cause in the communal riots which flared up in many parts of India in the years that followed the consolidation of these communal parties. The key slogan was *Sanghatam* (unification, integration). They aimed at functioning as an organic nation with a clear political self-consciousness. They effected the plan of reclaiming those who had left the Hindu fold as an important part of the Sanghatam programme. The suddhi (purification) ceremony was instituted to recover those who had been converted to Islam and Christianity or descendents of these converts.

Against this Hindu Communalist movement, other Hindu reformers and leaders proposed a spirit of not only tolerance but also of universalism that is characteristic, according to them, of true Hinduism. The Hindu religious genius was able to reconcile and harmonize all conflicting creeds. This daring concept of India's spiritual mission to the world has been voiced by many of her thinkers since the starting of the Brahmo Samāj. Keshub Chunder Sen develops this spirit of universalism thus: "In his Epistles to the Corinthians, "By one Spirit are we all baptized into one body, whether we be Jews or Gentiles", Paul was raised by God to break caste, and level the distictions of race and nationality; and nobly did he fulfil his mission. The Jew and the Gentile he made into one body. The modern Pauls of the new dispensation are carrying on a similar crusade against caste in India. The obnoxious distinctions between brāhman and sudra, between Hindu and Yavana, between Asiatic and European, the new Gospel of love thoroughly proscribes.

"In the kingdom of God there is no invidious distinction, and therefore this dispensation gathers all men and nations, all races and tribes, the high and the low, and seeks to establish one vast brotherhood among the children of the great God, who hath made of one blood all nations of men... We Hindus are specially endowed with, and distinguished for, the yoga faculty, which is nothing but this power of spiritual communion and absorption... How by yoga one nation becomes another! Cultivate this communion, my brethren, and continually absorb all that is good and noble in each other. Do not hate, do not exclude others, as the sectarians do, but include and absorb all humanity and all truth. Let there be no antagonism, no exclusion. Let the embankment which each sect, each nation, has raised, be swept away by the flood of cosmopolitan truth, and let all the barriers and partitions which separate man from man be pulled down, so that truth and love and purity may flow freely through millions of hearts and through hundreds of successive generations, from country to country, from age to age. Thus shall the deficiencies of individual and national character be complemented, and humanity shall attain a fuller and more perfect standard of religious and moral life"[35].

Rabindranath Tagore denounced strongly the evils of nationalism and materialism. He declared that mankind could only survive from destruction by a return to spiritual values which permeate all religions. Especially, Asia, the home of the world's great faiths, is under a special obligation to lead this religious revival. To India, the home of Hinduism and Buddhism, belonged the mission of reawakening Asia and the rest of the world. Tagore while stressing India's role as spiritual teacher to the world also reminded Indians that they also had to learn from the West's vitality and dedicated search for truth. Tagore was of opinion that the clamour for political rights distracted men from more fundamental tasks such as eradicating caste barriers, reconciling Hindus and Muslims, uplifting the poor and helpless villagers, and liberating men's minds and bodies from many self-made but unnecessary burdens. Tagore writes with insight: "In the evolving History of India, the principle at work is not the ultimate glorification of the Hindu, or any other race. In India, the history of humanity is seeking to elaborate a specific ideal, to give to general perfection a special form which shall be for the gain of all humanity, nothing less than this is its end and aim"[36].

Vivekananda gave his famous address at the Parliament of Religions in Chicago, in which he presented to the world an image of Hinduism as a religion tolerant of all faiths, profoundly spintual, yet utterly simple in its creed. He proclaimed that India had spiritual resources to cure the maladies of the West. He derives the attitude of tolerance from the Hindu idea of universal religion, as follows:

35 *Keshub Chunder Sen's Lectures in India*, Calcutta, 1899, pp. 484-5.
36 P. TAGORE, *Greater India*, Madras, 1921, p. 82.

"To him (Hindu) all the religions from the lowest fetichism to the highest absolutism, mean so many attempts of the human soul to grasp and realize the Infinite, each determined by the conditions of its birth and association, and each of these marks a stage of progress; and every soul is a young eagle soaring higher and higher, gathering more and more strength till it reaches the Glorious Sun... If there is ever to be a universal religion, it must be one which will have no location in place or time; which will be infinite, like the God it will preach, and whose sun will shine upon the followers of Krishna and of Christ, on saints and sinners alike; which will not be Brahmanic or Buddhistic, Christian or Mahommedan, but the sum-total of all these, and still have infinite space for development; which in its catholicity will embrace in its infinite arms, and find a place for every human being, from the lowest grovelling savage not far removed from the brute, to the highest man towering by the virtues of his head and heart almost above humanity, making society stand in awe of him and doubt his human nature. It will be a religion which will have no place for persecution or intolerance in its polity, which will recognize divinity in every man and woman, and whose whole scope, whose whole force, will be centred in aiding humanity to realize its own true, divine nature"[37].

3. Conclusion

The tolerant attitude of oriental religions in general and of Hinduism in particular, and the readiness of the Hindus to share activities with other religions results from a state of mind which is deep-rooted in Asia. As a result any kind of proselytism is repugnant to the Hindu mind, for there is no need of changing one's religion into which one is born, which is considered, if not better, at least equal to other religions. Besides, in India, whatever knowledge an individual or group may have about the nature of God and of man and of the cosmos, it is never taken to be final or definitive. Hence in the field of religion it has given birth to innumerable sects whose leaders have tried to work out a synthesis between the

37 *The Complete Works of Swami Vivekananda*, Vol. 1, Almora, pp. 16-17.

teachings of several great gurus (spiritual masters) in Hinduism. The borderline separating dogmas of different world religions appears much more vague than we could possibly imagine; and the spirit of integration or absorption of one religion or of one dogma into one's own religion or belief system is evident with regard to the Hindus. The consequences of this mental attitude with regard to practical life are a spirit of tolerance, of hospitality, and very often, if not always, of syncretism. Hinduism is always ready to accommodate other religious beliefs and derives pleasure from taking over the religious concepts of all the peoples of the world.

CHAPTER EIGHT

THE HINDU WAY TO PEACE

Introduction

Hinduism has been criticized as other-worldly and therefore indifferent to man's happy life on earth. It is presented as a religion of world-negation, instead of world-affirmation. It is claimed that it obscures the Hindu mind in its assessment of the human good such as peace and prevents it from taking an abiding interest in the welfare of the people and keeps it constantly pre-occupied with the prospect of man's liberation from bondage to the affairs of this world. This interpretation of Hinduism is one-sided and false, as will be seen in the following pages. Generally speaking, Hinduism recognizes four ends of human life and activity: wealth *(artha)*, enjoyment *(kāma)*, righteousness *(dharma)* and liberation *(moksha)*. While it proposes liberation as the highest end of man's life, the other three ends, wealth, enjoyment and righteousness are accepted for what they are worth and are subordinated to the highest end, namely, liberation. A man should so regulate the pursuits of wealth, enjoyment and virtue that they ultimately may lead to the attainment of liberation. In different systems of Hindu religion the present life and the present world have received due attention and recognition. Nowhere do we find the attempt made or advice given to dismiss the world or destroy human life in it. The ideal of perfection held before man does not imply any escape from life or negation of it.

To achieve the ultimate goal of liberation man has to get rid of the defects and imperfections in his life , for these lead to pain and misery. His base passions, selfish desires and egoistic activities cause human suffering and misery and do not contribute to the lasting peace and happiness both within man and within human society. The Hindu ideal of self-control and self-enlightenment, of love and service to all human beings is what generates and maintains peace among men; these are the moral and spiritual means of achieving what is essential to the building up of right human social order and to the achievement of the good of every human being.

I intend to treat the following subjects in this paper. 1) The ideal of peace as proposed in the Upanishads; 2) the doctrine of peace as found in the Mahābhārata; 3) the ideal of peace as expounded in the Bhagavad-gītā; 4) the teaching of the Bhagavad-gītā as interpreted by Mahatma Gandhi; 5) Vinoba Bhave's understanding of the teaching of the Bhagavad-gītā. I have chosen to study these texts because they not only belong to the core of the Hindu Scriptures but they envisage the background of the battle between the Pāṇḍavas and the Kauravas in which the whole discourse on peace and non-violence are treated and discussed. These texts are also within the reach of most Hindus who read them, especially the Bhagavad-gītā, and meditate on them as their guiding light.

1. Peace as taught in the Upanishads

Already in the Atharva Veda we come across the idea of peace as the goal of both the macro-cosmic and micro-cosmic order in its moral and religious aspect:

> "Peaceful be earth, peaceful ether, peaceful heaven, peaceful waters, peaceful herbs, peaceful trees. May all Gods bring me peace. May there be peace through these invocations of peace. With these invocations of peace which appease everything, I render peaceful whatever here is terrible, whatever here is cruel, whatever here is sinful. Let it become auspicious, let everything be beneficial to us"[1].

While the above passage is a prayer for peace, directed to the gods, the following is a peace chant from the Upanishad:

"May my speech be firmly established in my mind.
May my mind be firmly established in my spreech.
O Self-manifest One, be manifest to me.

1 Atharva Veda 19.9.

Be for me the cornerstone of the Veda.
May what I have heard not depart from me
By that learning I join days and nights.
I will speak the right.
I will speak the truth.
May that protect me.
May it protect my teacher.
Yes, let it protect me,
and protect my teacher.
May that protect him.
Om, peace, peace, peace[2].

The above passage represents the world as a "creation" of the Absolute *(Brahman),* and man as its highest manifestation. The Self *(Ātman)* is said to occupy three abodes in man, the senses, mind and heart, to which respectively correspond the three conditions of waking, dreaming, and deep sleep. The unity of all beings in the Absolute *(Brahman)* is the foundation of peace and order which results from the practice of speaking the truth.

If we ask why we should identify ourselves with our neighbours, with other human beings or with every living being, Īśa Upanishad gives a profound reason:

"Those who see all beings in the Self,
and the Self in all beings
will never shrink from it (or 'will never doubt it').
When once one understands that in oneself
the Self has become all beings,
when once one has seen the unity,
what room is there for sorrow? What room for perplexity?"[3].

The wise man who perceives all beings as not distinct from his own self at all, and his own self as the self of every one, will not, by virtue of that perception, hate any one. The basis of not hating anyone but of loving all is the universality of the self; it is the realization that all beings are the manifestations of the one Brahman.

---

2 Invocation, Aitareya Upanishad.
3 Īśa Unanishad 6-7.

The consequence of this realization is that there is no delusion or sorrow for the wise man who sees the unity of existence and perceives all things as his own self. The person who develops this attitude of *sarvātmabhāva* attains equanimity and overcomes delusion and passion which would lead him to hate others. He will not shrink from anything and will not feel any revulsion towards anybody. The vision of all existences in the Self and of the Self in all existences is the foundation of freedom, peace and joy. Lord *(Īśa)* is immanent in all that moves in this world.

Śaṅkara comments on these passages in the non-dualist sense:

> "Seeing them all in his own Ātman means seeing that they are not distinct from his own self. Seeing his Ātman in them all means seeing his Ātman as the Ātman of all. Just as he finds his Ātman the witness of all his perceptions, the thinking principle, pure and unconditioned, the soul of his body, which is a bundle of effects and causes, he finds his Ātman in the same unconditioned state, the life principle of all the universe, from the unmanifest *(avyakta)* down to the immovable. He who thus views does not turn with revulsion by reason of such view. This statement is only a declaration of a truth already known. All revulsions arise only when one sees anything bad, distinct from one's Ātman... Perplexity or grief, the seed of all desire and *karma,* affect the ignorant, but not him who sees the oneness, pure and like the sky"[4].

We know that Īśa Upanishad is theistic and the whole spirit of this Upanishad should be understood in the light of opening verse:

> "This whole universe is pervaded by the Lord,
> Whatever moves in this moving world.
> Abandon it, and then enjoy it:
> Covet not the goods of anyone at all".

Mahatma Gandhi himself was of opinion that the essence of Hin-

---

4 See S. SITARAMA SASTRI, *Īśa, Kena and Mundaka Upanishads, wiith Śaṅkara's Commentary,* Madras, 1923, pp. 10-12.

duism was contained in this first verse of the Īśa Upanishad which he translated as follows:

> "All this that we see in this great universe
> is permeated by God.
> Renounce it and enjoy it.
> Do not covet anybody's wealth or possession.
>
> God is the Lord who pervades the whole universe and all of it is his. Therefore we must renounce the world because it is not ours and then enjoy and work in it because it is his and he wishes us to co-operate with him in the destruction of evil"[5].

2. The teaching of the Mahābhārata on peace

In the celebrated Mahābhārata the golden rule of human conduct is enunciated as follows: "He who regards all creatures to be like his own self, who never does any harm and has his wrath under control, obtains great happiness both here and hereafter"[6]. The same rule, expressed differently, runs thus: "Endowed with self-restrain, and possessed of righteous behaviour, one should look upon all creatures as one's own self"[7]. This rule of conduct which excels all other rules is looked upon as the essence of all *dharma* in relation to one's duty to one's neighbour and expresses a fundamental ethical principle. The highest virtue consists in regarding all others as one's self *(ātmaupamya)*. Brihaspati tells Yudhishthira:

> "I shall tell thee what constitutes the highest good of a human being. He who practises the religion of universal compassion achieves his highest good... He who, from motives of his own happiness, slays other harmless creatures with the rod of chastisement, never attains to happiness in the next world. He who regards all creatures as his own self, and behaves towards them as towards his own self, laying aside the rod of chastise-

5 Harijan 30.1.1937.

6 Mahābhārata 12.66.36. All the references to the Mahābhārata are to the P.C. Roy edition.

7 12.292.

> ment and completely subjugating his wrath, succeeds in attaining to happiness. The very deities who are desirous of a fixed abode become stupefied in ascertaining the track of that person who constitutes himself the soul of all creatures and looks upon them all as his own self, for such a person leaves no track behind. One should never do to another what one regards as injurious to one's own self. This in brief is the rule of righteousness. One by acting in a different way by yielding to desire becomes guilty of unrighteousness. In refusals and gifts, in happiness and misery, in the agreeable and the disagreeable, one should judge of their effects by a reference to one's own self"[8].

This discourse teaches that the highest good of a human being consists in the practice of the religion of universal compassion. What does the religion of universal compassion mean? According to the teaching of the Mahābhārata, there cannot be true religion without compassion. Compassion must necessarily be towards all living beings. Compassion is the root of all religious faith. The means of achieving this universal compassion is the control one exercises over lust, wrath and cupidity. But the most effective means is to practise non-violence *(ahiṁsa)*. He who never harms other creatures out of selfish motives attains true happiness. The end of religion is to secure the well-being of the whole society, to make the individuals realize that the happiness of others is as important as their own. A community can live in peace only in so far as its member desires the happiness of his associates as much as his own. Hence, the golden rule is formulated both negatively and positively: "Do not do to others what one does not wish to be done to oneself"; "Do to others what one expects others to do to oneself". The reason why everyone should follow this golden rule is explained in the above text as follows: He who practises the golden rule constitutes himself the soul of all creatures and looks upon them all as his own self. The meaning is certainly that such a man identifies himself with Brahman (the Absolute) and hence leaves no trace of his own self, while the gods desire a fixed abode

8 13.113.6-9.

such as heaven or a region filled with happiness. More clearly, as all beings bear the essence of the Divine in them, they do not harm them; if you harm them it is as bad as harming God Himself. This is the profound reason to condemn all form of violence and to practise kindness to all human and living beings.

Among all the virtues non-violence is the highest (ahiṁsāivahi sarvebhyo dharmethyo)[9]. And where there is righteousness there is victory (yato dharma tato jayaḥ)[10]. That which is disagreeable to oneself should never be done to others. Briefly this is righteousness *(dharma)*. Other kinds of virtue proceed from desire or caprice (na tat parasya saṁdadhyāt pratikūlaṁ yad ātmanaḥ, saṁgraheṇaiṣa dharmaḥ syāt kāmāt anyah pravartate)[11]. Anger must be conquered by forgiveness; and the wicked must be conquered by honesty, the miser must be conquered by liberality; and falsehood must be conquered by truth[12].

Tulādhāra in the Mahābhārata, well acquainted with the truths about the interpretations of morality, speaks thus:

> "I know morality which is eternal with all its mysteries. It is nothing else than that ancient morality which is known to all, and which consists of universal friendliness, and is fraught with beneficence to all creatures. That mode of living which is founded upon a total harmlessness towards all creatures or (in case of actual necessity) upon a minimum of such harm, is the highest morality.. He is said to know what morality or righteousness is; who is always the friend of all creatures and who is always engaged in the good of all creatures, in thought, word and deed. I never solicit anyone, I never cherish desire for anything. I cast equal eyes upon all things and all creatures"[13].

The one who practises this morality which is the noblest attains the state of Brahman. There is no duty superior to the duty of not injuring other creatures. Of all gifts the promise of hamlessness

9 12.257.6.
10 11.14.
11 5.39.57.
12 5.39.58f.
13 12.262 5ff; 10ff.

to all creatures is the greatest. The Hindu ideal portrayed in the Mahābhārata is that one should be free from attachment and pride, never give way to wrath or hate, never speak an untruth, who though slandered or struck, still shows friendship for the slanderer or the striker, never thinks of doing ill to others, restrains speech, acts and mind, behaves evenly towards all creatures, succeeds in approaching the presence of Brahman.

Non-violence *(ahiṁsa)* has been practised in various ways in ancient India. The Mahābhārata mentions these ways and singles out the spirit of forgiveness as the most lauded way. When Draupati tried to persuade Yudhishthira to give up forgiveness towards the Kauravas and show his might, he replied that he could not afford to give up forgiveness that is the abode of truth, wisdom, three worlds and Brahmā himself[14]. Forgiveness means not to return evil for evil but to keep patience and perseverence and win the opponents by means of fortitude. Yudhishthira's answer to Draupati is again very significant. Anger in this world is the cause of destruction of every creature. The angry man is unable to discriminate between right and wrong and might kill him who was worthy to be adored. A self-controlled man does not act against those whose anger has been aroused and thereby saves himself as well as others, acting as a physician on both cases. The blessings of forgiveness are outlined in a forceful manner as follows:

> "A wise man should ever forgive his persecutor even when the latter is in difficulties... The honest and forgiving man is ever victorious. Truth is more beneficial than untruth and gentleness than cruel behaviour... They that are regarded by the learned of foresight, as possessed of true force of character are certainly those who are wrathful in outward show only. Men of learning and of true insight call him to be possessed of force of character who by his wisdom can suppress his risen wrath. The angry man seeth not things in their true light... If amongst men there were not persons equal unto the earth in forgiveness, there would be no peace among men but continued strife caused by wrath. If the injured return their injuries, if one chastised by his superior

---

14 3.29.44.

> were to chastise his superior in return, the consequence would be the destruction of every creature, and sin also would prevail in the world... The birth of creatures is due to peace... One should forgive under every injury. It hath been said that the continuation of the species is due to man being forgiving"[15].

The important message of the above passage is that the man who forgives others, especially his enemies, is ever victorious; that true peace will be obtained among men only if persons are as forgiving as the earth itself. Injury for injury, tooth for tooth, evil for evil, will result in the destruction of the living creatures; and that the continuation of the human species is due to forgiveness. An entire hymn is dedicated to the honour of forgiveness in the Mahābhārata:

> "Forgiveness is virtue; forgiveness is sacrifice; forgiveness is the Vedas; forgiveness is the Śruti (Revealed texts). He that knoweth this is capable of forgiving everything. Forgiveness is Brahman. Forgiveness is truth; forgiveness is stored ascetic merit... forgiveness is holiness, and by forgiveness is it that the universe is held together... How can one abandon forgiveness in which are established Brahman, truth and wisdom and the three worlds?"[16].

The moral concept of truth *(satya)* is very highly valued in India. The Mahābhārata exalts truth to the highest position. "There is nothing higher than truth, truth is everything; in truth lies immortality; so follow the path of truth"[17]. Here truth is understood not only as true speech but in a wider meaning. Truth is the Veda; austerity *(tapas)* is also equal to truth. It is by truth that people are protected; it is truth that leads to heaven. Any behaviour that goes against the Vedas is called untruth *(asatya)*. Truth is identified with *dharma; dharma* is identified with light which is identified with happiness; so is falsehood identified with *adharma*, *adharma* with darkness and darkness with unhappiness[18].

---

15 3.29.
16 Ibidem.
17 12.251.10; 12.169.26-27.
18 12.190.1ff.

What are the characteristics of truth? How can it be acquired and what are the merits that follow from the practice of it? Truth, it is said, is eternal duty; it is the highest refuge of all; it is penance; it is yoga; it is the eternal Brahman. Everything rests upon truth. Truth is of thirteen kinds: truth, impartiality, self-control, lack of envy, forgiveness, modesty, endurance, absence of jealousy, renunciation, nobility, patience, mercy and abstension from injury[19]. These thirteen attributes are only apparently distinct from one another but have one and the same form; namely, Truth. The characteristics of the thirteen attributes of Truth are purely moral in nature; and if they are developed either singly or in many together, they help one to be attached to truth. The moral development of an individual is a form of truthful behaviour. There is no religion higher than truth; there is no principle better than truth: there is no sin greater than falsehood. Truth is Brahman; it is the universal law[20]. Only that is truth which is beneficial to all creatures. Hence it is truth which obtains peace and harmony both within the community and within oneself.

3. The teaching of the Bhagavad-Gītā

The golden rule is enunciated as follows: One should behave towards all as one would towards oneself. One should behave in the same way towards friend and enemy, kinsman and stranger, good people and bad people[21]. More clearly it is stated:

"By analogy to one's self whoever sees the same in all beings, Arjuna, whether it be pleasure or pain, he is considered the supreme disciplined man"[22].

In the above verse it is important to note that the same expression *ātmaupamya* is used as in the Mahābhārata to indicate the golden rule: *as one's self* in all our dealings with others. Śaṅkara and Rāmānuja interpret the verse in the sense that by analogy with

19 12.162.
20 1.69.21-25; 3.43.42-49.
21 6.9.
22 6.32

oneself one sees that what is pleasant or painful to oneself must also be pleasant or painful to others and that one should hence refrain from harming others. Professor R.C. Zaehner justly remarks that this interpretation does not fit in with the doctrine which Krishna preached; namely, that it is impossible to hurt the embodied self since it is of its very nature inviolate[23]. The integrated man sees the same Brahman everywhere in pleasure as in pain. I am inclined to think that both the interpretations can be taken to be valid, as the humanitarian interpretation is the consequence of the most profound experience of the sameness of Brahman in all living beings.

As to the teaching of Krishna that it is impossible to hurt the embodied self, we have to note that it comes in the context of doing one's duty and Arjuna is urged to do his duty simply because it is *his* duty, and with perfect indifference to the results. Moreover we have to remember that the Bhagavad-gītā is not a logical or systematic philosophical work. It proposes a very high moral ideal, derived from the Hindu philosophical view. If God is present in all beings and if the real self of all beings is the Absolute (Brahman), then the wise hold as equal in their sight a wise and cultivated Brāhmana, a cow, an elephant, a dog and an outcaste[24]. By true knowledge "you shall see all beings without exception in yourself, and in me"[25]. "He who is disciplined, seeing the same in all things, perceives himself in all beings, and all beings in himself". "Who sees Me in all and sees all in Me, for him I am not lost; and he is not lost for Me"[26]. Hence one should behave in the same way towards all, friend or foe, as one would towards oneself. For those who behave thus will not "injure themselves (in others) by themselves"[27]. Since the same Lord is present in all beings and the self of others is one's own one cannot injure himself in others.

Thus the golden rule is accepted by the Bhagavad-gītā as a basis for a lofty ideal of morality. Man must treat of all creatures alike as himself. The morally perfect man "delights in the welfare of all

23 See his *Bhagavad-gītā*, Oxford, 1969, p. 237.
24 5.18.
25 4.35
26 6.29-30.
27 13.38.

beings"[28]. The practical conclusion of all this teaching is that one should avoid all kinds of injury to living beings. Non-violence or harmlessness finds expression in the attitude of peace and pacifism and "passive resistance". Non-violence *(ahiṁsa)* is taught in the Bhagavad-gītā, though not so emphatically and in a very conspicuous manner. In the first part of this book Krishna instructs Arjuna that he should not grieve for the soul because it is immortal and incapable of suffering.

> "Who believes him to be a slayer or who thinks him to be slain, both these do not understand; he does not slay or is slain. He is not born, nor does he ever die; never did he come to be nor will he ever come to be again; unborn; eternal, everlasting is this self, primeval. He is not slain when the body is slain"[29].

It is claimed that this doctrine implies a justification of war and of killing in general. Since the soul cannot be killed and the body itself has to die one day or other, Krishna urges Arjuna to fight[30]. Some interpret this teaching as a sort of concession on the part of Krishna to the dramatic situation of the work itself as inserted in the Mahābhārata. But there are various texts in the Bhagavad-gītā itself which are clearly against any kind of violence[31]. He who is wise is necessarity righteous and true knowledge includes harmlessness among virtues[32]. The good are characterised by harmlessness, truth, freedom from anger, etc.[33]. Whenever it teaches the doctrine of unselfishness and doing good to others, it certainly and necessarily implies in practice doing no harm to living creatures. Although many of the saymgs in the work are inconsistent with the dramatic situation of the war between the Pāṇḍavas and the Kauravas, yet we understand somewhat justly that Arjuna's business is to wage war, and war is the sacrificial fire of which the warriors are the prie-

28 5.25.
29 2.19-20.
30 2.18.
31 13.7; 16.2; 10.5; 17.14.
32 13.7.
33 16.2.

sts[34]; but whatever he does, he should do it in a spirit of detachment; fighting is the yoga most suitable to a member of the warrior class as Arjuna. It should be performed with sameness and indifference.

Krishna's advice to fight: "It is said that these bodies of the eternal, imperishable and incommensurable embodied souls come to an end, hence fight on", is interpreted as follows. Śaṅkara comments:

> "Since the Self is thus eternal and immutable, you must fight, and not withdraw from battle; this is the sense. Hence fighting is not enjoined as a duty. For Arjuna has already addressed himself to fight. But he remains immobilised due to grief and delusion. Therefore the Lord removes the impediment in his path to the performance of his duty. Hence, the term 'fight' is only a restatement of a given position and not an original injunction"[35].

Rāmānuja comments thus:

> "'Hence', for the reason that the body is by nature perishable and the soul is by nature eternal, both are not objects fit to be sorrowed over. Therefore bearing with fortitude the unavoidable descent of weapons and such other harsh contacts, received by you as well as by others, begin for the sake of attaining immortality the action known as war without being attached to the fruits"[36].

Both for Śaṅkara and for Rāmānuja, the real motive of Krishna's advice to fight is the removal of the impediment of grief and delusion on the part of Arjuna, who is reminded of his duty to fight without being attached to the fruits of his action. Arjuna's grief which deters him from his duty of fighting is born of ignorance as

---

34 Mahābhārata 5.139.29ff.

35 See A.G. Krishna Warrier (tr.), Śrīmad Bhagavad-gītā Bhasya of Śrī Śaṅkarācārya, Madras, 1983.

36 See M.R. Sampatkumaran (Tr.), *The Gītābhāsya of Rāmānuja,* Madras, 1969.

to the true nature of the soul. Hence Krishna's repeated attempt to instruct him on the subiect.

S.K. Belvalkar makes an interesting critical analysis of the argument of the second chapter of the Bhagavad-gītā, which throws much light on the problem of fighting[37]. Arjuna was struck with remorse under the influence of a somewhat sophistic pleading for peace and non-violence in order to justify his inaction. Hence one can recall one of the extreme trends of the Upanishadic philosophy which preached the ideal of a total abnegation of all activities. Krishna in the Bhagavad-gītā tries to prove the untenability of this position as a universal guide to conduct. There was also the other one-sided development of theism or Bhakti during the time of the Bhagavad-gītā which considered man as a mere tool in the hands of God and that man has no right to arrogate to himself God's own privilege to resist, to pardon, or to take revenge thereby justifying the ideal of peace and passivity. The mission of Krishna was to bring men back to a more realistic view-point.

If the theory of non-activism (*naiśkarmya*) was considered the highest ideal, knowledge and action are treated as contradictories that could never exist together in an individual. So when Arjuna by refusing to fight wanted to spurn all action and turned to knowledge, he was not yet qualified for knowledge for which disinterested action (in this case, fighting in a mood of equanimity) was a necessary preparation. This theory will not stand in the context of the passages[38] which is in support of action (i.e., killing in battle). The correct interpretation of the passage 2.11-38 is that it is a continuous argument in justification of action (fighting) performed in a mood of equipoise, grounded on the metaphysics of the immortality of the soul and of the distinction between the soul and body. Just as fire under all circumstances must burn, even though what is to be burnt is the hand of an innocent child, so with that same unconcern or indifference for consequences must the kshatriya fight and kill others in battle or be killed himself.

37 See S K. Belvalkar, *The Bhagavad-gītā,* Poona, 1943, pp. xv-xx.
38 2.11-30.

4. M.K. Ghandi's interpretation of the Bhagavad-Gītā

The most important lesson which Gandhiji draws from the Bhagavad-gītā is his Gospel of non-violence. He does not say that it teaches non-violence directly but that non-violence is the consequence of its teaching. He observes:

> "I do not believe that the Gītā teaches violence for doing good. It is pre-eminently a description of the duel that goes on in our own hearts. The divine author has used an historical incident for inculcating the lesson of doing one's own duty even at the peril of one's life. It inculcates performance of duty irrespective of the consequences; for, we mortals, limited by our physical frames, are incapable of controlling actions save our own"[39]. "I do not agree that the Gītā advocates and teaches violence in any part of it. See the concluding discourse at the end of Chapter Two. Although that chapter lends itself to a violent interpretation, the concluding verses seem to me to preclude any such interpretation. The fact is that a literal interpretation of the Gītā lands one in a sea of contradictions. The letter truly killeth, the spirit giveth life"[40].

Krishna was not discussing the question of violence and non-violence. Arjuna was not adverse to killing in general but only to killing his own relatives. Hence Krishna advised that one should do one's duty without consideration of one's relations.

The real theme of the Gītā is self-realization and its means, namely, renunciation of the fruit of action. The fight between the two armies is only an occasion to expound the theme. The Mahābhārata is a profoundly religious work in which the futility of war is demonstrated. If it is difficult to reconcile certain verses with the teaching of non-violence, it is far more difficult to set the whole of the Gītā in the framework of violence[41]. Violence is impossible without

39 *Young India*, 23.2.1921. See specially M.K. Gandhi, *The Teachings of the Gītā*, Bombay, 1971 for the collection of passages of Gandhi on this subject. See also J.T.F. Jordens, "Gandhi and the Bhagavad-Gītā", in: Robert Minor (ed.), *Modern Indian interpreters of the Bhagavad-gītā*, Albany, 1986, pp. 88-109.

40 *Young India*. 12.3.1925.

41 *Young India*, 12.11.1925.

anger, without attachment, without hatred; and the Gītā tries to carry us beyond the state of *sattva, rajas* and *tamas,* a state that evidently excludes anger, attachment and hatred. Again, the second chapter of the Bhagavad-gītā, instead of teaching the rules of physical warfare, tells us how a perfect man is to be known. In the characteristics of the perfect man of the Gītā there is nothing that corresponds to physical warfare. Its whole design is inconsistent with the rules of conduct governing the relations between warring parties[42].

It is interesting to note the comment which Gandhiji makes of the verse 2.18 of the Bhagavad-gītā:

> "Therefore fight, O Bharata. If we argue that since all bodies are perishable, one may kill, does it follow that I may kill all the women and children in the Ashram? Would I have in doing so acted according to the teaching of the Bhagavad-gītā, merely because their bodies are perishable? We believe the watchman to have been mad because he had killed a person; if, however, he were to cite this verse of the Gītā to justify what he did, we would call him wicked. What, then, shall we say of a person who mouths these seemingly learned arguments and then commits wickedness? To know the answer to this, we should go back to the first chapter. Arjuna had said that he did not want even the kingdom of gods if he had to kill his kith and kin for that. But he is bound, in any case, to kill them, for he has accepted the dharma which requires him to kill. This verse with the word *yudhyasva* applies to him, but it does not apply to others. In this verse Śrī Krishna wants to free Arjuna from his ignorant attachment"[43].

Finally, it is significant to note that Gandhiji himself has given a description of the Non-violent Volunteer Corps in a very practical manner. He says: "They must be small if they are to be efficient. The members must know one another well. Each corps will select its own head. One thing should be common to all members and that is implicit faith in God. He is the only companion and doer.

---

42 *Young India,* 6.8.1931.

43 See *Gandhi interprets the Bhagavad-gītā,* Delhi, 1984.

Without faith in Him these peace brigades will be lifeless"[44]. Then he outlines the rules of the peace brigades:

> "1) A volunteer may not carry any weapons.
> 2) The members of a corps must be easily recognizable.
> 3) Every volunteer must carry bandages, scissors, needle and thread, surgical knife, etc., for rendering first aid.
> 4) He should know how to carry and remove the wounded.
> 5) He should know how to put out fires, how to enter a fire area without getting burnt, how to climb heights for rescue work and descend safely with or without his charge.
> 6) He should be well acquainted with all the residents of his locality. This is a service in itself.
> 7) He should pray (with the name of God) ceaselessly in his heart and persuade others who believe to do likewise"[45].

5. Vinoba Bhave's interpretation of the Bhagavad-gītā

Acarya Vinoba Bhave is a remarkable personality, steeped in the learning and spirituality of ancient India, blending inner spiritual life with devoted work in the cause of the needy and poor. His early contact with Gandhiji wrought deep moral and spiritual changes in his life and mission. He not only preached but also practised the ideals taught in the Bhagavad-gītā.

Vinoba Bhave was not in favour of the view that the Gītā aimed at removing Arjuna's weakness and making him enter the battle; that the Gītā teaches both *karma-yoga* (the way of action) and the *yuddha-yoga* (the way of conflict). We cannot suppose that the whole of the Gītā was intended to make Arjuna worthy of the army. Arjuna was a great warrior and it was not fear that made him turn away from battle. Nor was the aim of the Gītā to cure Arjuna of his scruples based on non-violence and make him fight. Arjuna was quite ready to do his duty of fighting as a kshatriya but the sight of his own kinsmen and friends depressed him. He was not moved by

44 See M. K. Gandhi, *Non-violence in Peace and War,* Navajivan Publications, Ahmedabad, Vol, 2, 1960, 86-87.
45 *Ibidem.*

the spirit of non-violence but by his attachment to his own people. His attachment confused him and overshadowed his commitment to duty. He began to declare that war was a sin *(adharma)* and that it would bring disaster to his race and society and encourage moral anarchy. If Arjuna had been actually converted to non-violence, he would not have been satisfied until his real point had been met, however much he had been told of wisdom and knowledge. But the Gītā never answered this point of his, and yet Arjuna was satisfied. This implies that Arjuna's attitude was not that of non-violence, he certainly believed in fighting. He wanted to evade this duty because his vision was clouded by illusion.

Arjuna spoke the language of non-violence and of renunciation. But his own duty *(svadharma)* as a warrior was to fight. However unattractive his *svadharma be*, he has to find fulfilment by persisting in it, since it is only through this persistence that growth is possible. As the Gītā says, one's own *dharma*, even if devoid of merit, is the best for oneself. One may ask: if the way of renunciation (*sannyāsa*) is better than the way of conflict *(yuddha dharma)*, why did not Krishna make Arjuna a true sannyasin straightway? This was not impossible for Krishna. But in that case what would be the meaning and purpose of Arjuna's life? Every man is free to make his own efforts. The work of the teacher is to help the disciple with advice and instruction. God guides us all from within. From all this it follows that the purpose of the Gītā is to remove the illusion that stands between Arjuna and his *svadharma*, the sense of 'mine', this attachment. To the question: "Arjuna, have you got over the illusion?", Arjuna replies: "Yes, Lord. The illusion has left me; my *svadharma* is clear to me"[46].

The second chapter of the Bhagavad-gītā teaches three great truths: the spirit is immortal and indivisible; the body is transient; the *svadharma* cannot be thrust aside. Of these three truths, the *svadharma* is of the nature of a duty to be performed, while the other two have to be known and realised. The *svadharma* comes to one naturally. One has to serve one's parents in the family into which one has been born; so too one has the duty of serving the

---

46 See VINOBA BHAVE, *Talks on the Gītā*, Varanasi, 1964, pp. 3-11. See also Boyd H. Wilson, "Vinoba Bhave's *Talks on the Gītā*", in: S. Minor (ed.) *Modern Indian Interpreters, op. cit.*, pp. 110-130.

society in which one lives. As one cannot choose one's mother, no matter what sort of person she is, so also is the *svadharma* which is inescapable. Everyone has to keep his hold on *svadharma*. But in fulfilling one's *svadharma* there come many illusions; at the bottom of all these illusions is a restricted and shallow identification of oneself with the body. The sense of "me" and "mine" puts a wall around one and with it comes the attachment to one's family and nation, one's caste, one's religion and mode of life. In this way the germs of base thoughts are generated and the health which is *svadharma* is destroyed. In this situation it is not enough to perform one's *svadharma* with determination. One has to awake oneself to two other principles: "I am not this mortal body; the body is only the outer layer"; "I am the spirit that never dies, that cannot be destroyed; that pervades everything". The purpose of life consists in the awareness of the self that transcends the body[47]. The Gītā tells us how to realize these truths in our life. That is to say, we have to perform our duty but without being attached to its fruit[48].

It is the special responsibility of those persons who have taken a vow of self-less service to the community to create the necessary atmosphere to settle disputes through non-violent means. Non-violence should become the moral rule both in personal lives and in the social and political life of a community as a whole. The logic of non-violent behaviour is that no one likes to be injured or killed. Any one who aspires to spirituality and believes in the unity of all life cannot consent to kill other lives. Commenting on the Gītā's verse: the soul does not slay and is not slain and does not cause to slay, Vinoba says: the soul is never killed because it never kills. The inherent nature of the soul is that it is never involved in any action. He told the Bhoodan workers at Indore in 1960 that non-violence stems from the nature of the soul itself:

"The soul does not kill and is not killed. Such is the soul and this itself is non-violence. This thought later on took the shape of a social necessity and we have evolved out of it a social code, full of prescriptions and prohibitions. But the original, seminal idea is

47 *Ibidem*, pp. 12.21.
48 *Ibidem*, pp. 21-24.

that non-violence is a concomitant of the soul. Hence the more we seek the orginal nature of the soul, the more shall inner satisfaction and peace come to us"[49].

Once again, when the dacoits in Bhind-Morena area (Central India) surrendered their arms at the feet of Vinoba, he addressed them:

"Friends, if you are rebels, I too am one. I am your friend and well-wisher. I am also up in rebellion. My work consists in removing the curse of untouchability from society, to make land available to the landless, to banish poverty and undeserved affluence with a view to wipe out the distinctions of high and low. A revolt has to be undertaken with the aid of the soul force. If there were to be a revolt based on soul force, there would be no dacoits and no police either. There would be love and peace everywhere and consequently a healthy and happy society would emerge"[50].

Time and again Vinoba advocated and worked to establish a non-violent social order. "A non-violent social order implies the existence of public-spirited workers who will from day to day serve the people in their neighbourhood and be in intimate touch with them all. If everywhere there is a band of such workers, it would be quite easy, in case of a riot breaking out in one place, to quell it with readiness on their part for a little sacrifice"[51]. Under a non-violent social system there is no place for armed force or military; the work could be only undertaken by a Shānti Sena (Peace Brigade), an army of volunteers who believed in non-violence and who dedicated their lives to the service of the people. Vinoba established Shānti Sena in various parts of the country.

A shānti-sainik (a soldier of peace) must be ready to accept and observe the following obligations:

1) He should believe in the principles of truth, non-violence, non-property, physical labour, self-control.

---

49 Cited by VASANT NARGOLKAR, *The Creed of Saint Vinoba,* Bombay, 1963 p. 114.
50 Cited by Vasant Nargolkar, *op. Cit.,* p. 163.
51 Cited by Vasant Nargolkar, *op. Cit.,* p. 212.

He should engage himself to conform his own life to these principles.
2) He should believe that the world will attain peace only when every people will have a direct control over its own affairs. Consequently he will not take any part in political parties or parties of power, but engage himself to induce the members of all political parties to collaborate in the common work.
3) He should dedicate all his mental energy to the disinterested service of the people.
4) He will not concede the minimum of mental space and of behaviour to any spirit of exclusivism in matters of caste, class or religions.
5) He will dedicate all his time and the best of his energy to the duty of non-violent revolution of Sarvodaya, according to its concrete programmes of Bhoodanyajna (the gift of the land) and of the local industries of the village.
6)He will be available at whatever moment and everywhere to fulfil the service of Shānti Sena, and ready to give, if necessary, even his own life[52].

To realize concretely a non-violent social order Vinoba was convinced of the fact that the end and the means for achieving the end must be clean in an attempted revolution. There are three kinds of bringing about a social, economic or political revolution: the way of killing, the way of compulsion and the way of compassion; the way of loot, of legislation and of love. Vinoba adopted the way of love and compassion. The ultimate objective of the Bhoodan movement was to establish in India a non-violent, non-exploitive social order. He prevented at all cost any kind of violent revolution. He realized that the future peace and prosperity of the country depends upon the peaceful solution of the land problem, through non-violent revolution.

Addressing the land-owners, Vinoba Bhave said:

"If you will accept the path of love and non-violence, you will have to abandon the attachment to land. Otherwise the age of vio-

52 See VINOBA BHAVE, *La Legge dell'Amore,* a cura di Satish Kumar, Tr., Roma, 1973, pp. 80-81.

lence which is approaching will destroy not only the land but also those who are occupying it. Let us therefore realize that the problem has been presented to us by God Himself, and let us therefore give and give incessantly"[53].

Unless the existing social order which is based upon inequality, strife and conflict, is replaced by one founded on equality and mutual co-operation, there can be no salvation for mankind. The moral and spiritual basis of the Bhoodan movement is based on the Hindu way of thinking and living. Vinoba says: "People should accept the principle that all land belongs to God. If all land were socially owened, the present-day discontent would disappear and an era of love and co-operation would ensue"[54]. No force or legislation can effect this change.

6. Conclusion

The cardinal Hindu virtues are truth, non-violence, detachment, self-control and purity. It is these ideals that have given the Hindus a common idea of goodness and peace. Truth in Hinduism means far more than mere truthfulness; it means eternal Reality. The Mahābhārata insists that the pursuit of truth, wherever it may lead and whatever sacrifices it may entail, is indispensable to the progress of man and to obtain peace. Truth is always associated with non-violence in the Hindu Scriptures. The two are considered to be the highest virtues. Non-violence must be practised not only by individuals but also by communities and nations, in all spheres of life. The influence of this ideal of non-violence is seen in all aspects of Hindu life: compassion, forgiveness, respect for life, horror of violence, tolerance, etc. The sacred texts also enjoin the avoidance of certain vices, specially, lust, anger, and greed which represent 'the triple gate of hell'. Non-violence is the cosmic outlook which every Hindu should have, which teaches that everyman should see with equality everything in the image of one's own self

53 As cited by B.R. MISRA, *V for Vinoba,* Bombay, 1956, p. 36.
54 *Ibidem,* p. 36.

and do good to all creatures. This precisely is the golden rule: treat others in the same way as you treat yourself *(ātmaupamya)*. When one is established in non-violence human beings give up their mutual animosity in the presence of such a person. When one is established in truthfulness, the light of eternal Truth dawns on him and helps him work for the well-being of the whole society, realizing that the happiness of others is as important as his own. As all living beings bear the essence of the divine in them, one cannot hurt them in any way. Peace is the natural outcome of this attitude of universal benevolence. Unless people adopt the law of love there can be no hope of eliminating war and destruction. The only way to stimulate the inherent goodness in human nature is to adopt the spiritual discipline of non-violence, which arouses love in man and brings about the victory of love over hatred, of truth over untruth, of light over darkness, of righteousness over unrighteousness, and of immortality over death.

CHAPTER NINE

MEANING OF DEATH IN HINDUISM

Introduction

Of all forms of religious practice homage to dead relatives appears to be the most widely extended. It forms a part of nearly all religions, and is an important element in the belief system of nearly every culture. In India, especially in the Hindu India, there exists not only a reverence for the dead but a constant periodical performance of commemorative obsequies as a positive obligation incumbent on the relatives of the dead. They believe that it is their duty to support and contribute by offerings and homage to the happiness of the dead in the other world to which they pass after the death. They have elaborate funeral rites and attach great importance to these and to the subsequent ceremonies called Śrāddha. Funeral rites are called "the last sacrifice" *(antyeṣṭi);* that is to say, the sacrifice of the body in fire. Any contact with a dead body and any connection with the departed spirit are deemed impure. The departed spirit, though released from the body by fire is considered impure until the *śrāddha* ceremony is performed; impurity also results from any connection with a dead body. Hence the funeral ceremonies themselves are thought to be inauspicious (amaṅgala) but necessary. The *śrāddha* on the other hand is an auspicious *(maṅgala)* ceremony because it is performed for the benefit of a dead person after he has received an intermediate body and become a father *(pitṛi)*.

The mystery of death is probed into also from the mystical point of view, especially in the Upanishads. The spiritual self is ensnared in space and time and the sphere of action; it becomes subject to the cycle of re-births and re-deaths. Hence death is an event in the never-ending process of becoming; i.e., coming to be and passing away. The self's true salvation consists in returning to the original state which is beyond death, darkness and non-being.

The plan followed in this study is as follows: (1) The Vedic idea of death; (2) The *Upanishads'* teaching on death; (3) The meaning of death as found in the Law Books *(Dharma Sūtras* and *Śāstras)* and Ritual Books (Śrauta Sūtras and Gṛhya Sūtras); (4) The teaching of the *Mahābhārata* on death; (5) The idea of death according to the *Bhagavad-gītā*; and finally, (6) The doctrine of death in the *Purāṇas*. These treatises contain myths and rituals about death, mystical insights into the meaning of life and death, into the nature of human suffering and misery. I have adduced the texts extensively and preferred to let them speak for themselves to condensing their views in my own words, for the texts even in the English translation retain some of their originality and character. I have added two appendices at the end, which are the extracts from the *Garuḍa Purāṇa, Pretakalpa* and the *Atharva Veda*. *Garuḍa Purāṇa* is perhaps the best authority on the Hindu rite of death and on the right performance of funeral and *śrāddha* ceremonies. The *Atharva Veda* extracts reflect the early Vedic ideas on death.

1. The Vedic idea of death

According to the Vedic belief the separated spirit of the deceased man went to the realm of eternal light through the path followed by the Fathers who are depicted as revelling with Yama, the king of the dead, and feasting with the gods. The Rig Veda contains five hymns[1] which deal with death and future life. From these hymns it is evident that the Vedic Indians adopted the method of cremation usually for the disposal of the body, though burial of the

1 Rig Veda 10.14-18. Except the last one (10.18) which is a funeral hymn in the strict sense, all of them contain invocations of different gods connected with the future life. They are addressed to Yama (10.14), to the Fathers (10.15), to Agni (10.16), and to Pusan and Sarasvati (10.17). Agni conveys the corpse to the other world, the Fathers and the gods; Pusan protects the dead on its way to the heavenly world; Sarasvati comes to the sacrifice on the same chariot as the Fathers and seats herself on the sacrificial grass. Yama is the king of the dead.

corpse was also practised.

The following hymn describes the dead man's way to Yama's realm:

> Him who has passed away along the mighty steeps
> and has spied out the path for many,[2]
> him the son of Vivasvant, the assembler of people,
> Yama the king, so thou present with oblation.
>
> Yama has first found out the way for us:
> this pasture is not to be taken away.
> Whither out former fathers have passed away,
> thither those that have been born since [pass away] along their several paths.
>
> Mātalī having grown strong with the Kavyas, Yama with the Aṅgirases,
> Bṛhaspati with the Rkvans, whom the gods have made strong
> and who [have made strong] the gods, some rejoice in the call Svāhā,
> others in the offering to the dead.[3]
>
> Upon this strewn grass, O Yama, pray seat thyself,
> uniting thyself with the Aṅgirases, the fathers.
> Let the spells recited by the seers bring thee thither.
> Do thou, O King, rejoice in this oblation.
>
> Come hither with the adorable Aṅgirases; O Yama, with the sons of
> Virūpa do thou here rejoice. I call Vivasvant who is
> thy father, [let him rejoice], having set himself
> down on the strew at this sacrifice[4].

---

2 Yama is the deified lord of the dead; originally, he is considered to have been the first to die and to have shown to others who died after him the path to the abode of the departed.

3 Kavyas, Aṅgirases and Ṛkvans are different groups of ancestors. The ancestors strengthen the gods with their sacrifice and the gods in turn strengthen them with their help. Some ancestors delight in Svāhā, the sacrificial exclamation, worship or praise, addressed to the gods; others in the funeral oblations offered to them (Svadhā).

4 It is not the priest who sits down on the strew but the god.

The Aṅgirases, our fathers, the Navagvas, the Atharvans, the
Bhṛgus,[5]
the Soma-loving: we would abide in the favour, the good graces of them the adorable ones.

Go forth, go forth by those ancient paths on which our fathers
of old
have passed away. Thou shalt see both kings rejoicing in the
offering to the dead, Yama and Varuna the god.[6]

Unite with the Fathers, unite with Yama, with the reward
of thy sacrifices and good works in the highest heaven.
Leaving blemish behind go back to thy home;
unite with thy body, full of vigour.[7]

Begone, disperse, slink off from here: for him
the Fathers have prepared this place. Yama gives him
a resting-place distinguished by days and waters
and nights.[8]
Run by a good path past the two sons of Saramā,[9]
the four-eyed, brindled dogs; then approach the bountiful
Fathers who rejoice at the same feast as Yama.[10]

Give him over to those two, O King, that are thy dogs,
O Yama, the guardians, four-eyed, watchers of the path,
observers of men;
bestow on him welfare and health.

---

5 Navagvas, Atharvans and Bhrigus are priestly families of ancient times.

6 This and the following stanza are addressed to the spirit of the departed whose funeral rites are being celebrated.

7 Being free from disease and frailties, the dead man unites with a body that is complete and without imperfections.

8 This stanza is addressed to the demons to leave the dead man alone. The joys of the next world are described in Rig Veda 9.113: "where there is eternal light, in that immortal world place me"; "where are those swift waters, there make me immortal." Nights are mentioned as alternating with days.

9 Sarama is the hound of Indra.

10 The spirit of the departed is addresed here.

Broad-nosed, life-stealing, the two as messengers of
Yama wander among men; may these two give us back
here to-day auspicious life that we may see the sun.[11]

For Yama press[12] the Soma, to Yama offer the oblation;
to Yama goes the sacrifice well prepared,[13] with Agni
as its messenger.

To Yama offer the oblation abounding in ghee, and step forth;
may he guide us to the gods that we may
live a long life.[14]

To Yama the king offer the most honied oblation.
This obeisance is for the seers born of old,
the ancient makers of the path.

It flies through the three Soma vats. The six earths
the one great [world], triṣṭubh, gāyatrī and [the other] metres,
all these are placed in Yama.[15]

The above hymn is a funeral address, partly to Yama the god of the dead and partly to the soul of the departed whose body is being consumed on the pile. It describes Yama as the chief of the blessed dead, who is spoken of as the ruler of the departed and as the gatherer of the people, who gives the dead a resting place and prepares an abode for them. It was he who first discovered the way to the other world after death, and his messengers are two dogs which guard the way trodden by the dead proceeding to the other world.

11 As having already marked us for their victims, let Yama's messengers give back our life today.

12 The three following stanzas are addressed to the priests.

13 To Yama goes the sacrifice: the idea is that the smoke of the sacrificial fire goes up to heaven where Yama dwells.

14 Yama is implored to keep the survivors to the worship of the gods and not lead them to the Fathers, so that they may enjoy long life on earth.

15 Rig Veda 10.14.

The following hymn[16] is a funeral prayer. The relatives and friends of the dead man who is about to be buried are assembled around the corpse before placing it in the grave.

> Depart, O Death,[17] and go thy way far from us,
> Far from the path which by the gods is trodden.[18]
> Thou seest and hearst the words to thee I mutter;
> Harm not our children, harm not thou our heroes.
>
> Ye who have come here, blotting out Death's footprints,[19]
> and in your yet extended life rejoicing,
> in wealth and children's blessing still increasing,
> O righteous men, your minds be pure and spotless.[20]
>
> The living from the dead are separated,
> the sacred rite to-day has prospered for us,
> and we are here, prepared for mirth and dancing,[21]
> prolonging still the span of our existence.
>
> This boundary[22] I place here for the living,
> That to this goal no one of them may hurry.
> May they live on through full a thousand harvests,
> and through this rock keep death away far from them.
>
> As days in order follow one another,
> As seasons duly alternate with seasons,
> And as the later never forsakes the earlier,
> So settle thou the lives of these,[23] Ordainer.

---

16 Rig Veda 10.18. In this hymn there is no reference to any of the gods. It gives us more information about the funeral usages of the ancient times.

17 Mrtyu is the god of death, distinct from Yama who is the judge and ruler of the departed.

18 There is here a probable allusion to the way of the Fathers, opposed to the way of the gods; cfr. Brh. Up. 6.2.2.

19 A wisp or clog is fastened to the foot of the corpse which represented Death in order to prevent the dead from returning to carry off the living.

20 This stanza is addressed to the relatives of the deceased.

21 The enjoyment of ordinary life after the performance of the duties to the dead.

22 A fine of demarcation between the dead and the living, and limiting the jurisdiction of Death until the natural time for his approach.

23 Let them pass away in due order of seniority.

Do ye attain long life, old age selecting,
as many as you are combined in order.[24]
May Tvastar, well-disposed, the skilled creator,
produce forthwith long life for your existence.

The women here, still happy wives, not widowed,
shall come and bring rich oil and precious ointment;
and tearless, blooming, rich adorned, may they first[25]
approach the resting-place of the departed.

Rise to the living world thy mind, O woman;
his breath is fled and gone by whom thou sittest;
who took thee by the hand once and espoused thee,
with him thy plighted troth is now accomplished.[26]

From out his lifeless hand his bow I have taken,
a pledge to us of power, strength and honour.
Thou yonder, and we here below as brave men,
shall overcome the force of every onslaught.[27]

Return once more unto the earth, thy mother,
her arms she opens kindly to receive thee.
To good men kind and tender as a maiden,
may she henceforth preserve thee from destruction.[28]

Firm may his spaceless earthly home continue,
beneath supported by a thousand pillars,
let it henceforward be his house and riches,
a sure protecting refuge for him ever.

I settle firmly now the earth about thee;
I cast the clods on thee,-let this not harm me.

---

24 One behind the other, the oldest reaching the end of their journey first.

25 i.e., before the ceremonies proper begin.

26 This verse is to be spoken by the husband's brother to the widow, and he is to make her leave her husband's body.

27 This verse is applicable only to the deseased kshatriya.

28 This stanza is addressed to the dead body.

The Fathers shall uphold these columns for thee,
but yonder Yama shall prepare a dwelling.[29]

The hymn begins with the rite of adjuring death to depart, and summons those present to devotion. Then is expressed the feeling of joy that death has not befallen to any of the assembly and urges all gladly to enjoy life in the future. A stone laid between those present and the dead symbolizes the separation of the realms of life and death. It expresses the desire that a long life for all be decreed in the other world. The husband's brother or the priest summons the widow to separate herself from the corpse and himself takes the bow out of the hand of the dead man as the symbol of his ability. The hymn closes with the wish that the deceased may find a place in the other world.

In other hymns (Rig Veda 10.15-17) it is said that Agni carries the corpse to the other world of the fathers and the gods. They pray to Agni to preserve the body intact and to burn the goat that is sacrificed as his portion. Savitar conducts the dead on the path to the heavenly world and Pusan protects the dead. Passing along the path trodden by his ancestors the spirit of the dead man goes to the realm of light and enjoys life in the company of the Fathers with Yama. It is interesting to note that before the pyre is lighted, the widow, having lain beside the dead man, arises, and his bow is taken away from his hand. This suggests that in earlier times the widow and the weapons of him were burnt with his body.

2. The Upanishads' teaching on death

The legend of Naciketas provides a dramatic setting for expounding the doctrine of immortality. When told by his angry father to go to Death, the brāhman boy Naciketas goes to Yama's realm and finds him absent there. He remained there for three days unfed. On his return Yama, convicted of the sin of inhospitality to a brāhman offers three boons in recompense. Naciketas accordin-

29 This is addressed to the urn containing the bone and ashes. which is buried after the body has been burnt.

gly expresses his wishes: first, "let me return alive to my father"; second, "tell me how my good works may not be exhausted"; third, "tell me the conquest of re-death." In answer to the second and third questions Yama told him the Naciketa fire. Let us give the important texts of the Katha Upanishad:[30]

> Naciketas said:
> "In the heaven-world there is no fear whatever:
> Thou art not there,[31] nor does one fear old age:
> Having crossed over both hunger and thirst,
> Sorrow o'er-past, one rejoices in heaven.
>
> Thyself, O Death, knowest well the heavenly fire,
> To me do thou declare it, who have faith:
> (By it) heaven's people share immortal life:
> This choose I as the second of the gifts."[32]

Yama grants the boon and expatiates on the efficacy of the First-rite. Here is reflected the thought of the Brahmanas in which the sacrifice became more important even than the gods, and the gods themselves were said to have gained the victory over the asuras and to gave gained immortality through the power of the sacrifice. Naciketas said:

> "This doubt there is about a man departed, -
> Some say, "He is", some, "He does not exist";
> This would I know, instructed well by thee:
> Of the three gifts, this gift is the third.
>
> Yama said:
> Even the gods of old on this point doubted,
> For subtle is this truth and hard to know.

---

30 Chapters 1-3. The legend of Naciketas is also found in the Taittiriya Brahmana 3.2.8 in which is explained the origin and title of the Naciketa fire sacrifice and its blessings are extolled.

31 i.e., death, in the sense of the cause of decay and fear.

32 Katha Up. 1.12-13.

Choose then another boon, O Naciketas!
Do not entreat me, give this up I pray!"[33]

Naciketas persists in his question about death and is finally told this.

One thing is the good,[34] quite other the pleasant:[35]
Both these with different aim bind man [to action]:
Well is it for him who takes hold of the good;
He fails of his aim[36] who chooses the pleasant.

Both the good and the pleasant approach a man:
Going all round them the wise discriminates:
For good before pleasure a wise man chooses;
The fool, for property,[37] prefers the pleasant.

But thou, the pleasant and sweet-seeming objects,
Examining, O Naciketas, hast renounced,
Not having fastened on that chain of riches[38]
Wherein so many mortals sink to ruin.
Far opposite are these two and divergent, -
Ignorance[39] and what is known as knowledge:
Eager for knowledge deem I Naciketas;
Many delightful things did not distract you.

Abiding in the midst of ignorance,
Self-wise, thinking themselves learned,
Fools go about, rushing round and round,
Like blind men led by the blind.[40]

---

33 Katha Up. 1.20-21.

34 *Sreyas* from *sri*, 'splendour, beauty, fortune'; here it means the morally excellent, the good.

35 Preyas from priya; hence, 'the pleasant'.

36 i.e. he misses the goal *(hiyate arthad)*.

37 *Yoga-ksema* means property, possession, prosperity; i.e., for the sake of possessing and keeping the fool prefers the pleasant.

38 ZaeLner translates this as 'this garland of wealth'.

39 *Avidya* as opposed to *vidya*: unwisdom as opposed to wisdom.

40 The words refer to the obstinate self-conceit of fools.

The passing-beyond[41] is not clear to the childish,
Careless, befooled with the glamour of wealth:
"This world exists, there is no other", - thinking,
Again and again he falls within my power.

He whom many cannot even hear of,
Whom many, even hearing, do not know, -
Wondrous His teacher, skilful His attainer,
Wondrous His knower, skilfully instructed.

Not taught by an inferior man can He
Be truly understood, though much considered;[42]
Save by another taught there's no way thither,
For He is inconceivably subtler than the subtle.

Not by reasoning is this thought obtainable,
Though, by another taught, well may one know it, friend:
Thou hast obtained it, being true and steadfast; -
May we find, Naciketas, a questioner like thee![43]

I know full well that wealth, so called, is transient,
For not by the unsteadfast is what is firm obtained:
Yet is the Naciketa fire[44] laid by me, -
By transient things I have obtained the enduring.

The attainment of desire, the world's foundation,
The endless fruit of rites, the fearless shore,

---

41 i.e., death; the meaning of death is not clear to the child; child (bāla) is synonymous with fool; hence 'childish'.

42 No amount of individual thinking will supply the place of a good teacher.

43 The Supreme Self is quite unknowable if sought by argumentative reasoning and readily knowable if revealed by a true spiritual master. This is so because the object sought after is so 'subtle' as to be beyond the reach of the senses and of understanding based upon sense-perception; religious truth is of the nature of intuition.

44 The story of Naciketas first occurs in the Taittiriya Brahmana (3.2.8) in connection with the Naciketa fire sacrifice. Yama reveals the sacrifice to Naciketas and calls it after him. This sacrifice seems to have been a form of the Agnihotra; for a description of this sacriEce with three fires, see the second khanda of the Satapatha Brahmana. Yama eulogises Naciketas, saying that he himself knew of the ephemeral nature of karma and its results and of the inefficacy of the impermanent to obtain the permanent, still performed the sacrifice to attain the Yama state (i.e. the sovereignty of the heavenly world).

The exceeding praised, the far-stretching, the goal, -
Being wise, Naciketas, firmly hast thou let go.[45]

He who is hard to see, entered into the hidden,
Set in the cave, dwelling in the deep, ancient,[46] -
Perceiving God through spiritual concentration,
The wise man leaves behind both joy and sorrow."[47]

The main teaching of this Upanishad is as follows: There are two ways: the way of good and the way of pleasure. The way of pleasure is the way of illusion of an apparent material wealth, obtainable by the senses, which leads to repeated death. One enters the way of good, i.e., of knowledge of true reality, through the help of a spiritual teacher. One has to give up the way of pleasure and even the good which seeks the heavenly satisfaction, if the highest good of all is to be attained. The highest good consists in the vision of the inmost reality by *adhyātma-yoga.*

When a person dies, the various component parts of his body unite with their corresponding counterparts in nature, while the sum total of his karma remains attached to his self *(ātman).* The force of this karma decides the nature of his next birth where he reaps the fruit of what he merits. The whole cycle of rebirth is determined by the law of action, good or bad; and birth and death are in continuous succession for a man who is involved in this cycle and liberation consists precisely in escaping through spiritual means of knowledge and love of God from the round of birth and death and in the attainment of immortal state in identity with the Absolute *(Brāhman)* or in union with a personal God in love, as is evident in the theist trend of the Upanishads. The episode above narrated of the *Katha Upanishad* illustrates the attitude to be taken towards death. Death and other human problems belong only to the earthly sphere.

---

45 The passage deals with the sacrifice and the heavenly world obtained by it as given in the Satapatha Brahmana 1.9.3 Naciketa has renounced the old Vedic ideal of immortality and is seeking the new ideal of the Upanishads: the immediate realization of unity with the Supreme Being.

46 The mysterious divine being is hidden behind all the phenomenal world and in the depths of one's own being, so difficult of access by any ordinary means, yet accessible by *adhyatma-yoga.*

47 Katha Up. 2.1-12.

Death appears like other human earthly realities equally undesirable. The fire sacrifice is the sure means of gaining access to heavenly immortality. Since Naciketas is interested only in the absolute reality which is not subject to transmigration, Yama reveals the secret doctrine of the immortal self; "The knowing self is never born; nor does he die at any time... He is unborn, eternal, abiding and primeval. He is not slain when the body is slain"[48].

The passage of the soul at death is vividly described in the *Brihadāraṇya Upanishad:*

> As a heavily loaded cart goes creaking, just so this bodily self, mounted by the intelligent Self, goes groaning when one is breathing one's last.
> When he comes to weakness - whether he comes to weakness through old age or through disease - this person frees himself from these limbs just as a mango, or a fig, or a berry releases itself from its bond; and he hastens again, according to the entrance and place of origin, back to life...[49]
> As noblemen, policemen, chariot-drivers, village-heads gather round a king who is about to depart, just so do all the breaths gather around the soul at the end, when one is breathing one's last.[50]
> When this self comes to weakness and confusedness of mind, as it were, then the breaths gather around him. He takes to himself those particles of energy and descends into the heart. When the person in the eye turns away, back to the sun, he no longer recognizes forms.
> He is becoming one, they say; he does not see... he does not smell... he does not taste... he does not speak... he does not hear... he does not think... he does not touch... he does not know. The point of his heart becomes lighted up. By that light the self departs, either by the eye, or by the head, or by other bodily parts. After him, as he goes out, the life goes out. After the life, as it goes out, all the breaths go out. He becomes one with intelligence. What has intelligence departs with

48 Katha Up. 2.18.
49 Brh. Up. 4.3.35-36.
50 Ibid. 4.3.38.

him. His knowledge and his works and his former intelligence (i.e., instinct) lay hold of him"[51].

The above description of the departure of the self from the bodily frame is followed by the discourse on the transmigration of the self in accordance with his good or bad actions; namely, the self of the unreleased passes from one state of existence to another in the round of births and deaths. Death is also considered as the process of absorption into the Real, into the Self. "When a person here is deceasing, his voice goes into his mind; his mind into his breath; his breath into heat; the heat into the highest divinity. That which is the finest essence - this whole world has that as its soul. That is Reality *(satya)*. That is the self *(ātman)*. That art thou, Śvetaketu"[52]. Only ignorance and persistence in the thought of a separate self prevent one from actually being the Self. Death is hence the loosing of the cords of the heart which bind man to an illusory life and to the thought of a separate self-existence.

"Gone are the fifteen parts to whence they came;
[Gone] all the senses *(deva)* to their corresponding base;
[All] works *(karma)* and the self composed of consciousness *(vijñāna)*, -

All these become one in the beyond that knows no change"[53]. Thus to the spiritually enlightened man death is a passage from the unreal to the real, from darkness to light, and from mortality to immortality. It is by death that he detaches his true self from the evils of his current embodiment and when he dies he leaves all suffering behind. But the non-enlightened person becomes involved in the cycle of rebirth.

---

51 4.4.1-2
52 Chandogya Upan. 6.8.6.
53 Mund. Up. 3.2.7.

3. The Meaning of Death in the Law Books

We shall describe the main features of the funeral rites and oblations as found in the Law Books with the view of understanding the meaning of death and of its consequences for man. We shall focus our attention on the important aspects of the rites, leaving out the many minute descriptions that are secondary to our purpose.

I) Āpastamba Dharma Sūtra[54]

The relatives of the dead should bathe, and fast until the day after death. They shall show the signs of mourning such as dishevelling their hair; clothed with one garment, they step into the river and throw up water for the dead persons and then ascending the bank they sit down. They pour out water consecrated in such a way that the dead will know it to be given to them. Then they return to the village without looking back and perform the rites for the dead. At all religious ceremonies they shall feed the brāhmans who are pure and well-versed in the Vedas. They shall distribute gifts at proper places, at proper times, to proper recipients. They should not eat the food, of which no portion is offered in the fire and of which no part is first given to the guests. No food that has been mixed with pungent condiments or salt can be offered as a burnt-offering.

At *śrāddha* rite the Manes are the gods to whom the sacrifice is offered. But the brāhmans who are fed represent the Āhavanīya-fire.[55] The rite must be performed in each month. A *śrāddha* offered on any day of the latter half of the month gladdens the Manes; it also procures different rewards for the performers according to the time observed. He shall feed the brāhmans who know the Vedas, and who are not connected by any blood relationship.

54 Prasna 2, Patala 6, Khanda 15; S.B.E. Vol. 2, pp. 137ff.

55 Ahavaniya fire is the consecrated fire taken from the householder's perpetual fire and prepared for receiving oblations.

II) Gautama Dharma Śāstra[56]

The relative of the dead person shall offer *śrāddha* to the Manes on the day of the new moon. Let him select as good food as he can afford, and have it prepared as well as possible. He shall feed an uneven number of brāhmans, at least nine. Let him feed also persons endowed with goodness and talents. The Manes are satisfied for a month by gifts of sesamum, masha beans, rice, barley, and water. They are satisfied for three years by fish and flesh of common deer, etc.; for twelve years by cow's milk and messes of milk.

III) Vāsishṭa Dharma Śāstra[57]

Let the relative of the dead person present *śrāddha* to the Manes during the dark half of the month on any day after the fourth. He shall feed three ascetics or three virtuous householders, who are not very aged, who do not follow forbidden occupations, with the exclusion of his own pupils. Let him feed brāhmans well-versed in the Vedas. He shall feed two brāhmans at the offering to the gods, three at the offering to the Manes, or a single man on either occasion. Or he may entertain at a *śrāddha* just a single brāhman who has studied the whole Veda, who is distinguished by learning and virtue, and is free from all evil marks on his body. Let him offer food at the sanctuary of the gods.

IV) Āśvalāyana Gṛihya Sūtra[58]

When a man dies, his relative should have a piece of ground dug up for him. The "cemetery" should be free from all sides and be fertile in herbs. The waters of the "cemetery" flow off to all sides; this is a characteristic required for the "cemetery" where the body is to be burned. The technical word used for "cemetery" is *śmaśāna*, which includes both the place where the body is to be burned and the place where the gathered bones are deposited.

56 Chapter XV; S.B.E. Vol. 2, pp. 255 ff.
57 Chapter XI.16ff; S.B.E. Vol. 14, pp. 51ff.
58 Adhyaya IV, Khandika 2-8; S.B.E. Vol. 29, pp. 237ff.

They cut off from the dead body the hair, the beard, the hairs of the body and the nails. They should provide plenty of sacrificial grass and butter. The "spirnkled butter" is used for the Manes.

The relations of the dead person now carry his sacred fires and his sacrificial vessels in the direction to the south-east or to the south-west. After them aged persons forming an odd number, men and women separate, carry the dead body. Some say that the dead body should be carried in a cart with a seat, drawn by cows.

Some say that the dead body be covered by a she-animal: a cow or a she-goat. They tie a rope to its left fore-foot and lead it behind the dead body. Then follow the relations of the deceased, wearing their sacrificial cords below round their body, with their hair-locks untied, the older ones first, the younger ones last. Having arrived at the place, the performer of the rites walks three times round the spot with his left side turned towards it, and with a śamī branch sprinkles water on it reciting the verse: go away, withdraw, and depart from here. (R.V. 10.14.9) One who knows how to do it piles up between the fires a pile of fuel. They place the dead body, turning its head towards *Ahavaniya*, on the sacrificial grass and black antelope's skin spread out. To the north of the body the wife of the dead person is made to lie down on the pile. Her brother-in-law or a pupil of the dead or an aged servant, should cause her to rise from the place, with the words: Arise, O wife, to the world of life. (R.V. 10.18.8) He bends the bow, breaks it to pieces, and throws it on the pile.

He should then put the various sacrificial implements on the dead body. He gives order: light the fires together. If the *Ahavaniya* fire reaches the body first, he should know, "It has reached him in the heaven-world. He will live there in prosperity, and so will this one, i.e., his son, in this world," etc. While the body is burning he shall recite over it, "Go on, go on, on the ancient paths." (R.V. 10.14.7) After reciting the verse: "These living ones have separated from the dead" (R.V. 10.18.3), they turn round from right to left, and go away without looking back. When they come to a place where there is standing water, they plunge into it and emerge from it, pour out one handful of water, pronouncing the *gotra* name and the proper name of the dead person; they go out of water, wring out old garments and put on other garments. They enter their homes when still a part of the sun is seen; following the order, the younger ones first, the older ones last. At the house they touch a stone, the fire, cow's dung, fried barley, sesamum seeds, and water. That night they subsist only on bought or ready-made food. No saline food for three nights; for twelve nights they avoid distribution of gifts and the study of the Vedas.

The gathering of bones is performed after the tenth day from the death. The performer of the ceremony walks three times round the spot with his left side turned towards it and sprinkles on it with a śamī branch milk mixed with the urn, and places water. He puts the bones in the urn and places the urn in a pit. Having covered the urn with a lid, all should leave the place without looking back, bathe in water, and perform the *śrāddha* for the deceased.

A *śrāddha* ceremony is celebrated on the Parvan Day (New Moon Day), or for the attainment of special wishes, or when there happened some good luck, or for the *śrāddha* directed to a single dead person. The brāhmans, endowed with learning, moral character and correct conduct, who have been invited, are made to sit down, after their bath, washing of their feet and sipping of water. They sit down as representatives of the Fathers, with their faces turned to the north, one for each one of the Fathers, or two or three for each. The larger their number, the greater the reward for the sacrificer. Having given to the brāhmans water, double-folded darbha blades and a seat, again water; having poured water into three vessels over which he has put darbha grass, and having recited over the water the mantra: For luck and help the divine waters (R.V. 10.9.4), he pours sesamum seeds into it with the formula: "Sesamum art thou; Soma is thy deity; at the Gosava sacrifice[59] thou hast been created by the gods. By the ancients thou hast been offered. Through the funeral oblation render the Fathers and these worlds propitious to us. Svadhā! Adoration".

The performer offers with the left hand or with the right, the Arghya water to the Fathers with the words: Father, this is thy Arghya. Grandfather, this is thy Arghya, etc., having first offered ordinary water to the Fathers. Then he hands over the Arghya water[60] to the brāhmans who represent the Fathers. He recites the verse

59 Gosava sacrifice is a cow sacrifice.

60 *Arghya* water is water offered at the respectful reception of a guest.

over the Arghya water: "The celestial waters which have been produced on the earth, the aerial waters and the waters which are terrestrial, the gold-coloured ones, apt for the sacrifice, may these waters bring us luck and be kind to us." He moistens his face with the water left over, if he desires a son to be born to him. Then gifts of perfumes, garlands, incense, lights, and clothes are offered to the brāhmans. Taking some food, besmearing it with ghee, he asks the brāhmans permission by saying, "I shall offer it in the fire", or "I will sacrifice my offering in the fire". The permission is given by the words "offer it", and he then sacrifices in the fire. The brāhman says, "The mouth of the gods verily is the fire, the mouth of the Fathers is the hand" Then food is offered with the words: "What is given away and offered, that brings prosperity." When they have eaten and enjoyed, he should offer the remaining to the brāhmans. Then the spit-ox sacrifice is offered to Rudra.

V) Vishnu Smṛti (Vaishṇava Dharma Śāstra)[61]

A dead man shall be carried out by his own son who is equal in caste to the dead man. For instance, a member of the twice-born caste cannot be carried out by a śūdra though he be a kinsman of the dead.

After having carried out a dead man and burnt his corpse, the relatives or others shall walk round the pile from left to right, and then plunge into water, dressed in their clothes. After having offered a libation of water to the dead, they must place one ball of rice on blades of kuśa grass; they have to repeat this ceremony everyday during the period of impurity. Then having changed their dress, they must bite Nimba leaves between their teeth, and having stepped upon the stone threshold, they must enter the house. Then they must throw unbroken grains into the fire. On the fourth day they must collect the bones that have been left and throw them into water from the Ganges. As many bones of a man are contained in the water of the Ganges, so many thousands of years will he reside in heaven.

61 Chapter XIX ff.; S.B.E. Vol. 7, pp. 75 ff.

They must eat food which has been bought, or which they have received unsolicited; they must not eat meat. They must sleep on the ground, separately. Once the impurity is over, they must walk forth from the village, have their beards shaved, and having cleansed themselves with a paste of sesamum or of mustard-seed, they must change their dress and re-enter the house. There after reciting a propitiatory prayer, they must honour the brāhmans. The gods are invisible deities; the brāhmans are visible deities; when the visible gods are pleased, the invisible gods are surely pleased as well.

Every creature is seized upon by Kāla (Time) and carried into the other world. It is the slave of its action in a previous birth. Why then should one wail on its death? Those who are born are sure to die, and those who have died are sure to be reborn. This is inevitable, and no associate can follow a man in his passage through mundane existence. Since mourning will not help the dead in this world, the relatives should not weep but perform the obsequies to the best of their ability. Both his good and bad actions will follow the dead man after death like associates; there is no use mourning for him. But as long as his relatives remain impure, the departed spirit finds no rest and returns to visit his relatives who are bound to offer up to him the funeral ball of rice and the water libation. Until the performance of *Sapindikarana*[62] the dead man remains a disembodied spirit and is afflicted with hunger and thirst. *Sapiṇḍikarana* takes place when at the end of the year the relative gives food to the brāhmans, after having fed the gods first, in honour of the deceased and of his father, grandfather, and great grandfather. Until this rite is performed, the performer of the rite has to give the dead man rice and a jar with water. After the performance of the *Sapiṇḍikarana* the dead man passes into the abode of the Manes and enjoys his portion of the *śrāddha* in the shape of celestial food. Therefore his relatives have to offer him the *śrāddha*. Whether he has become a god, or stays in hell, or has entered the body of an animal, or of a human being, he will receive the *śrāddha* offered by

62 *Sapiṇḍikarana* or *sapiṇḍana* from *sapiṇḍa*, 'having the same piṇḍa (ball of food), a kinsman connected by the offering of the balls of food to certain deceased ancestors at the śrāddha ceremony; the kinship is through six generations in an ascending and descending line.

his relatives. Both the departed spirit and the performer of the *śrāddha* will benefit by it.

Virtue alone will follow the dead man wherever he goes. Therefore do your duty unflinchingly in this wretched world. Tomorrow's business should be done today and the afternoon's business in the forenoon; for death will not wait whether a man has done it or not. Time (Kāla) is no one's friend and no one's enemy. When the effects of his acts in the previous birth by which his present existence is caused, has expired, he snatches a man away forcibly.

Even as a calf finds his mother among a thousand cows, an act formerly done is sure to find the perpetrator. The self of man is immaterial and immutable. Hence, one should not grieve for the destruction of his body.

The first *śrāddha* takes place thus. When the impurity is over, the relative of the dead bathes, washes his hands and feet, sips water, and proceeds to bestow gifts upon brāhmans who have been invited, and who have cleansed themselves in the same way. These gifts are perfumes, garlands, clothes and other things; after giving these he entertains them hospitably.

At the *śrāddha* for one recently dead, he should refer to the dead person directly in the mantra thus: "This is your share, father, etc." He should offer a ball of rice, calling out at the same time the dead person's name. Let him offer water to the brāhmans, having called out the dead person's name. Let him make three oblations of boiled rice in each of the three fires which have been lighted, saying,

> "Svadhā and reverence to Soma, accompanied by the Manes,
> Svadhā and reverence to Agni, who conveys the oblations addressed to the Manes,
> Svadhā and reverence to Yama Angiras".

Then let him offer balls of rice as before. After having filled the three trenches with rice, sour milk, clarified butter, honey, and meat, let him mutter: "This is for you."

This ceremony has to be repeated every month on the day of his death. At the end of the year let him give food to the brāhmans, after having fed the gods first, in honour of the deceased. As he pours water for washing the feet and the water libation destined for the deceased, into vessels, he must mutter the mantra: "May earth unite thee" [with the ancestors] and "United your minds". Near the leavings he must place four balls of rice.

4. The Teaching of the Mahābhārata on Death

The solution to the problem of birth and death is one of the constant motifs in the myths of world religions and the *Mahābhārata* attempts to give an explanation of it in the spirit of Hinduism of its epoch. First we shall give a brief account of the myth of the origin of death and then the philosophical explanation of the origin of death that the great Epic indicates to us.

(1) The myth of the creation of death occurs in the Droṇa Parvan.[63] The context is that Yudhisṭhira is struck with sorrow by the death of Abhimanyu and that Vyāsa consoles him by recounting how Nārada comforted Akampana in a time of bereavement by the story of how Death was originally created and commissioned. In the beginning Brahma created all beings. Endowed with mighty energy he saw that the creation bore no signs of decay. He was dejected at this thought of not seeing the end of creation and became angry. And in consequence of his anger a fire sprang from the sky and spread in all directions and began to consume everything of the universe. Seeing this Rudra went to him and requested him to check this wrathful deed. Brahma accepted this request of Rudra and contracted the whole of the fire into his own body. While he was doing so, there came out from the doors of his diverse senses a damsel who was dark, red and tawny; and her tongue, mouth and the eyes also were red in colour. Brahma called her by the name Mrtyu (Death) and told her that she was produced for the sake of destroying the people. The lady on the other hand was sorry to hear about her task and began to weep. She said to Brahma: "How can I do such a cruel and evil act, knowing it to be cruel and evil? I fear unrighteousness greatly. I will not be able to take away the dear life-breaths of living creatures weeping in sorrow". Brahma gathered in his hands the tears that came from her eyes and consoled her and bade her again to destroy living beings.

---

63 Mahabharata 7.52-54; also 12.256 ff. Gr. ed. 248 ff.).

She however took leave of Brahma, went to Dhenuka and practised severe penance. Brahma again appeared before her and asked her the reason of her severe penance. She implored him to set her free from the cruel and sinful obligation of destroying living beings. Brahma said: "You shall commit no sin by slaying these creatures. Eternal virtue shall always be yours. That Regent of the world, viz., Yama, and the diverse diseases shall become your help-mates". To which she replied: "Listen however to what I say. Let covetousness, wrath, malice, jealousy, quarrel, folly and shamelessness, and other stern passions tear the bodies of all embodied creatures". Brahma finally said: "It will be as you say. Sin shall not be yours. Your tear-drops that are in my hands will become diseases, springing from living creatures themselves. If they will kill men then sin will not be yours. Casting off both desire and wrath, take the life of all living creatures. Death agreed to Rudra's request and began to take away the life of creatures, when the time came for their dissolution.

The concluding remarks of Vyāsa to Yudhisṭhira are worth noting. "Death has been ordained by the Creator himself for all creatures. When their hour comes, creatures are destroyed duly. The death of creatures arises from the creatures themselves. Creatures kill themselves. Death doth not kill anyone, armed with her bludgeon. Therefore they that are wise, truly knowing death to be inevitable, because ordained by Brahma himself, never grieve for creatures that are dead". The lady - Death - appears to be purposely thought of to give the idea of how reluctantly the destruction of life has to be done as a duty and no cruelty should be thought of in the action of death which is a necessity for creation to continue.

When Gautamī's son died in consequence of having been bitten by a serpent, an angry fowler bound the serpent with a string and wanted to kill it.[64] In the conversation that took place between Gautamī, the fowler, the serpent and Death, it is clearly illustrated that man's fate is due solely to his *karma* (action). Gautamī said: "By killing this serpent this my boy will not be restored to life, and by letting it live no harm will be caused to you... The death of the boy was predestined; therefore I am unable to approve of the destruc-

---

64 Ibid. 13.1 ff.

tion of this serpent". The serpent said: "I have no will of my own, and I am not independent. Death sent me on this errand. By his direction have I bitten this child, and not out of any anger or choice on my part. Therefore if there be any sin in this, O fowler, the sin is his". Death intervened to say that guided by Kāla he sent the serpent on this errand and that hence he was not the cause of this child's death. Kāla concluded the whole conversation by saying: "Neither Death, nor this serpent nor I am guilty of the death of any creature. We are merely the immediate exciting causes of the event. The *karma* of this child formed the exciting cause of our action in this matter... The child was killed as a result of its own *karma*. It has met death as the result of its *karma* in the past. We are all subject to the influence of our respective *karma*. *Karma* is an aid to salvation even as sons are, and *karma* also is an indicator of virtue and vice in man."

(2) As regards the nature of death the *Mahābhārata* teaches that the dissolution of the elements at death does not mean dissolution of the indwelling self *(jīva)*, which never dies, although it is invisible.[65] There is no destruction of the living creature, or of what is given, or of our other acts. The creature that dies only goes into another form. The body alone dissolves away. That which is called death is only the dissolution of the body. The Soul, wrapped in diverse forms, migrates from form to form, unseen and unnoticed by others. Death means the flight from the body of something that is different from the body.[66] When all are equal in death why should human beings, whose understandings are always deceived by the things of this world covet one another's rank and position? The learned say that the bodies of men are like houses. In time these are destroyed. There is one being, however, that is eternal. As a person, casting off one attire, whether old or new, wears another, even such is the case with the bodies of all embodied beings. Creatures obtain weal or woe as the fruit of their own acts... Creatures are born or destroyed according to their acts in previous lives. When such is the course of the world, why do you then indulge in grief? ... They that are wise, observant of virtue, and desirous of doing good unto all living creatures, they, acquainted with the real

65 Ibid. 11.3; 12.185 ff.218.
66 Ibid. 11.3.

nature of the appearance of creatures in this world, attain at last to the highest end".

(3) It is interesting to read the description of how death comes to a man, as given in the celebrated episode of Sāvitrī.[67] The sage Markandeya comforts Yudhisṭhira and other Pāndava princes during their exile in the forest by relating to them Sāvitrī's story of how she succeeded in delivering her huband from the fetters of Yama, the God of death. The death of a just man, Satyavant, her husband, is narrated thus:

> Then, in company with his wife, he energetically gathered fruits until he had filled a pot, then set to chopping wood. Then, as he was splitting the wood, a sweat broke out on him, and from his strenuous exertion there arose a pain in his head. And oppressed by weariness, he came and said to his dear wife: "Sāvitrī, from my exertion a pain has come in my head, and my limbs and heart ache. Lady of measured speech, I seem to be far from well. I feel that this head of mine is being pierced with sharp stakes, as it were. I wish to sleep, sweet one, I have no power to stand".
>
> Then Sāvitrī made her husband sit close to her, and sat down on the ground herself, taking him in her arms, and laying his head in her lap. Then, as the pious lady continued to ponder the prophecy of Nārada, she concluded that this was the very day, hour and minute. All of a sudden she saw a man, wearing a yellow garment and a turban. He was handsome, like to the sun in brilliance. His skin was clear, yet dark; his eyes red; in his hand he held a noose; he was terrifying; and he stood beside Satyavant looking down at him. When she saw him, she gently placed her husband's head on the ground, and quickly rose to her feet, and with hands clasped in reverence she addressed him, distressed and with trembling heart.
>
> Sāvitrī: "I recognise you to be divine. This form is not human. Tell me, I pray, who you are, and what the deed which you wish to do."
>
> Yama: "You are a faithful wife, Sāvitrī, and rich in penance. Therefore, I speak to you. Know me, fair lady, to be Yama.

67 Ibid. 3.293-99.

> This your husband, prince Satyavant, has finished his allotted span of life. I shall bind him and carry him off. Know that this is the task for which I have come."
> Thus speaking, the King of the Departed, the Blessed One, for her favour proceeded to tell her duly all that he was about to do. "This man is righteous and beautiful, an ocean of virtues. It would not be fitting for my servants to fetch him. Therefore I have come myself." Then Yama drew forth by main force from the body of Satyavant a man the size of a thumb, bound with the noose, and completely in his power.
> Then his body became motionless and sorrowful to look upon, the life drawn forth, the breathing stopped, the lustre destroyed. And when he had thus bound him, Yama set out with his face towards the south, followed by Sāvitrī[68]".

By her love and wisdom Sāvitrī recovers her husband's life from Yama after it had been taken. As Sāvitrī persistently follows Yama, he grants her various boons except the life of her husband, but finally yields to her importunities and restores the soul to the lifeless body of Satyavant.

The death of Droṇa is again an illustration of the last moments of a holy man.[69] Droṇa, informed falsely by Yudhisṭhira that his son Asvatthaman had been killed, grows weak rapidly in fighting; he sinks into yoga and his spirit ascends to heaven. The description of this moment is instructive: "As regards Droṇa himself, abandoning his weapons, he was then in a supremely tranquil state. Having said those words he had devoted himself to yoga. Endowed with great effulgence and possessed of high ascetic merit, he had fixed his heart on that Supreme and Ancient Being, viz., Vishṇu. Bending his face slightly down, and heaving his breast forward, and closing his eyes, and resting on the quality of goodness, and disposing his heart to contemplation, and thinking on the monosyllabe Om, representing Brahman, and remerbering the puissant, supreme, and indestructible God of gods, the radiant Droṇa of high ascetic merit, the preceptor (of the Kurus and pāṇdavas) repaired to heaven that is so difficult of being attained even by the pious"[70].

---

68 Ibid. 3.297.

69 Ibid. 7.192.

70 Ibid.

(4) Funeral obsequies and *śrāddha* rites: in the *Mahābhārata* we find on the occasion of the deaths of illustrious persons narratives which describe funeral obsequies and *śrāddha* ceremonies.

After Pāṇdu's death funeral rites were performed. "Celebrate the funeral ceremonies of Pāṇdu and of Madri in right royal style. For the good of their souls distribute cattle, clothes, gems and diverse kinds of wealth, every one receiving as much as he asks for. Make arrangements also for Kunti's performing the last rites of Madri in such a style as pleases her. Let Madri's body be so carefully wrapped up that neither the sun nor Vayu (god of wind) may behold it. Lament not for the sinless Pāṇdu. He was a worthy king and has left behind him five heroic sons equal unto the celestials themselves ... Then Vidura fixed upon a sacred spot for the funeral rites of Pāṇdu. The family priests went out of the city without loss of time, carrying with them the blazing sacred fire fed with clarified butter and rendered fragrant therewith. Then friends, relatives, and adherents, wrapping it up in cloth, decked the body of the monarch with the flowers of the season and sprinkled various excellent perfumes over it. And they also decked the hearse itself with garlands and rich hangings. Then placing the covered body of the king with that of his queen on that excellent bier decked out so brightly, they caused it to be carried on human shoulders. With the white umbrella (of state) held over the hearse with waving yak-tails and sounds of various musical instruments, the whole scene looked bright and grand. (Hundreds of people, of all the four castes followed)... The priests poured libations of clarified butter on the sacred fire blazing in an ornamental vessel. The people loudly wailed, saying: O prince, where do you go, leaving us behind, and making us forlorn and wretched for ever? At last they came to a wood on the banks of the Gaṅga. There they laid down the hearse... brought water in many golden vessels, washed the prince's body besmeared before with several kinds of fragrant paste, and dressed it in a white dress... When the other funeral ceremonies also were finished in consonance with the directions of the priests, the Kauravas set fire to the dead bodies of the king and the queen, bringing lotuses, sandalpaste, and other fragrant substances to the pyre. Then seeing the bodies aflame, Kausalya burst out: O my son, my son! All wept from grief and affection for their king... And people began to console the bereaved sons of Pāṇdu. The Pāṇdavas with their friends began to sleep on the ground, and all the citizens passed twelve days in mourning with the weeping Pāṇḍavas.[71]

Then Bhīsma and Kunti with their friends celebrated the *śrāddha* of the deceased monarch, and offered the *piṇḍa*. And they feasted the Kauravas and thousands of brāhmans unto whom also gave gems and lands. Then citizens returned to Hastināpura with the sons of Pāṇḍu, now that they had been cleansed from the impurity incident to the demise of their father. All then fell to weeping for the departed king. It seemed as if they had lost one of their own kin"[72].

The funeral rites for the slain in the war were performed thus. "Vidura and others, procuring sandal, aloe and other kinds of wood used on such occasions as also clarified butter and oil and perfumes and costly silken robes and other kinds of cloth, and large heaps of dry wood... caused funeral pyres to be duly made and lighted and then without haste burnt with due rites the slain kings in proper order. They properly burnt upon those fires that blazed forth with libations of clarified butter in torrents over them the bodies of the kings... The pitṛi-medha rites in honour of some of the illustrious dead were performed there, while some sang Sāmas and Ṛiks, and some uttered lamentations for the dead. The mourners proceeded towards the river Gaṅga, cast off their ornaments and upper garments. Crying, the Kuru ladies offered oblations of water unto their dear and near ones who are dead. Conversant with duties, they also performed the water-rite in honour of their friends.[73]

Bhīsma's death and the cremation rites for him are vividly portrayed thus. "The life-breaths of Bhīsma, piercing through the crown of his head, shot up through the welkin like a large meteor and soon became invisible. Even thus did he unite himself with eternity. Then the Pāṇdavas taking a large quantity of wood and diverse kinds of fragrant scents, made a funeral pyre. Then Yudhisṭhira and Vidura wrapped Bhīsma's body with silken cloth and floral garlands... The Pitṛi sacrifice of the high-souled Bhīsma was then duly performed. Many libations were poured upon the sacred fire. The singers of Sāmans sang many Sāmans. Then cove-

71 Ibid. 1.127.
72 Ibid. 1.128.
73 Ibid. 11.26.

ring the body of Bhīsma with sandal wood and black aloe and the bark wood, other fragrant fuel, and setting fire to the same, the Kauravas thus cremated his body... All the mourners arrived at the sacred river Gaṅga and duly offered oblation of water unto the dead. The goddess Bhagīrathi rose up from the Gaṅga and lamented very bitterly the death of her son. Krishṅa consoled her by saying "Thy son has in felicity gone to heaven. Do not grieve for him"[74].

Dhṛitarāshtra, as he took formal farewell of his subjects before retiring to the forest, performs a costly *śrāddha* for his deceased sons. "He gave the rich gifts away for the advancement of the dead, naming each of them in the order as the gifts were made. With the approval of Yudhisṭhira, that śrāddha sacrifice became characterised by large gifts of wealth and profuse presents of jewels and gems and other kinds of treasure. At the command of the king, gifts were made to people. (Even today on occasions of *śrāddhas,* gifts are made in a similar way. Instead of dedicating each gift with mantras and water and making it over to the receiver, all the articles are assembled in a heap and are dedicated with the aid of mantras. The superintendent calls out the receiver and the scribe notes it down). It was in this way that the king performed *śrāddhas* for the advancement in the other world of his sons and grandsons and Pitrus as also of himself and Gandhari.[75]

At the news of the death of Dhṛitarāshtra, Gandhari and Kunti, Yudhishthira ordered funeral obsequies to be carried out in their name. "All the Pandava brothers went out to the banks of the Gaṅga, every one clad in only single piece of raiment. Then all, having plunged into the stream, began to offer oblations of water unto the dead, mentioning each separately by name, and their families. Having finished those rites that cleanse the living, they came back but without entering their capital took up their residence outside of it. They also dispatched a number of trusted people to the place where the king died in order to perform the cremation rites of the dead. On the twelfth day the king, properly purified, duly performed the *śrāddhas* of his deceased relations, which were characterised by gifts in abundance"[76].

74 Ibid. 13.168.
75 Ibid. 15.11-14.
76 Ibid 15.37-39

5. The Teaching of the Bhagavad-gītā on Death

Since the spiritual self of man is eternal and immortal, it cannot be born or die and is above the process of becoming. But the self in as far as it is associated with the bodily conditions (the individual psycho-somatic mechanism) it is embodied and as such is said to be born and dying over and over again until it is ultimately released from the cycle of rebirth.[77]

> "For the death of all that is born is certain, as also is certain the birth of all that dies: so in a matter that no one can prevent you should not grieve.
> The beginnings of contingent beings are unmanifest; their middle course (their empirical life) is manifest; their ends are again unmanifest: what cause then for mourning here"[78].

Speaking of a dead person, the *Mābabhārata* observes, "He has come from the unseen *(adarśana),* and has gone back to the unseen. He is not thine, nor thou his. Why this vain lamentation?"[79] Krishṅa speaks of the two paths that are open to the soul at death.

> "Fire, light, day, [the moon's] light (fortnight), the six months of the [sun's] northern course, -dying in these knowers of Brahman go to Brahman.
> Smoke, night, [the moon's] dark (fortnight), the six months of the [sun's] southern course, -[dying] in these the yogi wins the light of the moon, and back he comes again"[80].

When men die at a time in the year that befits their own self-made destiny, they pass to the worlds of Brahman by way of the gods *(Devāyāna)* or to the moon by way of the Fathers *(pitṛiyāna)* in accordance with the merit or demerit of their deeds and knowledge and loving devotion.[81]

---

77 Bhagavad-gita 2.12-13.

78 Ibid. 2.27-28.

79 11.213.

80 Bhagavad-gita 8.24-25.

81 See Chand. Up. 5.10.1-6 and Brh. Up. 6.2.14-15.

Krishṅa instructs Arjuna of the supreme importance of one's last thoughts at the hour of death, for they in fact will determine one's future existence. The dead man's thoughts should be fixed on God, the highest Person, or on the Imperishable; this alone will release him from rebirth.

> "Whoso at the last hour, leaving his body, remembers me and passes on, come to my being; there is no doubt about this.
> Whatever state a man may remember when at the end he abandons his body, to that state he goes, for ever does that state make him grow into itself ...
> For if you fix your mind and soul on me, you will no doubt come to me. With thought integrated by spiritual exercise and constant striving, and seeking no other resort, let a man meditate on the divine exalted Person; he then goes to that Person. With mind unwavering at the time of passing on, integrated by love of God and by the spiritual exercise, forcing the breath between the eyebrows duly, this man will go to that divine exalted Person...
> Repeating Om, the Brahman, the One imperishable (or 'in one syllable,) let him keep me in mind then when he departs, leaving aside his body, he will tread the highest way"[82].

Every man becomes what he worships. The worshippers of the gods go to them; those who worship the Fathers will go to them in their realm. The worship itself depends on the nature of action one performs and of the faith one shows in worship. Those who worship Krishṅa with loving devotion, being fully integrated and possessing of knowledge, will go to Krishna and participate in his mode of being. When the moment of death approaches, a man is haunted by the thought of that object alone on which his mind has dwelt most deeply in the course of his life. Hence one should think of Krishṅa again and again in life; performing his duties in disinterested spirit he shall meditate on Krishna, keeping his mind and undestanding on Him; then at the hour of death he will attain Him, his mind ever fixed on Him alone.

---

82 Bhagavad-gita 8.2-13.

6. The Purāṇic Idea of Death

The Purāṇas contain legends that reflect the thinking of the Hindu people of their period on death and its meaning. Each of the Purāṇas extols one Deity as the most Supreme God and subordinates all others to him. Thus Śiva or Vishṇu takes the position of the Supreme God to whom Yama, the god of death, is subordinate, and who prevails over the powers of the fetters of Yama. The Purāṇas propose and insist on love of God *(bhakti)* as the only way to solve the problem of living and dying. The cycle of rebirth is an endless process, without beginning and end, and only a few liberated persons could escape from the fetters of time which is cyclic. Although time is the ultimate destroyer, it is the quality of the actions of a man's past life that determines the quality and status of his present life and so the process of rebirth goes on, death after death. We have the story of the king Nṛga which illustrates this.[83] The sons of Krishna went out to play in the forest and came across a huge lizard in a certain well. They wanted to rescue it by raising it but failed to do so, for the lizard was too big and heavy to be lifted. When Krishna heard of it, he came and raised it without effort with his left hand, The lizard assumed the form of a god. On inquiry from Krishna, the king related his own story. "I am king Nṛga of the line of Iksvatu. My charities knew no bounds and they have become proverbial. One cow belonging to a Brāhman got mixed with my cattle and, without knowing that, I gave her to another Brāhman. While he was taking away the cow, the owner found her out. The two Brāhmans quarrelled and they came to me. They said: you are a giver as well as taker. I became surprised and, when the facts were known, I offered one lakṣa of cows for the return of the mistaken cow. One of them however said: I am not going to take a gift from the king. The other said: I do not wish for other cows even if they be ten lakṣa. They both went away. Then the messengers of Yama came and carried me away. Yama said: I see no end of your merits and the places acquired by them. Do you prefer to suffer for your demerit first or to enjoy those heavenly things? I accepted the first choice and down I fell as a lizard into this well. See

83 Bhagavata Purana 10.64. See also 1.13.46-50; 5.26.38.

how I have suffered for taking a Brāhman's property. The king then thanked Krishna for his favour and ascended to heaven. Krishna then made a discourse to his followers to explain how iniquitous it was to take a Brāhman's property even unconsciously.

Yama, the god of death, appears gracious and gentle to a man of good actions, and terrible and fearsome to unrighteous man. Yama as righteousness *(dharma)* is a fair and impartial judge. The general Purāṇic teaching is that the man who has no loving devotion to his Supreme God will be caught up in the cycle of rebirth which is governed by the law of *karma* and impartially ruled by Yama, the god of death. When a man dies, Yama's attendants claim the soul of the dead. The *Śiva Purāna* gives a description of this naked soul which hungers, thirsts and experiences a burning sensation all over:

> "At places the path is strewn with sharp thorns, at places it is full of sand, elsewhere it is full of pebbles sharp like the razor-edge. In other places it is full of deep irregular chasms and canyons, elsewhere, of rugged lumps of clay; of burning sands here and sharp spikes there.
> Different places are invested with different terrible beasts of prey such as lions, wolves, tigers and huge pythons or terrible mosquitoes or huge leeches.
> The persons who go that way are tortured and harassed by big boars digging and butting against the path with their sharp fangs, buffaloes with sharp horns, all sorts of beasts of prey, terrible evil spirits like Dakinis, horrible Raksasas and pernicious diseases.
> They go on, burnt and scorched by lightning falls and pierced through by heavy showers of arrows.
> They cry when heavy showers of dust envelop them. They tremble with fear ever and anon at the terrible rumbling sounds of massive clouds.
> They shrink and wither when oppressed by the rough and chill wind all round"[84].

It is precisely the love of God *(bhakti)* that can release the soul

84 Siva Purana, Umasamhita 7.9-25.

from the inexorable fetters of Yama, i.e., from the cycle of rebirth, and enable the soul to attain to the abode of the Supreme God, Vishṇu or Śiva. Time as the symbol of destructive life process is subject to Almighty God who can by his grace free the soul from the cycle of rebirth. The God-lovers take a positive attitude toward death; they are deeply convinced that they will reach God's eternal abode (Vishṇu's Vaikuṇṭha or Śiva's Kailāsa) through their love *(bhakti)* without passing through the cycle of rebirth and the fetters of Yama and his attendants. The legend of Devarāja illustrates the remarkable power of the even accidental love of God:

> "In the small city of Kiratas lived a poor brāhmin named Devarāja who was unusually ignorant for someone of his social and spiritual rank. Opposite to the demands of his profession, he worshipped none of the gods and engaged in selling forbidden liquors.
>
> Devarāja forgot his daily prayers, deceived the persons with whom he dealt and gained an immense fortune through his deceitfulness in business. Furthermore, being ignorant of his duty, he did not use any of his wealth for virtuous causes.
>
> Once when bathing in a lake, Devarāja was sexually aroused by a prostitute named Sobhāvatī who had also come to bathe. Mistaking his infatuation for love, the wealthy brāhmin Devarāja asked Sobhāvatī to be his wife. Recognizing the increased status and wealth such a marriage would afford her, Sobhāvatī agreed.
>
> Engaged in amourous play for days on end, the newly weds flaunted all conventions ascribed for a householder brāhmin... He spurned the admonitions of his first wife, his mother and his father. He became so enraged that he killed his first wife, his mother and his father and took their possessions... He was the most degenerate of all brāhmins.
>
> While travelling in an unfamiliar place, Devarāja just by chance, passed a Śiva temple where men were congregating for daily instruction and prayer. Feeling ill, he stopped and was treated for a fever which had gripped him. While lying in a feverish state, he overheard a discourse on Śiva by a temple priest.
>
> After a month of suffering, Devarāja died from the fever. At the

> moment of death he was bound with nooses by Yama's attendants and forcefully dragged toward Yama's abode. Meanwhile Śiva's army, gleaming white from the sacred ashes of the burial grounds, with tridents in their hands, rushed to Yama's city and intercepted Yama's attendants and took Devarāja from them....
> Yama did not question Śiva's servants but honored Śiva's name and offered him adoration. Receiving Yama's blessings, Śiva's army with Devarāja departed for Kailāsa where Devarāja was received by the merciful Śiva"[85].

The story of Devarāja is an extreme example to demonstrate the power of loving devotion to God. There are also stories to show the contrary; namely, that some who were devotees but failed in loving devotion to God at the last moment had to undergo suffering and misery. All this intends to teach that liberation from fetters is effected only by God's grace. Without love of God, in the *bhakti* religions, continuous births and rebirths follow for the man who has no faith in God and relies on himself. Death is a terror for him. Sought after by the messengers of Yama those who lack love of God are caught up in the round of births and deaths.

7. Conclusion

Let us condense in brief the Hindu funeral rites as they are described in the sacred texts. The dead man is washed and annointed; the hair and the beard are cut off and the nails are closely trimmed. The dead is freshly clothed, garlanded, and carried, either in men's arms or on a cart, to the cremation ground. The procession, carrying fires at the head, consists of relatives and mourners with loosened hair. The footprints of the party are wiped out by means of a bundle of twigs tied to the corpse, so as to prevent the recurrence of the spirit of the dead. During the procession are repeated verses, which urge the dead to join the ancestral spirits and Yama, to leave sin behind, to avoid the dogs of Yama; some other formulas drive evil spirits away from the dead. The body is then laid on

85 See Siva Purana, introduction 2.11-36.

funeral pyre, situated in the midst of three fires. The widow is placed beside him, but she is soon asked to rise again with the words: "Arise, O woman, to the world of the living; departed is the life of him with whom thou liest; to marriage here hast thou attained with him as husband who graspeth thy hand." Here the husband's brother or some other (a pupil or aged servant) is meant to take the place of her dead husband. If the dead is a kshatriya, the bow is taken from his hand; in the case of a brāhman, the instruments of the sacrifice are placed on the pyre. A cow or a goat is burnt with the corpse to satisfy the dogs of Yama. The pyre is then lighted and Agni is invoked to take the dead safe to the ancestors. Other prayers and offerings are addressed to Yama, the Aṅgirases, and Sarasvati. The meaning of the ceremony is clear from the words of the prayer: "From him thou art born; may he in turn be born from thee."

Then follows the departure of the mourners who do not turn round; the relatives perform purificatory rites *(asaucha).* Namely, they bathe and offer libations of water for the dead, and change their clothes, sleep on the ground and refrain from eating flesh, etc. The fire of the dead man is taken out of the house otherwise than through the door. On the night after death a cake is offered to the dead, and a libation of water is poured out; a vessel with milk and water is also placed in the open air and the dead man is called upon to bathe in it. The third or tenth day is that of collecting the bones of the dead. The remains of the dead are taken before sunrise far from the village to a place free of thorny plants. The bones are placed in the ground, covered with stones and earth. Water and milk are poured in the place. Then the performers go away, not turning back, purify themselves and offer a *śrāddha* to the dead.

The *śrāddha* is complimentary to the funeral rites for the purpose of transforming the "dead", a vague and harmful spirit, into a "father", a strong and friendly ancestor. The *śrāddha* rite takes place usually on the day of the new moon after midday. It consists of offering of balls of food *(piṇḍa).* The brāhmans carefully chosen (usually three) represent the Fathers, i.e., the direct ancestors. The master of the house gives them food and gifts and honours them like fathers.

Funeral rites close the concluding chapter of a Hindu's one earthly life. During his life he consecrates his earthly life by performing diverse rites at the various stages of his growth. At his leaving from this world, his survivors consecrate his death for his future happiness in his next life. A Hindu text says: "It is well-known that through the sacraments after the birth one conquers this earth; through the sacraments after the death the heaven".

In the *Mahābhārata karma* is the cause of death, for every man meets with death as a result of his *karma* in the past. Death is merely a dissolution of the body; the self never dies but migrates from one body to another as a consequence of its past good or bad actions. The *Bhagavad-gītā* instructs people to direct the thoughts at the hour of death on God and meditate on Him in order to obtain salvation from rebirth. Those who love God during their life, especially at the time of death go to Him and participate in His mode of being. The Purāṇas again propose love of God *(bhakti)* which alone prevails over the powers of Yama's fetters. Although time is the ultimate destroyer, it is the quality of one's actions in the past that determine the present life and future life in the process of rebirth. From this inexorable cycle of rebirth it is the discipline of knowledge *(jnāna)* and love of God *(bhakti)* that enable one to attain to the abode of God. The God-lovers are confident of their final salvation because of God's grace which is infallible and efficacious. In the non-dualist trend of Hinduism death is a mere passage for the liberated man in life *(jivanmukta)* to leave the body and be totally identified with the Absolute *(Brahman)*.

APPENDIX 1
The ritual of the fathers in the Garuḍa Purāṇa

The second part of the *Garuḍa Purāṇa* forms the Pretakalpa (ritual of the dead). It contains discourses on the speculations, beliefs and practices concerning death and the destiny of the dead in relation to the world which he has left and to the world in which he arrives. An extract of this Kalpa has been compiled by Naunidhirama under the title of *Sāroddhara* ("extract of the substance" of Pretakalpa).[86] I am translating the section that describes the ritual of the Fathers or Ma-

86 The Uttarakhanda of Garuda Purana (35 chapters) forms the Pretakalpa, abridged under the title Sāroddhara.

nes, as contained in the 13th chapter, verses 2-126 of the Sāroddhara.

2) Listen, I am going to explain to you the whole rite *sapindana*, thanks to which [the dead], ceasing to carry the name of *preta*, enters into the class of Fathers.

3) Those whose funeral rice-ball has not been mixed with that of *Śiva* and other ancestors[87] cannot draw a part of the various gifts made by their sons.

4) If the son remains always impure, they are never purified. If the *sapinda* ceremony does not take place, impurity does not go away.

5) Therefore the son ought to perform the *sapinda* at the end of the period of impurity. I shall tell you which is the end of impurity, such that all have to observe.

6) A brāhman is pure at the end of ten days; a kshatriya after twelve days; a vaisya after fifteen days, a śūdra after a month.

7) The *sapinda* relatives are purified from the mortuary impurity in ten days, those of the same family [other than *sapinda* relatives] in three days, those of the same clan by a simple bath.

8) If someone, gone to a foreign country, learns the [death of a relative, his impurity lasts] one day and one night, or the remaining portion of ten days; if he learns of the death after ten days, he is impure for three days; if a year has past, a bath will be sufficient to purify him.

13) [For a child that is dead] before his teeth appeared, the purification is instantaneous; [for a child dead between the appearance of the teeth and] the tonsure, purification takes place the night following [the death]; up to the taking of the vow (i.e., the *brahmacarya*), it takes place at the end of three days; further [after the taking of vow] at the end of ten days.

14) If a daughter dies between birth and tonsure, purification is instantaneous, whatever be the caste.

15) From this up to the verbal promise [of the engaged] after one day; for an adult woman, at the end of three days: such is the rule.

16) When the verbal promise has taken place, a lapse of three days is incombant on the father and the to-be-spouse; if [the daughters] have been already given [in marriage] on the husband alone.

---

87 The father and the three ancestors are considered for the circumstance as Siva, Vasu, Rudra and Aditya respectively.

17) If there is a miscarriage in the first six months, the purity for women begins again in as many days as the months of the embryo.

18) After six months impurity lasts according to the rules foreseen for the caste. In the case of miscarriage the *sapinda* relatives are pure instantaneously.

19) During the Kali age, the purification of ten days is enjoined for all castes, both in the case of death and in the case of birth: such is the decision of the Śāstras.

34) The fruit which one derives [from the visit to] all the sacred places, the fruit of [the performance of] all the sacrifices is the same as that which one obtains by performing the *sapindana* on the twelfth day.

35) So then, after having bathed and having smeared with cow dung the place of death, the son will perform *sapindana,* as enjoined in the Śāstras.

36) He renders homage to Visvadevas with water for washing the feet, water for hospitality, and water for rinsing the mouth. For the bad manes he will throw grain, and then touch the water again.

37) He will offer in order the three balls of rice for his grandfather and his two ancestors, who has taken the form of Vasu, Rudra and Arka (Aditya) and a fourth for him who is dead.

38) He will honour them with sandal wood, basil leaves, incense, lamps, good food, perfumes for mouth, beautiful clothes, and other gifts.

39) With the help of a golden stem, he will divide into three the rice ball, then mix each of the parts with the rice balls of the grandfather and of the two ancestors.

49) After having performed *sapindana,* [the son] will offer the libation of water to the ancestors; he will pronounce the invocation svadhā, accompanied by Vedic formulas (mantras).

50) Then he will give to a gueat the offering called *hantakara*[88] to eat, at each time: it is by this that the Fathers, the ascetics, the gods and demons are satisfied.

---

88 *Hantakara* from *hanta,* an exclamation or inceptive particle (expressive of an exhortation to do anything or asking attention, and often translatable as 'come on', 'here', 'see'; in later language it expresses also grief, pity, joy; *hantakara* is the exclamation *hanta* (a particular formula of benediction or salutation).

51) One mouthful alone is alms; four mouthfuls is abundance, and four abundances is *hantakara*.

52) During the *sapindana* [the son] ought to honour a brāhman with sandal and unhusked rice grain, and bring him an imperishable gift so that he be satisfied.

53) He will maintain his spiritual master for a year, giving him butter, food, gold and silver, and a good cow, a horse, elephant, a wagon and a piece of land.

54) Then he will honour by formulas preceded by the svasti benediction, by safran, by unhusked grain and other alimentary gifts, the starks, the goddess (Durga) and Vinayaka (Ganesa).

55) The spiritual master himself will sprinkle him with the formulas, putting the thread around the hand and giving him grains consecrated by the formulas.

56) [The son] will nourish brāhmans with diverse dishes, good and tasteful. He will give them a dozen vessels of water and food, as well as the others there present.

57) Once the brāhmans are nourished, the members of each caste ought to touch water, an arm, a goad and a stick: thus each of them will be made pure.

58) After the *sapindana* has been terminated, one has to put aside the clothes which one wore during the rise: it is with a pure clothe that one has to present the bed.

59) For all the gods, with Indra at the head, exalt the gift of a bed. This is why a gift of a bed is necessary, either at the death [of the father] or even of his living.

81) Greater still than the merit which comes from the visit to all sacred places, at all the days of lunar phase, is the merit which one gains by making the gift of a bed.

97) Now I will tell you the particular rules for the annual and monthly funeral rites, and those for the rite of fifteen days and those for determined days.

98) He who is dead in one of the full moon days, the ceremony for him falls on the fourth day [of the fifteen]; he who is dead on the fourth day the ceremony falls on the ninth day.

99) For him who is dead on the ninth day, it will be the forteenth day; in this case one has to perform the bimonthly funeral rite on the twentieth day.

100) When during a month the sun enters in two stars, the fu-

neral rite valid for two months is performed in the irregular month.

101) When the year counts an intercalary month, the annual rite takes place on the thirteenth month.

102) It is thus that one performs the annual funeral rite at the end of the first year; one will give the brāhmans on this occasion specially food to eat.

107) At the end of the year, one ought always to offer three rice balls in the funeral rite, but one ceases to perform the *ekoddista*[89] rite; if not, one will become the murderer of his fathers.

108) But a funeral rite in a sacred place *(tīrtha)*, a rite at Gayā, a sacrifice to the fathers under the constellation of the Shade of Elephant, ought not to be performed during the year neither during the eclipse nor on the days of *yuga* and others.

109) If the son wishes to perform a funeral rite at Gayā, he will do it after the lapse of a year for the love of his ancestors.

110) By the funeral rite at Gayā the fathers are liberated from the ocean of existences, and by the favour of the carrier of Club (Vishṇu) they would go to the supreme abode.

111) Let him venerate the feet of Vishṇu by bouquet of basil flowers; let him offer rice balls, in the order at sacred rivers which serve him for washing feet. He who offers at Gayaśira[90] a rice ball, be it only of a slipping of a leaf of śamī, he liberates seven clans and a hundred families.

120) Thus a man ought to show with all his forces loving devotion to the fathers; by his loving devotion to the fathers he will be happy in this world and in the next.

121) I have therefore revealed to you all the funeral ceremonies: those which a son ought to perform, conferring merit on him and giving deliverance to the fathers.

122) He who hears this discourse, though poor he be, is absolved of all his sins and receives the price of his gifts.

123) He who performs according to the rule the funeral rite decreed by me, and who makes gifts and hears the Garuḍa Purāṇa, this is the recompense which will come to him.

124) The father gives him good sons, the grandfather gives him plenty of cows, the great grandfather gives him silver.

---

89 *Ekoddista* rite, rite performed for one single dead person.

90 Mountain of Gayā.

125-26) The great great grand father gives him abundant food. All, being satisfied by the funeral rite, granting the wishes of the son, go by the path of the Law to the palace of the king of Law (Yama). And they remain there, in the most profound respect, among the assembly of the King of Law.

APPENDIX 2
Incantations to save the dying in the *Atharva Veda*

The following two hymns of the *Atharva Veda*[91] contain incantations for the purpose of saving the dangerously sick persons from death when they are at the point of death; or perhaps for the purpose of recalling their spirits after their death. They give us interesting information concerning the ideas the early Indians had of death and life.

Atharva Veda 5.30

1) Let things near to you [remain] near, near also the far off things! Remain here; do not go away, do not follow the ancient Fathers. I firmly hold back your breath.

2) If any kinsman or stranger has uttered incantations against you, with my voice I declare your release and delivrance from them all.

3) Whatever hurt you have done, or curse you have spoken, in your folly, against woman or man, with my voice, etc.

4) If you lie there in consequence of any sin committed by your mother or father, with my voice, etc.

5) Receive the medicine which your father, mother, sister and brother offer you. I make you long-lived.

6) Remain here, O man, with your spirit intact; do not follow the two messengers of Yama; come to the abodes of the living.

7) Come back when called, knowing the outlet of the path, the ascent, the advance, the road of every living man.

8) Fear not, you will not die; I make you long-lived. I have exorcised out of your members the consumption by which they are wasted.

9) The consumption which racks and wastes your limbs and sickens your heart has flown away to a distance like a hawk, overcome by my word.

10) The two sages, Alert and Watchful, the sleepless and the vigilant, these the guardians of your life, are awake both day and night.

11) Behold Agni which you must approach with homage. Behold, the Sun rises for you. Rise up from deep death, yea, even from black darkness.

12) Reverence to Yama, reverence to Death, reverence to the Fathers, and to those who guide us. I place in front of this [sick] man, for his security, Agni, who knows how to carry him across.

13) Let his breath, let his thought, let his sight come, and then his strength; let his body acquire sensation, and stand firm upon its feet.

14) Provide him, Agni, with breath, and with sight; restore him, furnished with a body, and with strength. You know what makes one immortal; let him not depart, or become a dweller in a house of clay.

15) Let not your inhaled breath cease; let not your exhaled breath vanish. Let the sun, the lord, raise you up from death by his rays.

16) This tongue speaks within, bound, convulsive. By you I have exorcised away the consumption, and the hundred torments of the fever.

17) This world is the dearest, unconquered by the gods. To whatever death you were destined when you were born, O man, - we call after you, do not die before you are worn out by old age.

Atharva Veda 7.53

1) Bṛhaspati, you have delivered us from dwelling in the realm of Yama, from the curse. The Asvins who, O Agni, are the two physicians of the gods have repelled death from us by their powers.

2) Continue, associated, you two breaths, inspired and expired; forsake not his body: may they, united, remain with you here. Live prosperously a hundred autumns. Agni is your brilliant protector and lord.

3) May your life, which has been dissipated afar, may your breaths, come back to you again. Agni has snatched it from the lap of Nirṛiti (Destruction): and I introduce it again into yourself.

4) Let not his inspiration abandon him, nor his expiration quit him and depart. I commit him to the seven ṛishis; may they carry him on in health to old age.

5) Enter into him, you two breaths, like two steers forcing their way into a cow-pen. May this man flourish here, an unmolested depository of old age.

6) We restore your breath. I drive away consumption from you. May this excellent Agni sustain our life on every side.

7) Ascending from the darkness to the uppermost heaven, we have reached, among the gods, the god Sūrya, the highest luminary.

CHAPTER TEN

HINDU ESCHATOLOGY

Introduction

Eschatology ("the doctrine of last things") is a Christian theological term of recent origin, though deriving from New Testament phrases themselves and leading back to the Old Testament. It usually means both the final destiny of the individual and also the future of the universe. The term is also used in the history of religions since all religions in some form or another contain teachings about the goal of human life, human history and the universe, as they do about the origins of the things.[1] We have to note at once that this doctrine of last things is distinct from hypotheses about the end of the universe based on natural science or scientific historical study. Religious eschatology is based on the experience of the absolute in history. We can even say that the philosophical eschatology, in as far as it deals with the problem of the ultimate destiny of man, society and the cosmos, is religious in nature.

This widespread appearance of a common theme in world religions hides a profound difference in how the theme of 'last things' is understood and developed. Phenomenology of religion proposes three distinct forms of eschatology, which reflect three basic ways of understanding man and the universe. The first is the cosmobiologic eschatology, characteristic of the so-called primitive religions and of mass religiosity in many higher cultures. These religions present an orientation to life, a set of assumptions and ways of interpreting which mould

---

1 The *eschaton*, the utmost limit, is not conceived merely as referring to some remote future, but equally in some distant past; primeval time and the end of time are linked together. This time is God's time which refers to the earliest yesterday and the farthest tomorrow. A golden age lies behind man and an eternal realm of salvation confronts him. See G. Van Der Leeuw, *Religion in Essence and Manifestation*, Tr., New York, 1965, Vol. II, p. 583.

man's understanding of himself in relation to the cosmos. His understanding of the origin of the cosmos and of his place in the cosmos provides the pattern for defining the kind of destiny available to him in future experience. Religion is an active and voluntary attitude of harmony and of participation of the individual in the universe, an attentive effort to adopt a just conduct before the whole visible or invisible reality, God included, which his experience proposes to his consciousness.[2] Nature is engrossed in cyclical rhythms, and the pattern of eternal recurrence or return characterizes this eschatology. The vision of last things is a vision of harmony between man and cosmos beyond the threat of time and season.[3] Sometimes a mythical hero, divine or semidivine, is thought of as the restorer of the end-state after a period of cataclysms and disasters. The second can be called eternalistic, as is the case in oriental religions like Hinduism and Buddhism. This considers time as the endless cycle of births and deaths and seeks to escape from this cycle of rebirths. The 'last thing' consists in the deliverance of the individual from the unreal realm of the empirical and temporal to the timeless realm of the spirit.[4] While these two eschatologies are non-historical, the third can be termed historical, characteristic of Judaism, Christianity[5]

2 See Joseph Goetz, *Summi Numinis vel etiam Patris...*, in: "Studia Missionalia," Vol. XV (1966), pp. 54ff. The expression *Cosmobiologic* is borrowed from the same author; see his *Le Religioni dei Primitivi*, Cosmobiologia e Mistero, in: Bergounioux-Goetz, «Le Religioni dei preistorici e dei primitivi», Catania, 1959, pp. 126ff.

3 Mircea Eliade confronts "historical man" (modern man) who consciously and voluntarily creates history with the men of primitive cultures who have a negative attitude towards history. Primitive people either abolish history periodically, or devaluate it by perpetually finding transhistorical models and archetypes for it, or give it a metahistorical meaning (cyclical theory, eschatological significations). See his *Cosmos and History* (The myth of the eternal return), New York, 1954, p. 141.

4 R. C. Zaehner sees the practical technique of the Indian spirituality either by yoga or by any other sādhana as the means of transforming consciousness so that the yogin can experience a state of being which transcends space and time; namely it is a technique whereby it is possible to separate the eternal soul from all its mortal trappings. The world of time and space as we know it belongs to the never-ceasing change of all that is not the spiritual self of man. The eternal for the Buddhist is "deathlessness, peace, the unchanging state of Nirvāna." See R. C. Zaehner, *At Sundry Times*, London, 1958, pp. 38, 41, 45-6, 49.

5 For Christianity time is real because it has a definite meaning: redemption.

"A straight line traces the course of humanity from initial Fall to final redemption. And the meaning of this history is unique, because the incarnation is a unique fact. Indeed, as chapter 9 of the Epistle to the Hebrews and 1 Peter 3:18 emphasize, Christ died for our sins once only, once for all (*hapex, ephapex, semel*); it is not an event subject to repetition, which can be reproduced several times (*pollakis*). The development of history is thus governed and oriented by a unique fact, a fact that stands entirely alone. Consequently the destiny of all

and Islam. Here the ultimate destiny is seen as the fulfillment of history. In this article we treat of the Hindu eschatology both in the case of the universe and in the case of the individual's future life after death.

1. Cosmic Eschatology

The theory of Kalpas (cosmic eras) was not known during the Vedic period. In later literature, especially in the Epics and the Purāṇas we find it fully developed. Each of these Kalpas is conceived as measuring the duration of one single world, from creation to dissolution; it is equivalent to one day in the life of Brahmā. This in turn contains thousand great ages *(Mahāyuga)*, each of which consists of four ages (yugas): Kṛta, Tretā, Dvāpara and Kali yugas.[6] The development curve of the actual humanity as well as that of the past and of the future is a retrogressive evolution, leading to an 'intermediate dissolution' (fire followed by flood); at the end of time comes the 'great dissolution' *(mahāpralaya)* which coincides with the end of the life of Brahmā. The world will be reabsorbed into Brahmā by involution and remain in that state until the hatching of a new cosmic egg.[7]

---

mankind, together with the individual destiny of each one of us, are both likewise played out once, once for ali, in a concrete and irreplaceable time which is that of history and life." See HENRI-CHARLES PUECH, *La Gnose et le temps*, in: "Eranos-Jahrbuch," XX, Zürich, 1951, pp. 70ff. The translation is by MIRCEA ELIADE, *Cosmos and History*, op. cit., p. 143.

6 Each world cycle is subdivided into four yugas or world ages; they took their names from the four throws of the Indian dice game, *kṛtā, tretā, dvāpara* and *kali*. Kṛta is the perfect participle of the verb *kṛi*, to do; hence it means "done, made, perfect." This is the dice thrown which wins the jackpot, the total gain. The idea of totality, according to the Indian conception, is expressed by the number four. A thing is perfect when it is established on its four legs, or "fourquartered." Righteousness (*dharma*) is perfect in this period and stands on four legs, like the sacred cow; or effective on all four quarters of the world. *Tretā yuga* is named after the dice-cast of the three; tretā is the triad or triplet. *Dvāpara*, derived from *dvi* ("two") is the age of dangerous balance between virtue and vice; only two quarters of dharma are to be found in this age. *Kali* means "strife, quarrel" (related to *kal-aha*, "strife, quarrel"); during this age man and the world are at their lowest and worst; *dharma* stands only on one quarter. See H. ZIMMER, *Myths and Symbols in Indian Art and Civilization*, edited by J. CAMPBELL, New York, 1962, pp. 14ff.

7 In Sanskrit it is called *Brahmāṇḍa*, "Brahmā's egg," i.e., the universe. In Hindu mythology Brahmā personifies exclusively the positive aspect of the life process of the universe. Brahmāṇḍa simply means "mundane egg."

The Teaching of Mahābhārata

Hanuman describes the four yugas as follows. The Krta yuga is that in which there existed the one eternal religion.[8] Every one was so perfect in religious experience that there was no need of religious acts.[9] There was neither deterioration of virtue nor decrease of people. There were no gods, no demons, no gandharvas, no yakshas, no rākshasas nor nāgas.[10] No buying and selling. No Vedas like Rig, Sāma and Yajus. One could obtain the necessaries of life by just thinking of it without any labour.[11] The only merit consisted in renouncing the world. There was no malice of any kind. The Supreme Brahma was attainable to all. Nārāyaṇa was the soul of all creatures. The four classes of society such as the brāhmans, kshatriyas, vaiṣyas and the śūdras kept their respective duties perfectly without any constraint or conflict. Brahma was their sole refuge and all their acts were directed to Brahma. One uniform soul was the object of their meditation. There was only one Veda and one mantra (OM) and one ordinance. Their religion consisted in the identification of the Self with Brahma.[12]

In the Tretā Yuga, Hanuman continues, sacrifices came into existence and virtue decreased by a quarter. People began to devise various means for the attainment of an object; and they attain it through acts and gifts.[13] In the Dvāpara Yuga religion decreases by one half; and the Veda became divided into four parts.[14] People began to prac-

---

8 *Sanātana dharma* can be translated as eternal religion or eternal righteousness. Here in the context it signifies the totality of religion, and righteousnes is included in it. It is the sum-total of the duties and tasks divinely ordained by the eternal *dharma*.

9 Religious acts such as sacrifice which can gradually lead to perfection, since everybody in this age had already religious perfection.

10 Men worship in this period only one God, who manifests himself wearing a white hue.

11 Men made no efforts to obtain the fruits of the earth, for they could get them by their mere wish.

12 In this age people were unceasingly devoted to only one God, i.e., Nārāyaṇa, and used one formula, one rule, and one rite. Though they had separate duties in conformity with their castes, they had but one Veda and practised one duty.

13 In this period men were devoted to righteousness dependent on ceremonies. Sacrifices came to the foreground with holy acts and a variety of rites. Men had an object in view, seeking some benefit for their rites and gifts. They were not motivated by virtue for the sake of virtue and for the sake of duty as such.

14 Some men studied four Vedas, others only three; still others only two; others only one, and some none at all.

tise asceticism and give gifts, mainly through passion. As a consequence of the decrease of the intellect, few people were established in truth. When people fall off from truth they became subject to various diseases; then lust and natural calamities ensued. Some celebrated sacrifices with the desire of enjoying the good things of life or attaining heaven. On the advent of the Dvāpara Yuga men became degenerate as a consequence of impiety. And finally in the Kali Yuga a quarter only of virtue abides. In this age the Vedas, the Institutes, and virtue and sacrifices and religious observances fall into disuse.[15] As the Yugas wane, virtue dwindles.[16]

Another description of the four yugas is further instructive and illuminating. In the Kṛta yuga all the duties exist in their entirety along with Truth. No knowledge or object came to men through unrighteous or forbidden means. In other ages duty ordained in the Vedas gradually declines by a quarter in each age. While sinfulness increases,[17] the words of the Veda, the period of life, the blessings and the fruits of the Vedic rites decrease gradually by one fourth in every succeeding age. Again in the Kṛta age penance occupies the foremost place; in the Tretā age knowledge is foremost; in the Dvāpara sacrifice is said to be the foremost. In the Kali age only gift is the one thing laid down.[18]

---

15 In this age practices enjoined by the Vedas, works of righteousness, and rites of sacrifice ceased. Calamities of every kind prevail.

16 *The Mahābhārata* 3.148. The *Mahābhārata* references are to the Translation" edition of Munshiram Manoharlal, K. M. Ganguli, 1974.

17 Sinfulness grows in consequence of theft, untruth, and deception.

18 *The Mahābhārata* 12.231. See also *the Mahābhārata* 12.341 (Nārāyanīya section):

Idaṁ kṛtayugaṁ nāma kālaḥ śreṣṭhaḥ, pravarttitaḥ
ahiṁsyā yajñapaśavo yuge'smin na tad anyathā //
Catuṣpāt śakalo dharmo bhaviṣyaty atra vai surāḥ
tatas tretā yugaṁ nāma trayī yatra bhaviṣyati //
Prokśitā yajñapaśavo badhaṁ prāpsyanti vai makhe
yatra pādaś caturtho vai dharmasya na bhaviṣyati //
Tato vai dvāparaṁ nāma miśraḥ kālo bhaviṣyati.

"This present Kṛta age is the best of all the yugas, in it it is unlawful to slay any animals for sacrifice; in this age righteousness shall consist of all its four portions and be entire. Then shall follow the Tretā age, in which the triple Veda shall arise, and animals fit for sacrifice shall be slaughtered as oblations. In that age the fourth part of righteousness shall be wanting. Next shall succeed the Dvāpara, a mixed period".

Manu differs from the above statement of the *Mahābhārata* in making the Dvāpara the age of sacrifice. See *Manu* 1.85-86.

Once again, it is said that in the Krta age men worshipped only one Brahman and looked upon the three Vedas, rites and sacrifices which were performed for motives of gain as different from the object of their worship and hence practised only yoga by means of penance. In the Tretā age the Vedas, sacrifices, and the distinctions between several orders and the four kinds of life existed in a compact state. In the Dvāpara age because of decrease in life span of men these fall off from that compact condition; and in the Kali age all the Vedas became so scarce that they may not be even seen by men. Afflicted by iniquity they suffer extermination along with the rites and sacrifices. In this age righteousness is visible in such brāhmans as are of pure souls and devoted to penance and the study of scriptures.[19]

The duration of these ages and the evolution and dissolution of the universe are also described in the great Epic. Krta age lasts four thousand years (of the deities); its morning[20] consists of four hundred years and its evening[21] four hundred years. The duration of each of the other yugas gradually decreases by a quarter with respect to both the substantive period with the conjoining portion and the conjoining portion itself. Twelve thousand years (of the deities) constitute one four-age period and a thousand such yugas compose a single day of Brahmā. The same is the duration of Brahmā's night. The universe comes to life with the start of Brahmā's day. During the period of universal dissolution the Creator sleeps, engaged in Yoga meditation. When the period of sleep expires, he awakes and creation begins with this. Brahmā modifies the indestructible consciousness *(Cit)* by causing it to be overlaid with ignorance *(avidyā)*. He then causes consciousness to spring up; at first springs up Mahat which is speedily transformed into Mind which is the soul of the Manifest. Brahmā is the effulgent seed from which, existing as it does by itself, has sprung the whole universe consisting of mobile and immobile beings.[22]

---

19 *The Mahābhārata* 12.232.

20 Sandhyā ("twilight").

21 Sandhyānsa ("portion of twilight").

22 *The Mahābhārata* 12.231. In some texts we find the following version of 31-34:
Pratibuddho vikurute brahmākṣayyaṁ kṣapā-kṣaye
sṛjate ca mahad bhūtaṁ tasmād vyaktātmakaṁ manaḥ //
brahmā tejomayaṁ śukraṁ yasya sarvam idaṁ jagat
ekasya bhūtaṁ bhūtasya dvayaṁ sthāvarajaṅgamam

The universal dissolution is described in the following manner. A dozen Suns and Agni with his seven flames begin to burn. Wrapt by these flames, the whole universe is caught up in a vast conflagration. Both the mobile and immobile things of the earth disappear and merge into the substance of the earth. The earth shorn of trees and herbs, looks naked like a tortoise shell. Water then prevails. Surging into mighty billows and producing awful roars, only water fills the whole space.[23]

As it is said clearly in the *Bhagavad-gītā,* "For whenever righteousness declines and unrighteousness uprises, then I (Krishna) create myself, to guard the good, and to destroy the wicked, and to confirm the right, I come into being in this age and in that"[24]. This statement of Krishna applies also to other *avatārs* in different ages whenever *dharma* declines and *adharma* is in the ascendency. The great Epic contains interesting details in this respect. At those times when virtue and morality decrease, and sin and immorality increase, God creates himself in new forms. He is born in the families of virtuous men and assumes human body and exterminates all evils caused by the malicious Daityas and Rākshasas who could not be slain by other gods. Moved by his own *māyā,* God creates gods and men and all immobile things and then destroys them. For the preservation of rectitude he assumes many forms. In the Kṛta age he becomes white; in the Tretā age he becomes yellow; in the Dvāpara age he becomes red and in the Kali age he becomes dark in hue.[25]

Then is described the coming of Kalkin at the close of the general degeneracy in the Kali age, who will give the earth to the brāhmans. When the terrible times of the Kali age will be over, creation will begin again, and men will be created and distributed into four classes; everywhere there will be prosperity and abundance,

---

ahar-mukhe vibuddhaḥ, san sṛjate 'vidyayā jagat
agra eva mahābhūtam āśu vyaktātmakaṁ manaḥ //
abhibhūyeha cārciṣmad vyasṛjat sapta mānasān
dūragaṁ bahudhāgāmi prārthanā-saṁśayātmakam. //

The external world is nothing but Mind transformed. Mind is spoken of as *vyaktātmaka*, that which is the soul of the manifest, *Tejomayam* is explained as *vasanamayam*, "having the principle of wish within it." By *Mahat* is meant Pure Intelligence.

23 The *Mahābhārata* 12.233.

24 Chapter 4, verses 7-8.

25 *The Mahābhārata* 3.188.

health and peace. A brāhman by the name of Kalkin[26] will be born; he will glorify Vishṇu and possess great energy, great intelligence and prowess. He will restore order and peace in this world.[27]

The Teaching of the Purāṇas

First let us deal with the account of the yugas as exposed in the *Vishṇu Purāṇa*. Twelve thousand divine years, each consisting of three hundred and sixty such days, form the period of four yugas; Kṛta yuga has four thousand divine years; the Tretā yuga three thousand; the Dvāpara yuga two thousand; the Kali yuga one thousand. The period that precedes a yuga is called a Sandhyā and has as many hundred years as there are thousands in the yuga; the period that follows a yuga, called Sandhyānsa, is of similar duration. The four yugas constitute a great age; a thousand such great yugas are a day of Brahmā, and fourteen Manus reign within that period. At the end of Brahmā's day a dissolution of the universe takes place when all the three worlds, earth and the regions of space, are consumed with fire. When the three worlds are one mighty ocean, Brahmā who is one with Nārāyaṇa, satiate with the demolition of the universe, sleeps upon his serpent-bed, contemplated by the ascetic inhabitants of the Janaloka, for a night of equal duration as his day. At the end of this he creates anew. A year of Brahmā is composed of such days and nights; and a hundred such years constitute his whole life.[28]

"In the Kṛta age Vishṇu, devoted to the welfare of all creatures, assumes the form of Kapila and others to confer upon them the highest knowledge. In the Tretā age the Supreme Lord, in the form of a universal potentate, represses the violence of the wicked, and protects the three worlds. Assuming the form of Vyāsa, the all-pervading Being repeatedly divides the single Veda into four parts and multiplies it by distributing it into hundreds of sakhas"[29]. Vishṇu divides the

26 Kalkin is the name of the tenth avatāra of Vishṇu when he is to appear mounted on a white horse and wielding a drawn sword as destroyer of the wicked. This is to take place at the end of the four yugas.

27 *The Mahābhārata* 3.189.

28 *The Vishṇu Purāṇā* 1.3.

29 *The Vishṇu Purāṇa* 3.2.18:
Kṛte yuge paraṁ jñānam kapilādi-svarūpa-dhṛk
dadāti sarva-bhūtānāṁ sarva-bhūtathite rataḥ, //
cakravartti-svarūpeṇa tretāyām api sa prabhuḥ

Vedas into many parts for the good of all creatures, because he perceives the vigour, energy, and strength of men to be now but limited[30].

Here is a significant account of what happens in the Kali yuga, the age of universal degeneracy. There will be kings who are of churlish spirit, violent temper, and ever addicted to falsehood and wickedness. They will subject women, children, and cows to death; they will steal the property of their subjects, and their lives will be short, their desires insatiable, and they will show little piety. The world will be deprived of wealth and piety gradually. Property alone will confer rank and wealth will be the only source of devotion. Passion will be the sole bond of union between the sexes. Falsehood will be the only means of success in conflict. Women will be merely objects of sensual gratification. External signs will be the distinctive characteristics of several orders of life. Dishonesty, presumption, menace will be substituted for learning. Liberality will be devotion; simple absolution will stand for purification; mutual assent will be marriage; fine clothes will be dignity; and any water that is far off will be considered holy. At the end of the Kali yuga a portion of God will be born as Kalki who will destroy the wicked and re-establish righteousness upon earth.[31] Professor Wilson summarizes the general account of the cosmogony as found in the *Vishṇu Purāṇa:* there are two accounts of creation: primary and secondary. The first explains how the universe proceeds from Prakrti (eternal prime matter) and the second in what manner the forms of things are developed from the elementary substances previously evolved, or how they reappear after their temporary destruction. Both these creations are periodical, but the termination of the first occurs only at the end of Brahmā's life, when all the gods and all the forms are annihilated and all the elements are

---

duṣṭānāñ nigrahaṁ kurvan paripāti jagattrayam //
vedam ekaṁ caturbhedaṁ kṛtvā śakhā-śatair vibhuḥ
karoti bahulam bhūyo vedavyāsa-svarūpa-dhṛk. //

30 *The Vishṇu Purāña* 3.3.6f:
hitāya sarvabhūtānāṁ veda-bhedān karoti saḥ
yayā sa kurute tanvā vedam ekaṁ pṛthak prabhuḥ.

31 *The Vishṇu Purāña* 4.24. There will be no sacred places of pilgrimage and holy rivers; no place of the earth will be particularly sacred, or will have any special sanctity. Gifts will be made from the impulse of ordinary feeling without any connection with religious rites or as an act of devotion, Ablution will be performed for pleasure or for comfort without any religious purpose. One assumes the exterior garb of sanctity.

merged into primary substance. The latter takes place at the end of every Kalpa or Brahmā's day. It affects only the forms of inferior creatures and lower worlds, leaving the substance of the universe entire and the sages and gods unharmed.[32]

The dissolution of existing beings can be incidental, elemental and absolute. The incidental is related to Brahmā and occurs at the end of each Kalpa. The elemental takes place after two Parārddhas. The absolute is the final liberation from existence. Vishṇu in the form of Rudra destroys the whole world by entering into the seven rays of the Sun, by drinking up all the waters of the globe, and by causing all moisture in living bodies or in the soil to evaporate, and thus drying up the whole earth. The seven solar rays set the three worlds and the Pātāla on fire and reduce everything to ashes.[33]

The *Vāyu Purāṇa* describes how in the Dvāpara age the Vedas have been divided. Brahmā said to Manu: "Divide the Veda. The age is changed; through its baneful influence the Brāhmans have become feeble, and from the same cause everything has been gradually corrupted, so that little (good) is seen remaining.... The destruction of the Veda would involve the destruction of sacrifice; that again would occasion the annihilation of the gods, and then everything would go to ruin. The primeval Veda was four-footed and extended to one hundred thousand verses, while sacrifice was of ten sorts, and yielded every object of desire. Being thus addressed, Manu the Lord, devoted to the good of the world, replied, 'Be it so', and in conformity with the command of Brahmā divided the one fourquarted Veda into four parts"[34].

---

32 *The Vishṇu Purāṅa,* Tr. H.H. Wilson, Calcutta, 1961 (reprint), pp. LVIIff in Preface.

33 The *Vishṇu Purāṅa* 6.3.

34 *The Vāyu Purāṇa:*

Brahmā manum uvācedam vedaṁ vyasya mahāmate /
parivṛttam yugaṁ tāta svalpavīryā dvijātayaḥ, /
saṁvṛttā yugadoṣena sarvañcaiva jathākramam /
bhraṣṭamānaṁ yāgavaśād alpaśiṣṭaṁ hi dṛśyate /

. . . . . .

vede nāśam anuprāpte yajño nāśaṁ gamiṣyati /
yajñe naṣṭe deva-nāśas tataḥ sarvam praṇaśyati /
ādyo vedaś catuṣpādo śata-sāhasra-sammitaḥ /
punar dasa-guṇaḥ kṛtsno yajño vai sarva-kāma-dhuk /
evam uktas tathety uktvā manur loka-hite rataḥ /
vedam ekam catuṣ-pādaṁ caturdhā vyabhajat prabhuḥ. /

The above text is given: in Muir, *Original Sanskrit Texts,* Vol. III, London, 1861, p. 22.

The Bhāgavata Purāṇa, Book 3, chapter 11 gives the finalised shape of the eschatology of the cosmos and the duration of various periods.

"18) The four ages, namely, Kṛtayuga, Tretā, Dvāpara and Kali, along with periods which begin and terminate (each of them) have been declared as consisting of twelve thousand divine years.

19) The duration of the Kṛta and of the three following ages is successively of four thousand, of three thousand, of two thousand and of one thousand years; to these numbers it is necessary to add twice as many hundred years.

20) The time comprised between a Sandhyā (beginning of each age) and a Sandhyāṁsa (end of each age), periods whose duration is counted by hundreds, is called Yuga by sages conversant in these matters; each Yuga is the domain of (a special) Dharma.

24) During the Manvantaras there are Manus with their descendents, seers and gods; these diverse beings are born at the same time, as well as the chiefs of gods and their attendants.

25) Such is the creation of Brahmā, creation which is renewed each day of the life of this God, which produces the three worlds, and in which animals, human beings, manes and gods are born according to their respective action *(karma).*

26) During these Manvantaras it is the Lord who with the quality of goodness protects the universe...

27) ...After having with time absorbed all in his being, he remains in silence at the end of the day.

28) It is thus that the three worlds, that of the earth and others, disappear successively in his being, while the night having come, the universe is deprived of the light of the sun and of the moon.

29) When the three worlds are being consumed by the divine energy in the shape of fire from Sankarsana...

30) In an instant the seas swollen by the end of the kalpa, breaking their limits, cover the three worlds with their waves tossed by impetuous gusts of wind.

31) In the midst of this ocean resides Hari, couched on Ananta, his eyes closed by the sleep of meditation, amidst praises of sages who inhabit the Janaloka.

32) ... the hundred years even of Brahmā's life, the longest in this creation comes to an end.

33) The duration of the half of his existence is called Parārdha;[35] the first Parārdha has already expired, and the second is now running.

34) At the beginning of the first Parārdha took place the great Kalpa, named Brahmā, in which appeared Brahmā, whom the sages recognize as Śabdabrahma (the divine Word).

35) And at the end of the same Parārdha, appeared the Kalpa which is called Padma, in which sprang the lotus of the worlds from the pool of Hari's navel.

36) As to the Kalpa which has just commenced the second Parārdha, one names it Varāha, O descendant of Bhārata; it is then that Hari appeared in the form of a boar"[36].

Towards the close of *the Bhāgavata Purāṇa* is to be found a description of how Vyāsa arranged the Vedas and the Purāṇas. A sound issued forth from the sky of Brahmā's heart when he was in deep me-

---

35 The number of human days corresponding to 50 years of Brahmā's life.

36 *The Bhāgavata Purāña,* 3.11:

kṛtaṁ tretā dvāparañ ca kaliś ceti catur-yugaṁ
divyair dvādaśabhir varṣaiḥ sāvadhānaṁ nirūpitam.
catvāri trīṇi dve caikaṁ kṛtā'diṣu yathā-kramam
saṁkhyātāni sahasrāṇi dvi-guṇāni śatāni ca.
sandhyā-sandhyā'ṁśayor antar yaḥ kālaḥ śata-saṁkhyayoḥ
tam evā'hur yugaṁ taj-jñā yatra dharmo vidhīyate. (18-20)
manvantareṣu manavas tad-vaṁśyā ṛśayaḥ, surāḥ
bhavanti caite yugapat sureśāś cā'nu ye ca tān. (24)
eṣa dainandinaḥ sargo brāhmas trailokya-vartanaḥ
tiryaṅ nṛ-pitṛ-devānāṁ sambhavo yatra karmabhiḥ. (25)
manvantareṣu bhagavān bibhrat sattvaṁ sva-mūrtibhiḥ. (26)
. . . . . .
kālenā'nugatā'śeṣa āste tūṣṇīṁ dinā'tyaye. (27)
tam evā'nvapidhīyante lokā bhūr-ādayas trayaḥ
niśāyāṁ anuvṛttāyāṁ nirmukta-śaśi-bhāskaram. (28)
tri-lokyāṁ dahyamānāyāṁ śaktyā saṁkarṣaṇā'gninā. (29)
tāvat tri-bhuvanaṁ sadyaḥ kalpā'ntaidhita-sindhavaḥ
plāvayantyukaṭā'ṭopa-caṇḍa-vateritormayaḥ. (30)
antaḥ sa tasmin salile āste'nantā'sano hariḥ
yoga-nidrā-nimīlā'kṣaḥ stūyamāno janā'layaiḥ. (31)
. . . asyā'pi paramāyur vayaḥ-śatam. (32)
yad ardham āyuṣas tasya parā'rdham abhidhīyate. (33)
pūrvasyā'dau parā'rdhasya brāhmo nāma mahān abhūt
kalpo yatrā'bhavad brahmā śabda-brahmeti yaṁ viduḥ. (34)
tasyaivā'nte ca kalpo'bhūd yaṁ pādman abhicakṣate
yad dharer nābhi-sarasa āsīt loka-saroruham. (35)
ayaṁ tu kathitaḥ kalpo dvitīyasyā'pi bhārata
varāha iti vikhyāto yatrā'sīt sūkaro hariḥ. (36)

ditation. The devotees perceive this sound when they close their organs of sense; they destroy all their taints, extrinsic, inherent, and superhuman by adoring this sound and are freed from future birth. The triple oṁkāra, the emblem of the divine Brahmā, the supreme Spirit, sprang from this sound. The supreme Spirit hears this sound, though his ears are closed and his senses are inactive. Through this sound is speech revealed; there is a manifestation of it in the firmament of the soul. This oṁkāra is the sensible exponent of Brahmā, the supreme Spirit. It is the eternal seed of the Vedas, including all mantras and Upanishads. With the three letters of oṁkāra the omnipresent Being , desiring to reveal the functions of the four classes of priests, created from his four mouths the four Vedas with the three sacred syllables and the oṁkāra[37].

Synthesis of the doctrine

Time, like soul and matter, is a phase of the Supreme Spirit. As Brahmā wakes or sleeps, so also does the universe wake or sleep. Each day and each night of Brahmā is an 'aeon' *(kalpa)* and is equivalent to two thousand 'great ages' *(Mahayuga)*; that is to say, 8,640,000,000 human years.[38] During an 'aeon' fourteen Manus (Fathers of mankind) appear; each one presides over a period of seventy-one 'great ages' with a surplus. Each 'great age' is further divided into four ages (yugas) of progressive physical and moral deterioration of men. These are Kṛta, Tretā, Dvāpara and Kali yugas which are supposed to last respectively

---

37 *The Bhāgavata Purāṅa* 12.6.37ff:
Samāhitātmano brahman brahmaṇaḥ, parameṣṭhinaḥ /
hṛd-ākāśād abhūd nādo vṛttirodhād vibhāvyate /
yad-upāsanayā brahman yogino malam ātmanaḥ /
dravya-kryā-kārakākhyaṁ dhūtva yānty apanurbhavam /
tato 'bhūt trivṛd oṁkāro yo'vyakta-prabhavaḥ, svarāṭ /
yat talliṅgam bhagavato brahmaṇaḥ paramātmanaḥ /
sṛṇoti ya imaṁ sphoṭaṁ suptaśrotre ca śūnyadṛk /
yena vāg vyajate yasya vyaktir ākāśe ātmanaḥ /
svadhāmno brahmaṇaḥ sākṣād vācakaḥ paramātmanaḥ /
. . . . . .
tenāsau caturo vedāṁš cāturbhir vadanair vibhuḥ, /
sa-vyāhṛtikān soṁkārāṁś cāturhotra-vivakṣayā /...

38 Some authors take into account only the duration of the day of Brahmā and hence include only half of this period; i.e., 4,320,000000 human years. We include in the text the full duration both of the day and of the night of Brahmā.

1,728,000,1,296,000, 864,000 and 432,000 human years. Each of these yugas is preceded by a period called sandhyā (twilight) and is followed by another period of equal length called Sandhyāṅsa (portion of twilight), each being equal to one tenth of the yuga. A year of the gods (divine year) is equal to 360 human years.

1) Krta Yuga	4,000	
Sandhyā	400	
Sandhyāṅsa	400	
Total . . .		4,800
2) Treta Yuga	3,000	
Sandhyā	300	
Sandhyāṅsa	300	
Total . . .		3,600
3) Dvapara Yuga	2,000	
Sandhyā	200	
Sandhyāṅsa	200	
Total . . .		2,400
4) Kali Yuga	1,000	
Sandhyā	100	
Sandhyāṅsa	100	
Total . . .		1,200
GRAND TOTAL . . .		12,000

Creation of the universe takes place and lasts during Brahmā's day; at its close the universe is dissolved for the same length of time (Brahmā's night). 360 such days and nights make one year of Brahmā, and 100 such years make Brahmā's life span. A day of Brahmā has 14 manvantaras; a manvantara is a period of a Manu who is the mythical progenitor of the world in his period; a kind of secondary creator who exercises the function of a regent of the world during his manvantara. Present-day humanity is governed by the seventh Manu, Vaivasvata, the son of the solar god Vivasvant. We are at present living in the Kali Yuga which began at midnight between the 17th and the 18th of February 3102 B.C.[39]

39 According to the calculation of M. MONIER-WILLIAMS, *Sanskrit-English Dictionary*, see *Yuga*.

The way of representing history, as we see, in the Hindu context resembles an organic process. Time and history is cyclical, rhythmical; this conception allows for the periodical annihilation of both time and chronology. We can say that the mentality reflected in this conception of time and history is that which bases its attitude towards the world not on sense impressions and rational inference according to which time is linear and continuous and inorganic and history is scientific, but on metaphysical intuition into the impermanence and cyclical renewal of Nature and of empirical reality in general.

The universe according to the Hindu conception is called the "Cosmic egg" *(brahmāṇḍa)* which contains in its upper half seven celestial stories, the topmost of which is the dwelling place of Reality *(Brahman)*. The bottom half contains seven subterraneous stories *(Pātāla)*, which is the home of the Nagas and other fabulous beings; hell *(naraka)* is situated in the lowest part of the Pātāla, the place of punishment, itself being divided into seven regions.

The earth is between the two spheres, a sort of disc at the centre of which is the Mount Meru, the world's pivot, which shines like the morning sun or a smokeless fire. Around Meru are located four 'island continents' *(dvīpa)*, corresponding to the four cardinal points. This primitive geography developed into a system of seven concentric oceans and islands arranged around Mount Meru.[40]

2. Individual Eschatology

The Vedic religion:

Mostly the ninth and the tenth books of the *Rig Veda* contain some references to a life after death. The following funeral hymn[41] deals with death and the future life. From it we learn that the spirit of the dead man, passing by the path trodden by the Fathers, goes to the realm of light and meets with the Fathers who revel with Yama in the highest heaven.

---

40 See Louis Renou, *L'Hindouisme*, Paris, 1979, pp. 52-53. In the primitive geography Jambudvipa (The Island of the Rose-apple Tree) lies to the south of Mt. Meru; but in the developed system it has Meru as its centre and is the inhabited region of the earth or it represents India alone (according to some texts). Outside this lies the geography of the known world. Cfr. Ibid., p. 53.

41 Rig Veda 10.14 This hymn describes the way to Yama's realm.

"Him who has passed away along the mighty steeps[42]
And has spied out the path for many mortals,
Vivasvant's son, convener of the peoples,
Yama the King,[43] present thou with oblation.
Yama was first to find for us the pathway,[44]
A way that can never be taken from us,
Wither our former fathers have passed away
Thither those that have been born since (pass away) along their several paths. (1-2)

Go forth, go forth upon those ancient pathways[45]
By which our former fathers have departed.
Thou shalt behold god Varuna, and Yama,[46]
both kings, in funeral offerings rejoicing.
Unite thou with the Fathers and with Yama,
with *iṣṭapūrta*[47] in the highest heaven.
Leaving behind all blemish homeward return.
Unite with thine own body, full of vigour.[48] (7-8)
Past the two sons of Saramā, the two dogs,[49]
Four-eyed and brindled, hasten thou by pathway straight;[50]
Draw near thou to the Fathers rich in bounty,
Who at a common feast with Yama revel.
Thy two dogs, Yama, guardians are and four-eyed,
Mankind-beholding, watchers of the path-way;

---

42 The steep paths *(pravatas)* leading to the highest heaven where Yama dwells.

43 Yama is often called a king, but never expressly a god, though he appears as god.

44 Yama passed to the other world, finding out the path for many to where the ancient Fathers passed away. He was the first of mortals that died. As first and oldest of the dead he would easily be regarded as the chief of the dead.

45 Addressed to the dead man.

46 Yama and god Varuṇa are the two kings whom the dead man sees on reaching heaven. Note that Yama is not called god in this verse.

47 This word is interpreted as sacrificial merits *(iṣṭa)* and good works *(pūrta)*. These things meet the man after his death in his new life. This perhaps is a preparation to the later doctrine of action (karma). See BLOOMFIELD, *The Religion of the Veda,* New York, 1908, pp. 194f.

48 Being free from disease and frailties, the dead man unites with a body which is complete and without imperfection.

49 The two dogs, offsprings of Saramā, occupy the path and guard the entrance of paradise in order that no godless person may steal into the region of the blessed.

50 In the Avesta a four-eyed dog watches at the head of the bridge by which the souls of the dead pass to the other world, and scares away the fiend from the holy ones.

> Commit him to the care of these, King Yama,
> Welfare on him bestow and health abiding. (10-11)

Vivasvant's son, Yama, the first man, has been before the pathfinder for successive generations after him and has searched out a way to the 'world of the just' for the multitude after him. The spirit of the dead man, freed from all needs, passes through the air to new life. Led by Pūsan,[51] the spirit crosses the stream and passes by Yama's watchful dogs to the world of the spirits. The righteous dead pass over water to get to the paradise:

> "Mightily-saving Earth, incomparable Heaven, the good guide Aditi, who gives secure defence, the well-oared heavenly Ship that lets no water in, free from defect, will we ascend for happiness"[52].

The heavenly ship according to Sāyana is a metaphor which expresses sacrifice. Free from sin, the spirits of the dead embark on the divine ship with good oars. That the dead also pass through a bridge is mentioned thus:

> "Quelling the riteless Dasyu, may we think upon the bridge of bliss leaving the bridge of woe behind"[53].

This theme is quite common in Avesta: "May we succeed in passing over the bridge[54] hard to reach, after conquering the godless enemy"[55].

In the *Rig Veda* the term *asu* ('spirit', 'breath') expresses physical reality, while *manas* ('mind') expresses the seat of thought and emotion.[56] Human life depends on the presence of *asu* and *manas*. In the life after death *asu* and *manas* are united as while on earth; this indicates that all the functions of the mental life remain intact.[57] The body

---

51 Rig. Veda 10.17.3-6.

52 Ibid. 10.63.10.

53 Ibid. 9.41.2.

54 In the Avesta the Cinvat bridge leads from this world to the next.

55 See ADOLF KAEGI, *The Rigveda*, Boston, 1886, p. 159, note 273.

56 Besides *prāṇa* (respiration) and *ātman* (breath) the terms used for the animating principle are *asu* (spirit) which expresses physical vitality, and *manas* (soul) which seems to dwell in the heart. See Rig Veda 8.89.5.

57 The soul is not a mere shadow but regarded as retaining its personal identity.

also has a part in the after-life. Hence the full personality of the departed is believed to remain after death. Though men obtain immortality only after leaving the body in death, the corpse plays a part in the future life for the body shares in the existence of the other world.[58]

The dead are said to obtain immortality not by their own inherent capacity but by the gift of the gods. Agni is said to exalt a mortal to immortality and to be the guardian of immortality.[59] The worshipper prays to Agni, "May I, Agni, with my offspring attain immortality"[60]. Again they pray to Mitra and Varuna, "We ask of you twin rain, wealth, immortality"[61]. Many other prayers for immortality can be cited;[62] but the meaning of immortality is not the same in every case. It may mean a long life here on earth as in 7.59.12; it can mean the continued life of a man in his offspring as in 5.4.10; or it can also mean immortality after death as in 9.113.8ff. Hence the death from which a devotee prays to be delivered means often abrupt death or premature death. He yearns for a long terrestrial life.

Next comes the question about the Pitrs or Fathers. These are the ancestors who have passed through death and attained to life in the third heaven. These are the seers who made the paths by which the recent dead go to join them. They receive worship and are often requested to hear the prayers of the worshippers to protect them and their descendants.[63] The votaries pray to them for riches, offspring, and long life.[64] Father Manu[65] was the first 'Man' and subsequently the secondary parent. But Yama has taken his place and presides over the Fathers and rules the spirits of the dead. In post-vedic mythology he is the appointed judge or punisher of the dead, and hence is called dharmarāja or dharma. The Fathers are not gods but are still divine and possess many divine powers, granting prayers and lending aid.[66] The road to heaven or the abode of the Fathers is guarded by two

58 Rig Veda 10.16.5. Atharva Veda 18.2.26.
59 Rig Veda 1.31.7.
60 Ibid. 5.4.10
61 Ibid. 5.63.2
62 Ibid. 1.19.1; 1.125.5; 1.154.5; 1.179.6; 5.55.4; 7.57.6; 7.76.4; 8.58.7.
63 Ibid. 10.15.2, 5-6, 3.55.2.
64 Ibid. 10.15.7, 11. Atharva Veda 18.3.14; 18.4.62.
65 Ibid. 2.31.13 and 10.100.5.
66 Ibid. 10.57.5 and 10.15.

broad-nosed, four-eyed, spotted dogs, Yama's messengers. The dead man is exhorted to hasten straight past these dogs and to join the Fathers who rejoice with Yama.

The paradise in the Rig Veda is a place of bliss and happiness. The good dead revel in the company of Yama and partake of the funeral offerings and share in the feast of the gods. A detailed account of the joys of paradise is given in the following passage:

> Where radiance inexhaustible dwells, and the lights of heaven are set, place me, clear-flowing one, in that imperishable and deathless world. O Indu (Soma), flow for Indra's sake.[67]
> Make me immortal in the place where dwells the king Vaivasvata,[68] where stands the inmost shrine of heaven, and where the living waters are.
> Make me immortal in that realm, wherein is movement glad and free, in the third sky, third heaven of heavens,[69] where are the lucid worlds of light.
> Make me immortal in the place where loves and longings are fulfilled, the region of the ruddy (sphere) where food and satisfaction reign.
> Make me immortal in the place wherein felicity and joy, pleasure and bliss together dwell, and all desire is satisfied.[70]

Paradise is then a place of immense radiance and of living waters, of spirit-food and complete satisfaction, of glad and free movement, where happiness and joy, pleasure and bliss are abundant, and where loves and desires are fulfilled. The blessed dead are said to have fellowship with the gods and Yama in the realm of light. Those who risk their lives in battle, who bestow liberal sacrificial fees, practise auste-

---

67 The Rig Vedic ideas concerning the future life are connected especially with Vishṇu (1.154.5-6), Soma (9.113.7-11) and Yama. Soma grants the draught of immortality; Yama discovered the path to heaven and in the highest step of Vishṇu there is a well of honey.

68 I.e., Yama.

69 Paradise is situated in the midst of the sky, in the highest heaven, in the third heaven, in the inmost recess of the sky, where is eternal light. This is the abode of the Fathers and Yama who are united with the sun or are connected with the rays of the sun.

70 Rig Veda 9.113.7-11. The joys of paradise are eternal light, swift waters, unrestrained movement, spirit food and satiety, joy and fulfilment of all desires. The joys are those of love, love understood in an indefinite way. In the Atharva Veda it is said that in the heavenly world there is abundance of sexual gratification (4.34.2).

rity,[71] who gain merit through their offerings and pious gifts[72] are said to go to heaven.[73] The dead are said to be united not only with the gods and Fathers and with Yama but also with the rays of the sun and with what they have sacrificed and given *(iṣṭapūrta)* while on earth.[74]

If the righteous dead go to heaven, the wicked are said to go to an abode that can be termed hell.[75] If it is not a place of punishment for the wicked in the Rig Veda,[76] still the evil spirits are sent by the gods to a place of 'bottomless darkness', a 'deep place', as the portion of evil, false, untruthful men. Soma casts the irreligious into a 'hole' (abyss).[77]

> Roaming about, like brotherless young women,
> of evil ways, like dames that trick their husbands,
> as such being full of sin, untrue, unfaithful, -
> they for themselves this deep place have created.[78]
> O Indra- Soma , dash the evil-doers down
> into the pit, the gloom profound and bottomless,
> So that not one of them may ever thence emerge;
> Such be your wrathful might to overpower them.[79]

The Rig Veda expresses the wish that the thief and robber may lie under the three earths and that the demoness in the form of an owl may plunge down into the bottomless pits.[80] Every sinner creates his own hell, i.e., creates for himself this deep pit through his own evil deeds,[81] from which no exit is possible. Hell is darkness, and demons are spirits of darkness. Hell is a place either 'far away', or 'deep down', or 'under three earths'. But no torture of the sinner is indicated in the Rig Veda. Commonly the gods are entreated simply to an-

71 Rig Veda 10.154.2-5.

72 Ibid. 1.125.5; 10.107.2; 10.154.3.

73 Ibid. 10.14.8.

74 Ibid. 1.109.7.

75 *Naraka*.

76 In the Avesta it is a place of punishment of the wicked. The torments of hell are described in the *Atharva* Veda 5.19 and with greater detail in the *Śatapaha Brāhmaṇa* 11.6.1.

77 Rig Veda 2.29.6; 7.104.3, 17; 4.5.5; 9.73.8. *padam gabhīram* (deep place); *vavra* (pit).

78 Ibid. 4.5.5.

79 Ibid. 7.104.3.

80 Ibid. 7.104.11, 17.

81 Ibid. 4.5.5.

nihilate the wicked. But this idea of annihilation does not exclude the other passages where some kind of hell as an underground darkness is described, as we have shown.

In the *Brāhmaṇas* immortality, or at least longevity, is gained by those who rightly understand and perform sacrifice, while those who are deficient in this respect die before their time and go to the next world where they are weighed in a balance and receive good or evil according to their deeds.

> "For in the next world they place (his good and evil deeds) in a balance. Whichever of the two shall outweigh (the other), that he shall follow, whether it be good or evil. Now whosoever knows this places himself in the balance in this world, and is freed from being weighed in the next world; it is by good deeds and not by bad that (his scale) outweighs"[82].

The pious man is promised the highest reward in the next world with his entire body.[83] Here certainly the personal immortality is involved. Hence the loss of a dead man's bones is regarded by his friends as disgraceful. The doctrine of the Brāhmaṇas is that after death all are born again in the next world where they are recompensed according to their deeds, the good being rewarded and the wicked punished.

> "Hence they say that a man is born into the world which he has made." [84]
>
> "Now truly this man is composed of sacrifice. So many sacrifices as he has performed when he departs from this world, with so many is he born in the other world after his death"[85].

82 *Śatapatha Brāhmaṇa* 11.2.7.33:
atha ha eṣā eva tulā yad dakṣiṇo vedyantaḥ /
sa yat sādhu karoti tad antarvedi atha yad
asādhu tad bahirvedi tasmād dakṣiṇāṁ vedyantam adhispriśya iva āsīa /
tulāyāṁ ha vai amuṣmin loke ādadhati /
yatarad yaṁsyati tad anveṣyati yadi sādhu vā asādhu vā iti /
atha yaḥ evaṁ veda asmin ha eva asya yacchati na pāpakṛtyā.
83 sarvatanūr eva sāngah.
84 *Śatapatha Brāhmaṇa* 6.2.2.27:
tasmād āhuṁ kṛtaṁ lokam puruṣo'bhi jāyate.
85 Ibid. 10.6.3.1:
atha khalu kratumayo 'yam puruṣaṁ /
sa yāvatkratur ayaṁ asmāt lokāt praiti evaṁkratur ha amuṁ lokam
pretya abhisambhavati. /

There is also a conception of a higher state beyond that of desire and gratification. The following passage bears witness to this:

> "This (soul) is free from desire, and (yet) possesses all the objects of desire, for it desired nothing... By knowledge men ascend to that condition in which desires have passed away. Thither gifts do not reach, nor austere devotees who are destitute of knowledge. For a person who does not possess this knowledge does not attain that world by gifts or by rigorous abstraction. It pertains only to those who have such knowledge"[86].

The souls of the departed are spoken of as rays of the sun[87] or the stars[88], or as uniting with the gods and living in the world of the gods.[89]

> "He who sacrifices thus obtains perpetual prosperity and renown, and conquers for himself an union with these two gods (Aditya and Agni) and an abode in the same sphere."[90]

Again it is stated that the possessors of particular kind of knowledge attain to union with Āditya (the Sun), and union with Agni, Vāyu, Indra, Brhaspati, Prajāpati and Brahmā.[91]

But the *Brāhmaṇas* are not explicit with respect to the duration of

---

86 Ibid. 10.5.4.15-16:
sa eṣa akāmaḥ sarvakāmo na hy etaṁ kasyachana kāmaḥ /
tad eṣa śloko bhavati "vidyayā tad ārohanti yatra kāmāḥ parāgatāḥ /
na tetra dakṣiṇāḥ yanti nāvidvāṁsaś tapasvinaḥ" iti /
na ha eva taṁ lokaṁ dakṣiṇābhir na tapasā 'nevaṁvid aśnute /
evaṁvidāṁ ha eva sa lokaḥ /

87 Ibid. 1.9.3.10:
yaḥ eṣa tapati tasya ye raśmayas te sukṛtaḥ /
atha yat param bhāḥ prajāpatir vā svargo vā lokaḥ /
"The rays of him who shines (the sun) are the pious.
The light which is above is Prajāpati, or the heavenly world".

88 Ibid. 6.5.4.8:
ye hi janāḥ puṇyakritaḥ svargaṁ lokaṁ yanti teṣāṁ etāni jyotīṁṣi /
"These (the stars) are the lights of the practisers of holy acts who go to heaven".

89 Ibid. 2.6.4.8: eva sāyujyaṁ salokatāṁ jayati.

90 Ibid. 11.6.2.2.3: sāyujya (union) used here in this text seems to prepare the way for later conceptions like *laya* (dissolution) and *mukti* (liberation) into the Supreme Spirit.

91 *Taittirīya Brāhmaṇa* 3.10.11,6ff; *Śatapatha Brāhmaṇa* 11.4.4.1: so 'gninā brahmaṇo dvāreṇa pratipadya brahmaṇaḥ sāyujyaṁ salokatāṁ jayati: "... he attains to union with Brahmā, and abides in the same sphere with him".

the reward or punishment in the life after death. It is perhaps in this context that we can trace a beginning of the doctrine of the transmigration in different births after death. The common belief as expressed in the *Śatapatha Brāhmaṇa* is that the dead pass between two fires which burn the wicked but let the good go through. The good proceed either by the path leading to the Fathers or by paths that lead to the Sun.[92] The spirit or the man in body after death is represented as going up one of these two paths. He goes either to the Fathers through the path which passes southeast through the moon, or he goes northwest (the gods' direction) to the sun. The torments of hell are described in the *Śatapatha Brāhmaṇa*[93] but nothing is said of the eternity of this hell. Varuna sends his son Bhrgu to hell to find out what happens after death: there is suffering of torture, and avenge on those who wronged.[94]

One of the most significant doctrines of the *Upanishads* is the development of the idea of transmigration under the law of action *(karma)*. The early Indians had the apprehension that the life of the dead in the worlds of bliss may not be everlasting. Sacrifice secured for the believer admission to the sphere of the deity whom he served. The mystical interpretation of sacrifice supposed that a new body was prepared to fit him for ascension to the world above. There he dwelt in the happy fellowship with the deity of his devotion. Already in the Brāhmaṇas the idea of a post-mortem judgement occurs for the first time, as we have seen above, according to which men's deeds are weighed in a balance and are rewarded or punished as merit or demerit for good or bad actions respectively. In the *Bṛhadāranyaka Upanishad* a distinction is made between the way of the gods *(devayāna)* and the way of the Fathers *(pitṛyāna)*.

> "Those who know this and those too who in the forest revere faith as truth, merge into the flame; from flame into the day... into the world of the gods *(deva-loka);* from the world of the gods into the sun; ... A person who is (all) mind draws near to these realms of lightning and leads them on to the Brahman-worlds. In those Brahman-worlds they live for long ages. For them there is no return.

92 *Śatapatha Brāhmaṇa* 1.9.3.

93 Ibid. 11.6.1.

94 Ibid. 1.4.3.11-12; 9.6.1.

> But those who win for themselves many a world by sacrifice, the giving of alms and self-mortification merge into the smoke ... to the world of the ancestors, from the world of ancestors to the moon"[95].

The way of the gods is that of those who have faith, the way of this spiritual élite; purified by the fire that has consumed their gross bodies, they pass on into the flame and to the world of the gods. A spiritual person conducts them to the world of Brahman; from this there is no return. They have achieved eternal bliss. The way of the Fathers is that of those who have duly offered sacrifices, shown generosity in almsgiving, and performed austerities. This is the way of the righteous men who have only followed the ordinances of traditional religion. These followers of sacrificial cult pass on into smoke, the night and into the world of the Fathers and finally into the moon. Rising up into the worlds, they circle round within them. But those who do not know these two ways become worms, moths, and biting serpents.[96]

In the *Upanishads* three classes of souls are distinguished. Those that rely on faith in the eternity of the Ātman are released from the cycle of rebirth. Those who perform Vedic duties of sacrifice, almsgiving, and austerity return to the world in human form after being in the world of the Fathers. Those who do not know both these ways are condemned to a life of insect or reptile. For the first time in the history of Brahmanism the Upanishads teach explicitly the doctrine of transmigration as a consequence of the law of action, which becomes

95 6.2.15-16. See also *Chāndogya Upanishad* 5.10, a parallel passage. In the doctrine of the two ways both the way of man from the world to heaven and his way from heaven back to this world again are included. The one who goes to the Brahman world does not return to earthly life. This is the way of the forest hermits who possess the right knowledge. Instead those who have not abandoned ritual and social duties go to the world of the Fathers and to the moon and return to earth.

96 See *Chānd. Up.* 4.15.5-6; 5.10.1-8; *Maitri* Up. 6.30; *Prāśna Up.* 1.9-10 *Kauśītaki Upanishad* 1.2 is an important text on this subject: "Those who depart from this world they all go to the moon. (The moon puts questions.) Whoever answers him, him he lets go further. But whoever answers him not, him having become rain, he rains down here. Either as a worm, or as a moth, or as a fish, or as a bird, or as a lion, or as a wild boar, or as a snake, or as a tiger, or as a man *(purusha)* or as some other in this or that condiction, he is born again according to his work, according to his knowledge". Here it is said that *Karma* together with knowledge *(vidyā)* determines the kind of rebirth.

a distinctive feature of Hinduism itself. A man becomes what he does. He becomes good by good deeds, and evil by evil deeds, because every action leaves in man effect that is proportionate to the action. The root-cause of man's action is desire. The law of action is a universal law of immanent retribution according to which every good act meets with reward and every evil act meets with punishment either in this life or in the next. Such a law demands that man be reborn to reap the fruit of his action. The soul's reward in heaven or punishment in hell is only temporary, for once the retribution is over, it reverts to earthly life.[97] Here we see that the Vedic conception of the afterlife in heaven or in hell is combined with the new doctrine of cycle of rebirth and of final liberation from this cycle itself through higher wisdom.

The Teaching of Mahābhārata

There are many descriptions of heaven *(svarga* or *paraloka)* in the great Epic, some of which are very sensual and form the subject of most voluptuous narratives of the heavenly bliss.[98] But other passages portray heavenly blessedness without holding out any promise of any sensual gratification. We have the whole episode of the holy man Mudgala[99] who was persuaded to go to heaven bodily and to see the state of complete perfection that reigns there. The sage wanted to know however the advantages and drawbacks of the heavenly state. The messenger began telling him what kind of people went there. Only men of virtue who have subdued their spirit, controlled their faculties, free from malice, intent on practice of charity, and heroes and men of battle who have subdued their senses and performed most meritorious rites attain to heaven. There are established separately myriads of beautiful, shining, and resplendent worlds bestowing every object of desire, owned by celestial beings. There is seen the glorious mountain Meru and the holy garden Nandana, where the ri-

---

97 *Bṛh. Up.* 4.2.2-6; 3.2.13.

98 For example 3.42-46 (Indraloka). Indra and Varuṇa and other gods are sometimes represented in the *Mahābhārata* as leading a sensual and immoral life and as seducing austere sages.

99 The *Mahābhārata* 3.259-61.

ghteous sport. There hunger, thirst, weariness, cold, heat, fear are unknown. There is nothing disgusting or disgraceful; the scents are delightful; sounds are pleasant to the ear and mind. There is no sorrow, nor lamentation, nor decay, nor labour, nor envy, nor jealousy, nor delusion. There the blessed are clothed with glorious bodies which are produced by their works. Their garlands are fragrant and unfading; they ride in aerial cars. Beyond these there are higher regions to which seers who have been purified by their deeds proceed; beyond these are those gods, where there is no annoyance occasioned by women, or by envy arising from worldly grandeur. The gods do not desire pleasure. They do not experience joy, pleasure, delight, happiness, suffering, love, hatred. This state beyond the reach of those who seek pleasure is desired even by the gods. The disadvantages of heaven are explained thus. As the fruit of works done on earth is enjoyed in heaven, while no other work is newly performed there from which new reward could arise, this enjoyment is cut off from its root, and must come to an end[100]. The loss of gratification and the dissatisfaction and pain of those who have descended to lower state mark these souls who are fading slowly. The state of those who have fallen from heaven is not without compensation. As a result of their previous good deeds they are born in a condition of happiness. Hearing this the sage replies that he can have nothing to do with the state of happiness which is vitiated by so great defects and the end of which is followed by so great a misery. He has therefore no desire for heaven and will seek only the eternal abode where there is no sorrow, no distress, no change. The messenger further instructs him that above the abode of Brahmā is the pure eternal light, the highest sphere of Vishnu, the supreme Brahman. The sage after dismissing the messenger began to practise ascetic virtues, becoming indifferent to praise and blame, etc. Pure knowledge led to fixed contemplation;

100 kṛtasya karmaṇas tetra bhujyate yad phalaṁ divi /
na cānyat kryate karma mūla-ccedena bhujyate. 3.259

"In the celestial regions a person while reaping the fruit of his acts he has already performed, cannot be engaged in any others, and he must enjoy the consequences of the former until they are completely exhuasted, that he is subject to fall after he has entirely exhausted his merit".

karmabhūmir iyam brahman phalabhūmir asau matā: "this world is the place of works while the other is the place for reward". Ibid.

and that again imparted strength and complete comprehension whereby he attained supreme eternal perfection.[101]

The fate of the wicked is described in a significant passage thus: The region for the sinful is hell. Darkness and ceaseless pain accompany them and they are full of sorrow. Sinking in infamy, the sinful man is wrung with remorse there for many years.[102] The region of the sinful was enveloped in thick darkness, and covered with hair and moss forming its grassy vesture. Polluted with the stench of sinners, and miry with flesh and blood. Rotting corpses lay here and there. Overspread with bones and hair, it was noisome with worms and insects. It was skirted all along with a blazing fire. It was infested with crows and vultures, as also by evil spirits. There was a river full of boiling water and a forest of trees whose leaves were sharp swords and razors. There were many jars of iron all around with boiling oil in them. Cruel tortures were there on sinful men[103].

In the great Epic the two beliefs, namely of the *karma* doctrine and that of heaven and hell, sometimes stand separate; that is to say, an abode in Indra's heaven without any allusion to rebirth, or one is promised a high or lower birth hereafter without allusion to heaven or hell. Ordinarily the two beliefs are combined by proposing that rebirth follows the penalty of hell or reward of heaven. Final liberation consists precisely in being released from bondage of the cycle of rebirth. This state is described in different ways. The soul becomes Brahman, infinity, deathlessness, or the one Self of all things; it is free from all thought of 'I' and 'mi-

101 jñānayogena śuddhena dhyānanityo babhūva ha /
dhyānayogād balam labdhvā prāpya buddhim anuttamām /
jagāma śāśvatīṁ siddhim parāṁ nirvāṇa-lakṣaṇām. 3.259

102 12.73. In the chapter 190 of the same section hell and darkness are identified.
anṛtaṁ tamaso rūpaṁ tamasā nīyate hy adhaḥ, /
tamo-grastāḥ na paśyanti prakāśaṁ tamasā vṛtāḥ //
svargaḥ prakāśaḥ ity āhur narakaṁ tamaḥ eva ca /
"Untruth is only another form of darkness, By darkness a man is carried downwards.Those who are seized by darkness, being enveloped in darkness, do not see the light. Heaven they say is light, and hell is darkness."

Compare *the Vishṇu Purāṅa* 2.6.40:
manaḥ,prīti-karaḥ svargo narakas tad-viparyayaḥ /
naraka-svarga-sañjñc vai pāpapuṇye dvijottama:
"Heaven is that which delights the mind;
hell is that which gives it pain; hence vice is
called hell; virtue is called heaven."

103 18.2.

ne'; it casts off its lower self and takes possession of the higher self; it transcends all the opposites, fear and time, sorrow and joy. It goes to a state where it does not grieve or die, where it is neither born nor reborn, where it does not change, where is the highest Brahman, unmanifest, unmoving, steadfast, immortal and eternal, where all are like-minded and friendly and where they rejoice in the well-being of all creatures.[104] In the ultimate state of liberation *(moksha)* whether souls become Brahman or enter into God in union, it is not clear that anything of their personality remains, after their empirical self has been destroyed. The liberated soul is like a fish in the sea, permeated with water within and without; or like a maggot in a fig, enveloped by the fig; or purified from all stain it unites permanently with the permanently pure and 'isolated'; or in theistic trend the soul is united with God as two suns might unite in the sky.[105]

The Teaching of the Purāṇas

In the *Purāṇas* very often the cycle of rebirth is proposed as a spinning wheel which leads to misery and hence as an endless trap. The *Bhāgavata Purāṇa* records an interesting story which illustrates in allegory the truth about rebirth and redeath[106] There lived a well-known king, named Puranjana. He roamed all over the earth, hoping to find a suitable place to live. Being disappointed in his endeavour, he thought to himself: "I have seen many cities but none appears good to me. I want to live in one where all my desires may be satisfied; but none of these would be sufficient for the purpose." Finally he arrived at a city in Bhārata-varsha, south of the Himalayas. This magnificient city with its nine gates, its stately palaces, its beautiful gardens, and crystal lakes, appeared to have all the advantages he had been seeking. He felt assured that at last his wanderings were over since here all his desires could be gratified.

Then one day Puranjana saw a beautiful young lady with her attendants walking in a garden. They met and fell in love and within a short time they were married. They continued to live in the city of ni-

---

104 12.241 (Gv.)

105 12.310 (Gv.)

106 *The Bhāgavata Purāña* 4.25ff.

ne gates. Puranjana found he could indulge his many desires by passing through these gates, although he never found a real satisfaction in so doing. He loved his wife deeply and was happy only when he was in her presence. He shared her happiness and sorrow, and was slavishly responsive to her every whim and fansy; he was on the way to loosing the last vestige of his independence. For many years he lived in that city, gratifying his desires but never obtaining any lasting pleasure or comfort from his way of life.

Now it so happened that while Puranjana was immersed in pleasures and was forgetful of everything else, a mighty general attacked the city. This general possessed a certain magical charm by which he had the power to do great havoc. He demolished the city of nine gates and Puranjana could not escape. He lost everything, even the stronghold of consciousness, his memory. He forgot his past, his kingship, his magnificient city. Only the thought of his beautiful wife was left to him. This thought possessed him so completely that he did not notice his loss of memory for the rest of the world. His whole being became obsessed by her image, and like a madman who losing his identity becomes the object of his fixation, he found himself transformed into a lovely young girl like his wife. The young girl he had become forgot her past identity to such an extent that when she met king Malaydhwaja, she fell in love with him and married him. After the king's death, she was left alone, lamenting his death and her bereavement. At this time an unknown brāhmin came to her and said, "My friend, why are you grieving? Do you not know me, your dear friend. Try to remember who and what you are. I have been your friend always, but you neglected me, and forgetting me entirely went away in search of pleasure and enjoyment. You and I are friends, united in eternal bonds. Though you forgot me I have been with you all the time. You and I are not separate. Know yourself as me. Just as one sees himself as two when reflected in a mirror, so do you appear as you and I, but in reality we are one."

Nārada then explains the allegory.[107] Puranjana stands for the Purusha, the divine in man; the unknown friend is Brahman or God. None knows him; no deeds or attributes can express or reveal him. The cities are of various kinds, of which the human body is a suitable

107 Ibid. 4.29

instrument for the enjoyment of all desires. The human body is the city of nine gates such as eyes, ears, nose, etc. through which the self goes out to enjoy the objects of sense. The wife is the intellect, united with whom man enjoys the world and worldly goods. In thus identifying itself with the intellect or ego, the divine self forgets its true nature and becomes immersed in ignorance and vanity. The great general is all-destructive time, whose charms are disease and death, which ultimately destroy the body. Man is divine and free and blissful; but being deluded he forgets his real self and identifies himself with non-self. He thus becomes attached to the world and its pleasures. He is bound by his deeds and undergoes the birth that is the result of his deeds. Man carries the burden of misery in his life in an endless manner.

The lesson taught by the above allegory is that the embodied self is born again and again according to its actions of the past life and assumes one body after another in various but endless existences. Nārada concludes: "So long as action exists there is ignorance, too, and so long as ignorance exists, bodies are tied to actions"[108]. Through the destiny of *karma* (action) the mind *(manas)* meditates on things seen and heard and gradually loses its memory with regard to them. This mind *(manas)* entering into another body ceases thus to remember all the experiences of the previous bodies. Hence we can define death as absolute forgetfulness[109] Birth is regarded as acceptance of new experiences. As Śridhara, the commentator of the *Bhāgavata* explains, the function of the ego with respect to the experiences of the past bodies ceases and the function of the ego with respect to the experiences of the new body begins in the new birth. The mind of man is permeated by deeds and their causes, and it is this mind that passes from one body to another. The *ātman* follows this manas.[110]

Besides these views, the *Bhāgavata Purāṇa* also teaches that those who perform sacrifices and make offering to gods and forefathers after death go to the lunar world from which they return again to the earth. Those who do their own duties and surrender all their actions to the gods, who are pure in mind and heart, and are unattached to

---

108 Ibid 4.29.78

109 Ibid. 11.22 39.

110 Ibid. 11.22.37.

worldly things, go to the solar world and hence to the universal being. Those who meditate on duality or whose spiritual life is determined by dual relationship between them and God pass into the nature of the qualified Brahman, and are then born again in the world in accordance with their past actions. People who lead an ordinary life, who make offerings to the forefathers first go by the southern way of smoky path to the region of the forefathers and then are born again in the line of their own progenies[111].

Vaikuṇṭha, the abode of Vishṇu

According to the *Vishṇu Purāṇa,* there are seven worlds *(lokas)* or spheres above the earth: Prajāpatya or Pitr loka, Indra loka or Svarga, Marut loka or Diva loka (heaven), Gandharva loka, the region of celestial spirits (also called Maharloka), Janaloka or the sphere of the saints, Tapaloka, the world of the seven sages, and Brahmaloka or Satya Loka, the world of infinite wisdom and truth.[112] The eighth, the highest world of Vishṇu (*visnoḥ paramaṁ padaṁ*) is considered to be a sectarian addition, which later on is called Vaikuṇṭha[113] and Goloka.[114]

Vaikuṇṭha-dhāman, the state of existence free from worldly limitations, the highest region of Vishṇu, is described very vividly in the *Bhāgavata Purāna*[115] as follows. The people whose mind and body are purely divine (free from the taint of *māyā*) went there. All the people living there are endowed with a form similar to Vaikuṇṭha-Vishṇu. This region is attained by those alone who have worshipped Śrī Hari (Vishṇu) through disinterested performance of their duty. There the most ancient

---

111 Ibid. 3.32.

112 *The Vishṇu Purāña* 1.6. See H. H. WILSON, *The Vishṇu Purāña,* op. cit., p. 42, n. 10.

113 It is often the title of Vishṇu, though it is also of Indra. W. Hopkins cites the South Indian Version of the *Mahābhārata* 1.95,7 where Vishṇu is called the "divinity of the gods"; Devānāṁ daivataṁ Viṣṇur, viprāṇām agnir brahmā ca.

As such he is called Vaikuṇṭha by the gods, while the Vedas call him Vishṇu. All texts place him in the local habitation north of the Sea of Milk. There he rides in the car of eight wheels (elements). See his *Epic Mythology,* Strassburg, 1915, p. 207.

114 "Cow-world," a part of heaven of Vishṇu. It is sometimes translated as "the realm of light" in which resides Bhagavat, Śrī Krishṇa, or Vishṇu-Vaikuṇṭha, the land of freedom from limitations.

115 3.15.16-25; see also 2.9.10-17.

Person (Nārāyaṇa) who is righteousness personified, dwells, having assumed a form which is made of *sattva* alone (i.e., purely divine), and delighting his devotees. In this realm there is an orchard called Naiḥṣreyasa which is liberation *(kaivalya)* incarnate. This region is resplendent with trees which yield all that is desired and are laden with fruits and flowers in every season. The gandharvas there sing the praise of Lord Vishṇu, that is capable of wiping out the sins of the whole world. Birds of innumerable variety raise a tumultuous symphony; but it is silenced by lyrical hymn of bees, tuned to the laudation of Vishnu. *Tulasi* flower which Vishṇu has chosen as his adornment has an exalted position over other flowers. The splendour and fragrance of these flowers, and the presence of beautiful women, do not stimulate baser feelings.

In the royal palace of Vishṇu moves Śrī, the beloved of Vishṇu, with a lotus in her hand and jingling anklets at het feet. Her pure and beautiful form is reflected on the crystal floor to give the impression of showing her unqualified service to the Lord. During the worship of the Lord her beautiful face is mirrored in the pool which is located in the garden of Śrī. In the royal hall of the seventh chamber is seated Vishṇu, the Paramātman, on the hood of Ananta,[116] with all his grandeur and the great congregation assembled to his service. They have all assumed the four-armed form of Vishṇu, all except the exclusive qualities of Śrivatsa[117] and Kaustubha.[118]

Only those attain to this heavenly realm of Vishṇu, who have reached beyond the jurisdiction of Yama (the god of retribution) by virtue of their loving devotion to Vishṇu, who possess an enviable character, whose eyes stream with tears and whose body is thrilled when they are united with Him in love while talking to one another about the glories of the Lord.

In the *Pāñcarātra*[119] the highest heaven or Vaikuṇṭha has nothing to do with any of the temporal heavens which form the upper spheres of the Cosmic Egg. The Vaikuṇṭha is described as Tripādvibhūti, manifestation of

---

116 The snake-god who symbolises eternity.

117 Śrīvatsa, "favourite of Śrī," a name of Vishṇu. A particular mark or curl of hair on the breast of Vishṇu or Krishna. It is seen on the right chest of Vishṇu, representing the radiance of non-dual consciousness and his divine splendour.

118 Kaustubha is the precious jewel occupying the most prominent place in the body of Vishṇu, symbolizing his self-luminosity *(ātmalyotis)*.

119 See F. Otto Schrader, *Introduction to the Pāñcarātra and the Ahirbudhnya Saṁhitā*, Adyar, 1916, pp. 49ff, 58ff, 106ff.

the three-forths of the Lord, whereas it is only one-fourth with which the Cosmic egg is created. In a later view it is said that Vaikuṇṭha is not affected by the great dissolution.[120] Here the distinction between master and spirit is admitted but the master is considered pure, *śuddha-sattva,* not a mixture of three guṇas. Pure master is spiritual, i.e., of the nature of knowledge and bliss. Souls without this master would not have any object of enjoyment. This pure matter does not come in the way of the spirit to enjoy or to fulfil its desires.

God in his highest form lives in the Vaikuṇṭha. God as Para[121] is said to be always in company with his consort Śrī. The liberated live as free beings, and their mode of life differs according to the devotional inclinations preserved from their last earthly existence. As inhabitant of Vaikuṇṭha the devotee beholds that kind of form to which he has been attached while he lived on earth. The saints in Vainkuṇṭha are intent upon nothing but service *(kainkarya)* to God.

According to the Pāñcarātra the general view is that at the time of dissolution souls return to God and remain in a potential form in Him but again become separate from God at the time of new creation. However at the moment of final liberation they enter into God, and remain in Him for ever. In this union between God and souls, there is no question of identification between them; they have independent existence in God and enter into the abode of Vishṇu, the Vaikuṇṭha which is often regarded as identical with Him.[122] The liberated man can realize true nature with reference to God only in Vaikuṇṭha, the abode of God where he is accepted as the servant of the Lord; only such a state can be called eternal.[123]

---

120 With this idea is perhaps connected also the distinction between *nityavibhūti,* i.e., the highest heaven or *Vaikuṇṭha,* and *līlā-vibhūti,* i.e., the world (eternal manifestation and play-manifestation).

121 God as Para, i.e., as the highest form.

122 In the 14th chapter of the *Ahirbudhnya-saṁhitā* liberation is described as the attainment of the Godhead (bhagavattā-mayi mukti, or vaiṣṇavaṁ tad viśet padam). See 16.3.4 and 41. The means of attaining this final end is said to be the virtuous action without self-seeking. Sādhanaṁ tasya ca prokto dharmo nirabhisandhikaḥ. Ibid. 14.4. The souls are beginningless, infinite, and pure consciousness and bliss, and being largely of the nature of God *(bhagavanmaya);* but they are said to own their existence to the spiritual energy of God *(bhagavadbhāvitāh sada).* See Ibid.

123 The ultimate goal, according to Śrī Vaishṇavism, is self-surrender to God. It consists in the servitude *(kaiṅkarya)* to God roused by love of Him, due to the knowledge of one's own nature and the nature of God in all his majesty, power and supreme excellence. See PILLAI LOKĀCĀRYA, *Tattva-śekhara,* ch. 4.

Later Śrī Vaishṇavism explains the Śrī Vaikuṇṭha and its symbolism more philosophically. The form, flavour and fragrance of *Brahmānuhbava* are not physical or psychical, but super-sensuous *(aprākṛta)*.[124] In the world of Brahman or Paramapada, matter shines without change and time exists under the form of eternity. The eternals are not qualities *(viśeṣanas)* housed in the Absolute as its elements, but are its members revelling in the rapture of union.[125] The liberated soul gloriously enters into Śrī Vaikuṇṭha, the heart of Brahmaloka, reaches the hall of *ānandamaya*, the sphere of bliss, and has direct insight of the Supreme Light *(paraṁjyotis)*. The throne in which is seated Brahman is wisdom *(prajñā)* and Brahman is the True of the true *(satyasya satya)*. The released soul realizes the unitive consciousness. The *Brahmavit* enjoys all the perfections of Vaikuṇṭha like *Sālokya* (identity of abode), *sāmīpya* (proximity), *sārūpya* (similarity of form) and *sāyujya* or intimate union. It is ever immersed in the eternal bliss of Brahman. Co-existence leads to nearness and fellowship and this leads to transformation and deification, and is consummated in the bliss of communion.[126]

Strictly speaking Vaikuṇṭha is not like any of the heaven *(svarga)* described in the Hindu mythology but the sphere of the Absolute Brahman with whom Vishṇu is identified, with whom the liberated soul remains eternally united in love of perpetual service to and fellowship of God. This state of union is final liberation itself from which there is no return to the cycle of rebirth or to the worldly existence. Such a conception of the abode of Vishṇu, which is called by some highest Heaven is characteristic of *bhakti* religion in Hinduism.

Every religion for Vedānta Deśika is a means for the attainment of Parama Pada, Tripād Vibhūti, Parama Vyoma, Vaikuṇṭha. God in his full divine state in the Divine Abode (Vaikuṇṭha) is the same as the immanent Being in the material world of ours. The divine Abode is

---

124 Strictly speaking the nature of the attainment of liberation and bliss *(parama-pada)* cannot be described or defined, because the categories used to express them are human and finite and the supreme state is transcendental. From the religious point of view God reveals himself to whom he chooses as he is Himself the means and the end of all religious experience. The *brahmavit* needs the divine eye to apprehend God and his nature.

125 The sun does not shine there, nor the moon, nor the stars; by His light everything is lighted. Brahman is before and behind, above and below.

126 On this later development of the concept of Vaikuṇṭha in Vaishṇavism, see P. N. SRINIVASACHARI, *The Philosophy of Viśiṣṭādvaita*, Adyar, 1946, pp. 474ff.

transcendent, but essentially immanent in the empirical existence. But the distinction between the transcendent realm of God (vaikuṇṭha) and the immanent realm of the transient world is necessary because God remains the inexhaustible Great Being, the Transcendent Absolute in whom all that is and has its being is eternally contained and composed. The Parama Pada is meant for devout meditation. The fulness of love and devotion and service which must be the essential nature of the Parama Pada must find an expression, however incomplete, in the empirical world of men and ordinary life.[127]

The state of final liberation consists in the rise of the ultimate expansion of the intellect. Such a state is effected as a result of loving devotion to Vishṇu and remains for ever without end. For it is the state of the ultimate dissociation of all causes such as sins or virtues which can produce a contraction of the mind and thus terminate such a state. The state of final liberation is a state of perfect bliss through a continual realization of Brahman to whom the liberated man is attached as a servant.[128] He is omnipotent in the sense that God never frustrates his desires. He can assume bodies at will, which is not a source of bondage to him. He beholds all things as contained as being held in Brahman as its parts without any pain or misery. Such an emancipation can be brought about only by *bhakti* which is love of God in the sense of meditation or thinking with affection.[129] Such a love of God also produces knowledge, and such a knowledge is also included in the love of God. *Bhakti* is defined as unceasing meditation and hence it has to be practised always.[130]

---

127 Life-divine: the ultimate ideal, in: SATYAVRATA SINGH, *Vedāntadeśika,* Varanasi, 1958, pp. 426ff.

128 This servitude is not one of misery, for servitude can be a misery only when it is associated with sin.

129 mahanīya-viṣaye prītir bhaktiḥ, prīty-ādayaś ca jñāna-viśeṣa iti vakṣyate snehapūrvam anudhyānaṁ bhaktiḥ. See Vedāntadeśika, *Sarvārtha-siddhi,* p. 190.

130 bhakti-sādhyaṁ prāpaka-jñānam api bhakti-lakṣaṇo-petam. Ibid. p. 191.

3. Conclusion

Cosmic eschatology in Hinduism is cyclical and therefore we may begin with the smallest time units, the yugas, and the great yuga *(mahāyuga)* which is comprised of four ordinary yugas. The great yuga is the basic cosmic cyclic entity, for it is at this level that we find the grand cyclic pattern in its full scope: creation, gradual diminuition in vitality and virtue, final dissolution, recreation and so on around again and again.

Diagram of a Hindu Cosmic Age

Cosmic Age *(kalpa)*
= Life-span of a world from creation to dissolution.
= A day in the life of Brahmā.
= 1000 great ages *(Mahāyuga).*

Each Great Age
= *Krta yuga:* 4800 God's years. Perfect, golden age, total *dharma.*
Tretā yuga: 3600 God's years. Three-fourths of *dharma.*
Dvāpara yuga: 2400 God's years. Half of *dharma.*
Kali yuga: 1200 God's years. one-fourth of *dharma.*

Great Dissolution *(Mahāpralaya)*: end of the life of Brahmā.

By involution the world is re-integrated into Brahmā until the hatching of a new cosmic egg.

The process is conceived by the Vaishnavites thus: The day of Brahmā dawns and God awakes. During the night of Brahmā Vishṇu lies, unconscious and recumbent, on the cosmic serpent Sesha, and as dawn approaches a lotus blooms miraculously from his navel, and from this lotus springs the creator-god Brahmā, while Śiva, the destroyer or rather the agent of reabsorption *(saṁhara)* springs from his head. From these beginnings the universe evolves. According to Vaishṇavism again, there is periodic intervention of Vishṇu in the form of an *avatāra* (descent) to restore order and righteousness in the universe, to punish the unrighteous and to reward the righteous, and to show men the way of liberation and union with God.

Although time is subordinated to Brahmā and Siva in various aspects of creation and dissolution respectively, the Hindu aspiration is precisely to transcend time and its cyclic round of rebirths. Time itself has no ultimate meaning and purpose except to bind man to misery and suffering. Hence the religious quest of the Hindus in various spiritual paths that make them get out of this time-bound cycle of existence, is to reach the state of eternal and blissful existence either in union with a personal God or in complete absorption with the Absolute (Brahman).

This precisely leads to the view of individual eschatology of the Hindu, which consists in various conditions of rebirth either in heaven *(svarga)* or in hell *(naraka)* or on earth in different states of human or even animal existence, until in the human form one is liberated from the whole cycle of rebirth. Release from the chain of cosmic existence and rebirth is the ultimate goal of every Hindu. Even though the two doctrines of rebirth and of heaven-hell appear inconsistent, they are joined together by imagining that rebirth follows the penalty of hell or reward of heaven. As we know from the Hindu sacred texts themselves, *moksha or mukti* (liberation) has both a negative and a positive meaning. Negatively it means release not only from the enchainment to a transitory and suffering form of existence but also from enchainment to a worthless cycle of rebirth. Positively it has the meaning of bliss, union with the Supreme Being: in the theist context it means union with the Personal God in love and surrender; in the absolutist or non-dual context, it means total identity of the individual self with the Absolute Self. Hinduism in all its forms endorses these views.

BIBLIOGRAPHY

1) Hinduism in general

W.G. ARCHER, *The loves of Krishna in Indian painting and poetry,* New York, no date.

K. BALASUBRAHMANIA IYER, *Hindu ideals,* Bombay, 1969.

N. V. BANERJEE, *The spirit of Indian philosophy,* New Delhi, 1974.

P. BANERJEE, *Early Indian religions,* Delhi, 1973.

L. D. BARNETT, *The heart of India,* London, 1924.

———, *Brahma knowledge,* London, 1911.

———, *Hindu Gods and Heroes,* London, 1922.

A. BARTH, *The religions of India,* London, 1882. (Tr.)

T. DE BARY, *Sources of Indian tradittion,* Delhi, 1965.

H. BATTACHARYA (ed.), *The cultural heritage of India,* 4 vols., Calcutta, 1961 ff.

S. K. BELVALKAR-R. D. RANADE, *History of Indian philosophy:* 1. *The creative period,* Poona, 1927; 2. *Mysticism in Maharashtra,* Poona, 1955.

A. BERGAIGNE, *La religion védique d'après les hymnes du Rigveda,* Paris, 1878-83, 3 vols.

A. BESANT, *Sanatana Dharma,* Adyar, 1967.

BHAGAVAN DAS, *An advanced textbook of Hindu religion and ethics,* Adyar, 1940.

R. G. BHANDARKAR, *Vaiṣṇavism, Saivism and minor religius systems,* Strassburg, 1913.

M. BIARDEAU, *Clefs pour la pensèe hindoue,* Paris, 1972.

———, *L'Hindouisme,* Anthropologie d'une civilisation, Paris, 1981.

M. BLOOMFIELD, *The Atharva-veda,* Strassburg, 1899.

———, *Religion of the Veda,* New York, 1908.

J. L. BROCKINGTON, *The Sacred Thread,* Hinduism in its continuity and diversity, Edinburgh, 1981.

N. BROWN, *Man in the Universe (Some continuities in Indian thought),* Berkeley, 1966.

A. C. BOUQUET, *Hinduism,* London, 1948.

J. E. CARPENTER, *Theism in medieval India,* Delhi, 1977 (reprint).

S. C. CHATTERJEE, *The fundamentals of Hinduism,* Calcutta, 1950.

S. C. Chatterjee-D. M. Datta, *Introduction to Indian philosophy,* Calcutta, 1950.
S. Chattopadhyaya, *Evolution of Hindu Sects,* New Delhi, 1970.
S. Chattopadhyaya-D. Datta, *Indian Philosophy,* Calcutta, 1962.
Sarasvati Chennakesavan, *A Critical Study of Hinduism,* Delhi, 1980.
A. K. Coomaraswamy, *Hinduism and Buddhism,* New York, no date.
———, and Sister Nivedita, *Myths of the Hindus and Buddhists,* New York, 1967.
A. Daniélou, *Le Polytheisme hindoue,* Paris, 1960.
S. N. Dasgupta, *History of Indian philosophy,* 5 vols., Cambridge, 1961 f.
———, *Hindu mysticism,* Chicago, 1927.
S. K. De, *Vaishnava Faith and Movement,* Calcutta, 1947.
P. Deussen, *Indische Philosophie,* 3 parts, Leipzig, 1922.
———, *The system of Vedanta,* Chicago, 1912.
———, *The philosophy of the Upanishads,* New York, 1966.
P. D. Devanadan, *Living Hinduism,* Bangalore, 1959.
M. Dhavamony, *Love of God according to Śaiva Siddhānta,* Oxford, 1972.
———, *Classical Hinduism,* Ed. PUG, Roma, 1982.
———, *La Luce di Dio nell'Induismo,* Ed. Paoline, Milano, 1987.
———, *L'Induismo,* Cittadella Editrice, Assisi, 1991.
———, *Hindouisme et foi chrétienne,* Coll. "Christus" Desclée de Brouwer, Paris, 1993.
———, *La spiritualité hindoue,* Bibliothéque de Spiritualité 14, Beauchesne, Paris, 1997.
J. Dowson, *A classical dictionary of hindu mythology,* London, 1950.
Abbé Dubois, *Hindu manners, customs and ceremonies,* Oxford, 1959.
F. Edgerton, *Beginnings of Indian philosophy,* London, 1965.
W. Eidlitz, *Der Glaube und die heiligen Schriften der Inder,* Olten, 1957.
C. Eliot, *Hinduism and Buddhism,* 3 vols., London, 1921.
A. T. Embree (ed.), *The Hindu Tradition,* New York, 1966.
A.-M. Esnoul, *L'Hindouisme,* Textes et Traductions sacrées, Paris, 1971.
J. N. Farquhar, *An outline of the religious literature of India,* London, 1920.
———, *A primer of Hinduism,* London, 1912.
———, *The crown of Hinduism,* London, 1913.
J. Filliozat, *Inde. Nation et tradition,* Paris, 1961.
E. Frauwallner, *Geschichte der indischen Philosophie,* 2 vols., Salzburg, 1955 ff.
E. Gathier, *La pensée hindoue,* Paris, 1960.
B. G. Gokhale, *Indian thought through the ages,* Bombay, 1961.
J. Gonda, *Die Religionen Indiens,* 2 vols., Stuttgart, 1960 f.
———, *Selected Studies,* Vol. IV: *History of ancient Indian Religion,* Leiden, 1975.
———, *Change and continuity in Indian religion,* The Hague, 1965.
———, *Aspects of early Visnuism,* Utrecht, 1954.

———, *Viṣṇuism and Sivaism,* London, 1970.
H. von Glasenapp, *Entwicklungstufen des indischen Denkens,* Halle, 1940.
———, *Die Religionen Indiens,* Stuttgart, 1943.
———, *Die Philosophie der Inder,* Stuttgart, 1949.
———, *Der Hinduismus,* München, 1922.
Govinda Das, *Hinduism,* Madras, 1924.
H. D. Griswold, *The religion of the Rigveda,* Patna, 1971 (reprint).
R. Grousset, *Les philosophies indiennes,* 2 vols., Paris, 1951.
P. Hacker, *Kleine Schriften,* Wiesbaden, 1978.
———, *Vivarta,* Wiesbaden, 1953.
B. Heimann, *Facets of Indian thought,* London, 1964.
J. Herbert, *Spiritualité hindoue,* Paris, 1947.
———, *L'Hinduisme vivant,* Paris, 1975.
A. Hillebrandt, *Ritual-Literatur,* Strassburg, 1897.
———, *Vedische Mythologie,* 2 vols., Breslau, 1927-29.
M. Hiriyanna, *Essentials of Indian philosophy,* London, 1951.
———, *Outlines of Indian philosophy,* London, 1964.
———, *The quest after perfection,* Mysore, 1952.
E. W. Hopkins, *The great Epic of India,* Calcutta, 1969 (reprint).
———, *Epic Mythology,* Strassburg, 1915.
V. Ions, *Indian mythology,* London, 1967.
C. V. N. Iyyar, *Origin and early history of Saivism in South India,* Madras, 1936.
P. T. S. Iyengar, *Outlines of Indian philosophy,* Benares, 1909.
S. Jaiswal, *The origin and development of Vaiṣṇavism,* Delhi, 1967.
Jesuit Scholars, *Religious Hinduism,* Allahabad, 1964.
P. Johanns, *La pensée religieuse de l'Inde,* Louvain, 1952.
J. Jolly, *Hindu law and custom,* Calcutta, 1928.
P. V. Kane, *History of Dharmaśāstras,* 5 vols., Poona, 1950-62.
A. Kaegi, *The Rigveda,* Boston, 1886 (Tr.).
A. B. Keith, *Religion and Philosophy of the Veda and and the Upanishads,* 2 vols., Cambridge (Mass.), 1925.
S. V. Ketkar, *An essay on Hinduism,* London, 1911.
W. Kirfel, *Der Hinduismus,* Berlin, 1934.
———, *Symbolik der Hinduismus und des Jinismus,* Stuttgart, 1959.
K. Klostermaier, *Hinduismus,* Köln, 1965.
S. Konow-P. Tuxen, *The religions of India,* Copenhagen, 1949.
O. Lacombe, *Indianité,* Paris, 1974.
———, *L'Élan Spirituel de l'Hindouisme,* Paris, 1986.
———, *L'Absolu selon le Vedānta,* Paris, 1937.
S. Lemaitre, *Hinduism,* New York, 1959 (Tr.).
A. A. Macdonell, *Vedic Mythology,* Varanasi, 1963 (reprint).
N. MacNicol, *Indian Theism,* London, 1915.
———, *The living religions of the Indian people,* London, 1934.
T. M. P. Mahadevan, *Outlines of Hinduism,* Bombay, 1960.

———, *Invitation to Indian Philosophy,* New Delhi, 1974.
P. MASSON-OURSEL, *Esquisse d'une historie de la philosophie indienne,* Paris, 1923.
MAX MULLER, *Heritage of India,* Calcutta, 1951 (reprint).
———, *The six systems of Indian philosophy,* Varanasi, 1962 (reprint).
P. D. MEHTA, *Early Indian religious thought,* London, 1956.
N. D. METHA, *Facets of Hinduism,* Bombay, no date.
J. MILLER, *The Vedas,* Bombay, 1974.
K. W. MORGAN (ed.), *The religion of the Hindus,* New York, 1953.
M. MONIER-WILLIAMS, *Brahmanism and Hinduism,* London, 1891.
———, *Hinduism,* Calcutta, 1877.
———, *Religious thought and life in India,* New Delhi, 1974 (reprint).
P. NAGARAJA RAO, *Fundamentals of Indian philosophy,* New Delhi, no date.
K. A. NILAKANTA SASTRI, *Development of religion in South India,* Madras, 1963.
SWAMI NITYABODHANANDA, *Mythes et religions de l'Inde,* Paris, 1967.
HANS OERTEL, *Zur indischen Apologetik,* Stuttgart, 1930.
W. D. O'FLAHERTY, *Hindu myths,* Hammondsworth, 1975.
———, *Asceticism and Eroticism in the Mythology of Śiva,* Oxford, 1975.
H. OLDENBERG, *Die Religion des Veda,* Berlin, 1923.
P. OLTRAMARE, *L'histoire des idées théosophiques dans l'Inde,* 2 vols., Paris, 1906.
T. W. ORGAN, *The Hindu quest for perfection of man,* Ohio, 1970.
———, *Hinduism,* its historical development, New York, 1974.
R. OTTO, *Viṣṇu-Nārāyana,* Jena, 1917.
R. PANIKKAR, *Vedic Experience,* London, 1977.
———, *Spiritualità indù,* Brescia, 1977.
C. PAPALI, *Hinduism (Religion and philosophy),* 2 vols., Alwaye, 1977.
SWAMI PRABHAVANANDA, *The spiritual heritage of India,* New York, 1964.
M. QUEGUINER, *Introduction à l'Hindouisme,* Paris, 1958.
S. RADHAKRISHNAN, *Indian philosophy,* 2 vols., London, 1958.
———, *The Hindu view of life,* London, 1963.
S. RADHAKRISHNAN-C. A. MOORE, *A source book in Indian Philosophy,* Princeton, 1957.
V. RAGHAVAN, *The Indian heritage,* Bangalore, 1958.
B. C. RAJAGOPALACHARI, *Hinduism: doctrine and way of life,* Bombay, 1959.
C. P. RAMASWAMY AIYAR, *Fundamentals of Hindu Faith and Culture,* Madras, 1959.
R. D. RANADE, *Mysticism in Maharashtra,* Poona, 1933.
———, *Pathway to God in Marathi literature,* Bombay, 1961.
———, *Pathway to God in Hindi literature,* Allahabad, 1954.
———, *Pathway to God in Kannada literature,* Bombay, 1960.
———, *Essays and reflections,* Bombay, 1964.
———, *A Constructive Survey of Upanishadic Philosophy,* Poona, 1926.

H. RAYCHAUDHURI, *Materials for study of the early history of the Vaishana-va sect,* Nex Delhi, 1975 (reprint).
L. RENOU-J. FILLIOZAT, *L'Inde classique,* 2 vols., Paris, 1947-53.
L. RENOU, *Religions of ancient India,* London, 1953.
———, *L'Inde fondamentale,* Paris, 1978.
———, *L'Hindouisme,* Paris, 1979.
GLYN RICHARDS (ed.), *A Source-book of Modern Hinduism,* London, 1985.
A. DE RIENCOURT, *The soul of India,* London, 1961.
W. RUBEN, *Geschichte der indischen Philosophie,* Berlin, 1954.
D. S. SARMA, *Renascent Hinduism,* Bombay, 1966.
———, *A primer of Hinduism,* Madras, 1929.
———, *Hinduism through the ages,* Bombay, 1973.
———, *Pearls of wisdom,* Bombay, 1962.
C. SHARMA, *A critical survey of Indian philosophy,* London, 1960.
N. J. SHENDE, *The religion and philosophy of the Atharva-veda,* Poona, 1952.
J. SINHA, *The foundation of Hinduism,* Calcutta, 1955.
———, *History of Indian philosophy,* 2 vols., Calcutta, 1956.
M. SIRCAR, *Hindu Mysticism,* New Delhi, 1974 (reprint).
S. SIVAPADASUNDARAM, *The Saiva school of Hinduism,* London, 1934.
K. SIVARAMAN, *Saivism in philosophical perspective,* Delhi, 1973.
V. S. SRINIVASA SASTRI, *Lectures on Ramayana,* Madras, 1977 (reprint).
O. STRAUSS, *Indische Philosophie,* München, 1925.
Ramananda Sarasvati SVAMINATH, *THe Hindu ideal,* Calcutta, 1970.
I. K. TAIMNI, *An introduction to Hindu symbolism,* Adyar, 1965.
P. THOMAS, *Hindu religion, customs and manners,* Bombay, 1961.
———, *Epics, myths and legends of India,* Bombay, 1960.
S. C. VIDYARNAYA, *The daily practice of the Hindus,* New Delhi, 1979 (reprint).
WILKINS, *Hindu Mythology,* Calcutta, 1882.
A. A. WILSON, *Religious sects of Hindus,* Calcutta, 1958.
H. H. WILSON, *Essays and lectures on the religion of the Hindus,* London, 1862.
P. ZACHARIAS, *Studies on Hinduism,* 5 Vols., Alwaye, 1945-50.
R. C. ZAEHNER, *Hinduism,* London, 1962.
———, *Hindu and Muslim mysticism,* London, 1960.
———, *Hindu Scriptures,* London, 1966.
H. ZIMMER, *Myths and symbols in Indian art and civilization,* New York, 1962.
———, *Philosophies of India,* New York, 1961.

2) Morality

A. S. ALTEKAR, *Sources of Hindu Dharma in its socio-religious aspects,* Sholajur, 1952.

A. B. Creel, *Dharma in Hindu Ethics,* Calcutta, 1972.
G. A. Chandavarkar, *A manuel of Hindu ethics,* Poona, 1925.
S. Dasgupta, *Development of moral philosophy in India,* Bombay, 1961.
J. D. Derret, *Hindu Law, past and present,* Calcutta, 1957.
B. K. Ghose, *Hindu ideal of life,* Calcutta, 1947.
E. W. Hopkins, *Ethics of India,* New Haven, 1924.
B. Khan, *The concept of dharma in Valmīki Rāmāyana,* Delhi, 1965.
R. Lingat, *Les sources du droit dans le système traditionnel de l'Inde,* Paris, 1967.
S. K. Maitra, *The ethics of the Hindus,* Calcutta, 1925.
J. McKenzie, *Hindu Ethics,* London, 1922.
G. H. Mees, *Dharma and Society,* The Hague, 1935.
I. C. Sharma, *Ethical philosophies of India,* New York, 1965.
P. S. Sivaswamy Iyer, *Evolution of Hindu Moral Ideals,* Calcutta, 1925.
D. P. Vora, *Evolution of morals in the Epics,* Bombay, 1959.

3) Prayer

A. J. Appasamy, *The Temple Bells,* Calcutta, no date.
A. K. Datta, *Bhaktiyoga,* Bombay, 1971.
A. Deleury, *Toukaram: Psaumes du pélerin,* Paris, 1956.
W. S. Deming, *Eknāth,* Bombay, 1931.
———, *Rāmdas and the Rāmdasis,* Bombay, 1930.
———, *Selections from Tukāram,* Madras, 1932.
W. D. P. Hill, *The holy lake of acts of Rāma,* translation of the Ramayana of Tulsi Das, Oxford, 1945.
J. Gonda, *The Indian mantra,* in his Selected Studies, IV, Leiden, 1975, 248-301.
F. Kingsbury-G. E. Phillips, *Hymns of the Tamil Saivite Saints,* Calcutta, 1921.
S. Krishnaswamy, *Thyagaraja, Saint and Singer,* Bombay, 1968.
A. A. Macdonell, *Hymns from the Rig Veda,* Delhi, 1968 (reprint).
N. MacNicol, *Psalms of Maraṭha Saints,* London, no date.
J. C. Oman, *The Mystics, ascetics, and saints of India,* London, 1903.
V. Raghavan, *The great integrators (The saint singers of India),* Delhi, 1969.
L. Renou, *Hinduism* (tr.), New York, 1967.
E. J. Thompson, *Bengali religious lyrics,* Calcutta, 1953.
K. C. Varadachari, *Alvārs of South India,* Bombay, 1970.
W. H. Westcott, *Kabīr and Kabīr Panth,* Calcutta, 1953.

4) Meditation

K. T. behanan, *Yoga, a scientific evaluation,* New York, 1964.

G. Coster, *Yoga and western psychology,* Glasgow, 1957.
A. Daniélou, *Yoga, méthod de réintégration,* Paris, 1951.
S. N. Dasgupta, *A study of Patañjali,* Calcutta, 1920.
M. Eliade, *Technique du yoga,* Paris, 1948.
———, *Patañjali and Yoga* (tr.), New York, 1969.
G. Feuerstein, *The essence of yoga,* London, 1974.
———, *Textbook of Yoga,* London, 1975.
——— and J. Miller, *A reappraisal of Yoga,* London, 1971.
J. W. Hauer, *Die Anfänge der Yoga-praxis,* Stuttgart, 1922.
———, *Die Yoga: ein indischer Weg zum Selbst,* Stuttgart, 1958.
R. Manheim-R. F. C. Hull (tr.), *Spiritual disciplines, papers from Eranos yearbooks,* New York, 1970.
P. Masson Oursel, *Le Yoga,* Paris, 1954.
J. Masui (ed.), *Yoga, science de l'homme intégral,* Paris, 1953.
H.-U. Rieker, *The secret of meditation,* London, 1974.
K. L. Reichelt, *Meditation and piety in the Far East,* New York, 1954.
Srinivasa Aiyengar, *Haṭha-yoga Pratīpikā,* Adyar, 1933.
C. Trungpa, *Meditation in action,* Berkeley, 1970.
G. Tucci, *Teoria e pratica del Maṇḍala,* Rome, 1969.
E. Wood, *Great systems of Yoga,* New York, 1968.
———, *Yoga,* Hammondsworth, 1962.
J. H. Woods, *Yoga system of Patañjali,* Harvard, 1914.
J. Varenne, *Yoga and the Hindu tradition* (tr.), Chicago, 1973.

5) Mysticism

B. Behari, *Sufis, mystics and yogis of India,* Bombay, 1971.
J. A. Cuttat, *Expérience chrétienne et spiritualité orientale,* Paris, 1967.
S. N. Dasgupta, *Hindu Mysticism,* New York, 1959.
M. Dhavamony, *Love of God according to Saiva Siddhānta,* Oxford, 1972.
———, *A bibliography on bhakti in Hinduism,* "Studia Missionalia", 30 (1981), 279-306.
M. Eliade, *Yoga, immortality and freedom,* New York, 1958.
L. Gardet, *Expériences mystiques en terres non chrétiennes,* Paris, 1953.
Le Vide, expérience spirituelle en Occident et en Orient, Paris, 1965.
R. Otto, *Mysticism, East and West,* New York, 1939.
A. Ravier (ed.), La *mystique et les mystiques,* Paris, 1965.
M. Sircar, *Hindu Mysticism (according to the Upanishads),* New York, 1974.
R. C. Zaehner, *Hindu and Muslim Mysticism,* London, 1960.

6) Monasticism

M. G. Bhagat, *Ancient Indian Asceticism,* New Delhi, 1976.

G. W. BRIGGS, *Gorakhnath and the Kamphanta Yogis,* London, 1938.
H. CHAKRABORTI, *Asceticism in Ancient India,* Calcutta, 1973.
L. DUMONT, *World Renunciation in Indian Religions,* in "Religion, Politics and History in India", Paris, 1970, chapter 3.
J. N. FARQUHAR, *The Organisation of the Sannyāsis of Vedānta,* in : JRAS, 1925, pp. 479-86.
———, *The Crown of Hinduism,* London, 1915, Ch. 7: "The Yellow Robe".
A. S. GEDEN, *Asceticism (Hindu),* Encyclopedia of Religion and Ethics, Edinburgh, 1909, Vol. 2.
JAN GONDA, *Change and Continuity in Indian Religion,* Ch. 7 Gifts; Ch. 9 Brahmacarya: Ch. 10 *Dīkṣā,* The Hague, 1965.
R. S. HARDY, *Eastern Monasticism,* London, 1850.
H. D. SHARMA, *History of Brahmanical Asceticism (Sannyāsa),* Poona, 1939.
SWAMI SIVANANDA, *Necessity for Sannyāsas,* The Yoga-Vedānta Forest Society, 1963.
L. SKURZAC, *Études sur L'origine de l'ascétisme indien,* Wroclaw, 1948.
———, *Étude sur l'Épopée Indienne,* Wroclaw, 1958.
———, *Indian Asceticism in its historical development,* in: "The Adyar Library Bulletin", Vol. 31-32 (1967-68), pp. 202-210.

7) Salvation and ways of salvation

Books

N. K. BRAHMA, *Philosophy of Hindu Sādhana,* London, 1932.
SYDNEY CAVE, *Redemption, Hindu and Christian,* London, 1919.
H. VON GLASENAPP, *Immortality and Salvation in Indian Religions,* Trans. by E. F. J. Payne, Calcutta, 1963.
A. G. KRISHNA WARRIER, *The Concept of Mukti in Advaita Vedanta,* Madras, 1961.
A. K. LAD, *A Comparative Study of the Concept of liberation in Indian Philosophy,* Burhanpur (M.P.), 1967.
T. M. P. MAHADEVAN (Edit.), *Proceedings of the Seminar on the concept of liberation and its relevance to philosophy,* in: "Indian Philosophical Annual", Vol. 5, Madras, 1969.
UNTO TÀHTINEN, *Indian Philosophy of Value,* Turku, 1968.
RODHE STEN, *Deliver us from Evil,* Lund, 1946.
R. OTTO, *India's Religion of grace and Christianity,* London, 1930.
H. LEFEVER, *The Vedic Idea of Sin,* Travancore, 1935.

Articles

R. VAN BELLINGEN, *The concept of mokṣa in the philosophy of Rāmānuja,* in: "Orientalia Lovaniensia Periodica", 5 (1974), pp. 139-152.
J. A. R. VAN BUITENEN, *Dharma and Mokṣa,* in: "Philosophy, East and West", 1959, pp. 33-40.

D. DATTA, *Mokṣa or the Vedic Release,* in: "Journal of Royal Asiatic Society", 1888.

A. S. GEDEN, *Salvation (Hindu),* in: "Encyclopedia of Religion and Ethics", Vol. 11, pp. 132 ff.

RHYS DAVIDS, *Mokṣa,* in: "Encyclopedia of Religion and Ethics", Vol. 8, pp. 770 ff.

DANIEL H. H. INGALLS, *Dharma and Mokṣa,* in: "Philosophy, East and West", 1959, pp. 41-48.

S. K. MAITRA, *Mukti and bhakti as the highest values,* in: "The Journal of Indian Academy of Philosophy", Vol. II, 1963, pp. 14-28.

MARIASUSAI DHAVAMONY, *The Quest for salvation in Hinduism,* in: "Religions", Secretariatus pro non-Christianis, Rome, 1970, pp. 175-203.

———, *Hinduism and Christianity* (under the aspect of salvation), International Congress of Missiology, Rome, 1976, Vol. III, pp. 151-161.

T. R. V. MURTI, *The concept of freedom as redemption,* in: "Types of Redemption", edited by R. J. Zwi Werblowsky and C. J. Bleeker, Leiden, 1970, pp. 213-222.

R. PANIKKAR, *The myth of incest as symbol for redemption in Vedic India,* in: "Types of Redemption", op. cit., pp. 130-143.

HENRY H. PRESLER, *Indian aborigene contributions to Hindu ideas of Mukti liberation,* in: "Types of Redempition", op. cit. pp. 144-167.

A. B. SHIVAJI, *The concept of salvation in Christianity and Vaishnavism,* in: "The Vikram", Vikram University, Ujjain, 1963, pp. 51-55.

O. STRAUSS, *Relation between Karma, jñāna and mokṣa,* in: "Kuppuswami Sastri commemoration Volume", Madras, 1960, pp. 159-166.

A. B. KEITH, *Sin (Hindu),* in, "Encyclopedia of Religion and Ethics", Vol. 11, pp. 500-502.

T. N. SIQUEIRA, *Sin and salvation in the early Rig-Veda,* in: "Anthropos", 28, pp. 179-188.

R. C. ZAEHNER, *Salvation in the Mahābhārata,* in: "The Saviour God", edited by S. G. F. Brandon, Manchester, 1963, pp. 218-225.

8) Hindu-Christian spirituality

1. Robert Vachon, *Pour une foi chrétienne à la lumière hindoue, Eglise Vivante* 21, 1969, 117-134.
2. Louis Gardet, *Etudes de Philosophie et de Mystique comparées,* Paris 1972.
3. Joseph de Sainte-Marie, *Sur les «voies» de la Mystique. Orient et Occident, Ephemerides Carmeliticae,* XXIII (1972), 101-170.
4. Sydney Cave, *Redemption: Hindu and Christian,* Oxford University Press, 1919.
5. Branden S.G.F., *Man and his Destiny in the Great Religions,* Manchester University, 1962.

6. John Bowker, *Problems of suffering in religions of the world,* Cambridge, 1970. (edit.)
7. R.C. Chalmers and J. A. Irving, *The Meaning of life in five great religions,* Philadelphia, 1965.
7b. S.C. Thakur, *Christian and Hindu Ethics,* London, 1969.
8. J. Neuner, *Avatara Doctrine and the Christ Mysterium,* in *Man and Religion,* München, 1967.
9. S.G.F. Brandon, *Hinstory, Time and Deity,* Manchester Univ. Press, 1965.
10. Suzanne Siauve, *Vers une liturgie indienne,* in *Axes,* Juillet-Août 1962.
11. Jules Monchanin, *Yoga et Hesychasme,* in *Axes,* Avril 1969.
12. S. Kulandran, *Grace in Christianity and Hinduism,* London, 1964.
13. P. De Letter, *The Christian and Hindu Concept of Grace,* Calcutta, 1958.
14. Olivier Lacombe, *Chemins de l'Inde et Philosophie chrétienne,* Paris, 1956.
15. G. Parrinder, *Upanishads, Gita and Bible,* London, 1962.
16. G. Parrinder, *Avatar and Incarnation,* London, 1970.
17. A.J. Appasamy, *The Gospel and India's Heritage,* London, 1942.
18. J.A. Cuttat, *Expérience chrétienne et Spiritualité orientale,* Paris, 1967.
19. P.D. Devanandan, *Christian Concern in Hinduism,* Bangalore, 1961.
20. M. Dhavamony, *Christian Experience and Hindu Spirituality,* in *Gregorianum,* 48 (1967).
21. M. Dhavamony, *Hinduism and Christianity,* in *Theology,* 70 (1967).
22. B. Griffiths, *Christian Ashram, Essays towards a Hindu-Christian Dialogue,* London, 1966.
23. O. Lacombe, *Le Brahmanisme,* in *La Mystique et les mystiques,* Paris, 1965.
24. R. Panikkar, *The Unknown Christ of Hinduism,* London, 1964.
25. J.C. Winslow, *The Christian Approach to the Hindu,* Edinburgh, 1958.
26. R. C. Zaehner, *At Sundry Times,* London, 1958.
27. « *Mysticism Sacred and Profane,* Oxford, 1957.
28. « *Hindu and Muslim Mysticism,* London, 1962.
29. « *The Convergent Spirit,* London, 1963.
30. « *The Catholic Church and World Religions,* London, 1964.
31. R.C. Zaehner, *Concordant Discord,* Oxford, 1970.
32. P.D. Devanandan, *Preparation for Dialogue,* Bangalore, 1964.
33. F. Whaling, *An Approach to Dialogue with Hinduism,* Lucknow, 1966.
34. E.J. Sharpe, *Not to destroy but to fulfil,* Uppsala, 1965.
35. Varii, *Rethinking Christianity in India,* Madras, 1938.
36. K. Klostermaier, *Vrindavan,* London, 1970.
37. *Rythmes du Monde,* XV (1967).
38. J.B. Chettimattam, *The Christian Approach to Hinduism,* Bangalore, 1962.

39. J. Monchanin et H. Le Saux, *A Benedictine Ashram,* Tiruchirappalli, 1964.
40. H. Le Saux, *Sagesse Hindoue, Mystique Chrétienne,* Paris, 1965.
41. M.A. Amaladoss, *Vers une Spiritualité Chrétienne-Indienne,* in *Axes,* XVI (190).
42. S. Kappan and Kayan (Edit.), *India and the Eucharist,* Ernakulam, 1964.
43. P. Fallon, *Catholicism and Hinduism in modern times,* in *Studia Missionalia,* Rome, 1963.
44. Ram Moyan Roy, *The Precepts of Jesus,* 1820.
45. P.C. Mazoomdar, *The Oriental Christ,* Boston, 1894.
46. « *The Spirit of God,* Boston, 1894.
47. Keshub Chunder Sen, *Lectures in India,* London, 1909.
48. Vivekananda, *Christ, the Messenger,* Vol. 4 of Complete Works.
49. Abhedananda, *Why a Hindu accepts Christ and rejects Christianity,* 1946.
50. Akhilananda, *Hindu View of Christ,* New-York, 1949.
51. Ranganathanda, *The Christ we adore,* Calcutta, 1955.
52. Radhakrishnan, *Eastern Religions and Western Thought,* London, 1939.
53. Sivananda, *Life and Teachings of Lord Jesus Christ,* Rishikesh, 1959.
54. Manik Lal Parekh, *A Hindu Portrait of Jesus Christ,* Rajkot, 1953.
55. M.K. Gandhi, *What Jesus means to me,* Ahmedabad, 1959.
56. Prajnanada, *Christ, the Saviour,* Calcutta, 1961.
57. N.K. Devaraja, *Hinduism and Christianity,* Asia Publishing House, 1969.
58. J.M. Dechanet, *Christian Yoga,* London, 1960.
59. O. Lacombe, *Sur le Yoga indien,* in *Etudes Carmélitaines,* 1937.
60. O. Lacombe, *Technique et Contemplation,* in *Etudes Carmélitaines,* 1949.
61. J. Neuner, *Indische und Christliche Meditation,* in *Geist und Leben,* 1953.
62. J. Monchanin, *Problèmes du Yoga chrétien,* in *Axes,* VIII, 1969.
63. A.J. Appasamy, *The use of Yoga in prayer,* Madras, 1926.
64. P. Johanns, *La Pensée Religieuse de l'Inde,* Paris, 1952.
65. Varii, *Religious Hinduism,* Allahabad, 1964.
66. R. Antoine, *Where we all meet,* Calcutta, 1958.
67. J.A. Cuttat, *The Spiritual Dialogue between East and West,* Delhi, 1961.
68. Swami Abhishiktananda, *Hindu-Christian Meeting Point,* Bangalore, 1965.
69. Camille Drevent, *Gandhi interpelle les chrétiens,* Paris, 1965.
70. J. Monchanin and H. Le Saux, *Ermites du Saccidananda,* Essai d'intégration chrétienne de la tradition monastique de l'Inde, Bruxelles, 1957.
71. J. Monchanin, *Ecrits spirituels,* Présentation d'Edouard Duperray. Paris, 1965.